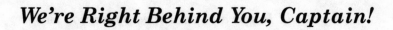

We're Right Behind You, Captain!

Also by David Hopps and published by Robson Books

Free As A Bird

We're Right Behind You, Captain!

The Alternative Story
of an Ashes Year

David Hopps

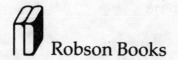

Robson Books

First published in Great Britain in 1997 by
Robson Books Ltd, Bolsover House,
5–6 Clipstone Street, London W1P 8LE

British Library Cataloguing in Publication Data
A catalogue record for this title is available from the
British Library

ISBN 1 86105 113 1

Printed in Great Britain by Butler & Tanner Ltd,
London and Frome

Contents

Foreword

David Hopps is what is known in the trade as a young cricket writer. That is to say, he is worried about turning forty, rather than sixty, eighty or a hundred. EW Swanton (aged ninety), it has to be said, has a more impressive head of hair.

We first met when he really was a young cricket writer, on the *Yorkshire Post*. He fed me a very choice titbit of gossip, which I duly printed in the *Guardian*. It turned out to be complete bunkum, and came as near as anything has so far (touch wood) to landing me in a full-blown libel action. We have, for some reason, been firm friends ever since.

It is a fairly spiky sort of friendship. Most days, we disagree on everything, from whether the County Championship should be split into two divisions to whether it is his turn to get the coffee. We once quarrelled formally, in print, about the merits of Ray Illingworth as supreme master of the England team. Hopps thought he was wonderful; I thought he was a disaster. A few months later, Hopps issued a grovelling apology.

Once we had a proper row, in the Headingley press box, which was so loud that heads turned several blocks away and I am surprised the charming Headingley security men did not arrive to follow their normal practice and kick our heads in. I have no idea what we were arguing about. Anyway, a few minutes later, I apologized.

He is, of course, a Yorkshireman, which means he has difficulty relating to lesser breeds, i.e. non-Yorkshiremen. But he is a very modern sort of Yorkshireman. He is aware that there are eighteen counties in the Championship, not one. He is aware that the population of Bradford has changed in the last fifty years, and does not entirely regret it. He is aware of women, and believes that they have feelings, emotions and rights.

That doesn't actually stop him exasperating Mrs Hopps by

playing and watching cricket all the time. For he is also an enthusiast and, specifically, an enthusiast for cricket. Seems barmy to me. War correspondents don't stage mock battles on their day off, unless they're completely crazed. Political correspondents, after spending a week at Westminster, don't spend their Saturday afternoons at local council meetings. Why on earth would anyone who spends his working week watching professionals play cricket want to play it himself at the weekend? Hopps does.

The effect is that his colleagues have to field calls in the middle of a Test match about who might and might not be available to play for him on Saturday and (on at least one occasion) whether or not another batch of hamburgers was needed for the post-match barbecue. It also gives him an unusual, maybe unique, perspective. Anyone is likely to be able to write about Mike Atherton's difficulties with captaincy more sympathetically if they have to wrestle with different versions of the same problems themselves. And England captains are not expected to worry about the hamburgers. There is a phrase the administrators at Lord's like to use these days, about improving cricket 'from the village green to the Test arena'. Hoppsy is a sort of walking embodiment of the idea.

He has one further attribute. He is a skilful, funny, well-informed, imaginative writer. He is, in one sense, unique, because he is the product of two very different cricket-writing traditions. On the one hand, he worked at the *Yorkshire Post*. His predecessor but one was JM Kilburn, a forbidding, silent man who wrote immaculately crafted reports in longhand for more than forty seasons up to 1976, and hardly ever crossed anything out. He occasionally mentioned the name of the obscure county Yorkshire happened to be playing, but didn't seem to think it mattered much.

Cricket on that side of the Pennines was something to be treated seriously, accurately and respectfully. Entertainment? What's that got to do with it? Across the mountains, Neville Cardus, far more famously, was writing scintillating pieces in the *Manchester Guardian* that touched the hearts of people who might otherwise have cared nothing for cricket. If the fact happened to coincide with his fancy, so much the better.

Hopps moved from Kilburn's job to join the *Guardian*, now long since emigrated from Manchester. He has been an adornment to the paper and provided a sort of synthesis of the two styles: Yorkshire sturdiness and Lancastrian whimsy. Yet he has never physically moved from Yorkshire, and so has never lost touch with his own roots. It makes him a remarkable cricket writer, and makes this a remarkable book.

Matthew Engel
Guardian writer.
Editor of *Wisden*.
September 1997

For Janice, Richard and Jennifer.

We have a great opportunity for the rebirth of English cricket...the creation of one happy and successful family from the village green to the Test arena.'

AC Smith, retiring chief executive of the Test and County Cricket Board, September 1996

'English cricket is an irrelevance on and off the ground. And this is not the ramblings of an Anglophobe. It is a statement of fact.'

Mike Coward, Australian sports writer, January 1997

AUTUMN 1997

1
Raking The Ashes

BEWARE the image makers! Now that sport is often presented as the dominant culture of the Nineties, surreptitiously seeking to tweak your emotions and rule your life, you can't even pick up a cricket book without wondering about hidden agendas. What have we here? The predictable utterings of an avowed traditionalist, or a cock-eyed collection of conspiracy theories and dreary anecdotes? Can *you* trust a sports writer these days, even one wearing a dust jacket?

It's best to come clean. What you actually have is a man who has just smashed down his own stumps. Well, that's not entirely accurate, the off-stump having been conveniently flattened by the bowler a second or two earlier, but you get the drift. The pitch, belonging to a comprehensive school, was a disgrace, which just about made it possible to depict the whole regrettable incident as a moral crusade on behalf of England's youth, but no one really believed it. If you come across any pompous paragraphs about English cricket's collapsing standards of behaviour, you will be forgiven a cynical chuckle.

But what *you* don't appreciate is the pressure Michael and I have been under this summer. I'll tell you, we've had it tough. He was the captain of England, trying to win back the Ashes, and he always knew how hard that would be. But I was just planning another aimless season of village cricket and then suddenly up popped the new-fangled England and Wales Cricket Board to announce that we were all part of a great national pyramid, and that we were all in this Ashes-winning business together. Bloody 'ell! It sounded like the calling up of the Home Guard.

Thankfully, by the end of the season, the ECB had supplied two large blue management manuals to tell us how to go about it. Admittedly, the Ashes series had already been lost by then, but at least the code of conduct proved useful. We adopted it immediately, apologized for my stump smashing, and voted to award me a one-match ban. As I ricked my knee around the same time, it didn't really matter.

At times in the past year, I imagined I was writing a novel. A book that was assembled week by week as events unfurled might have been written in hindsight, so conveniently did many outcomes fit my prejudices, or satisfy my whims.

I was adamant about England's unenlightened attitude to touring, and they provided ludicrous evidence of it in Zimbabwe. The debate about the future of English cricket focused attention on a domestic structure in crisis. As I occasionally praise Australia enough for nationalistic Brits to exhort: 'Well, go and bloody live there, then,' it was convenient, if not particularly welcome, that Australia retained the Ashes, just as it was heartening to see England make their best fist of it for a decade. Even the village season sparkled with comedy, but then what's new?

But *can* you trust a journalist? As the summer closed to the sound of Australian celebrations, Michael Atherton's resignation as England captain was widely perceived as inevitable. Some commentators regretted Atherton's impending departure, others demanded it so rabidly that they lost touch with reality. It was scapegoat time again.

Ahterton spoke to team-mates, selectors, his family and his closest confidants and then chose to soldier on. But it was a darn close-run thing. Even twenty-four hours before the media conference at Lord's which confirmed that Atherton would lead England in the West Indies, his mind was not entirely settled. But he retained a stubborn desire for his own self-determination, and was certainly not about to abandon a job half done on the grounds that the media suspected that his time was up.

I saw few reasons why Atherton should resign, contending that personalities are too often blamed for deep-seated problems for which many share responsibility. But any normal man would have long sickened of the criticism. His resignation would have been a thematically satisfying conclusion, especially as I had just resigned at village level, pleading incipient insanity. I told him as much at the Cricket Writers' Club dinner in London at the end of the season and he laughed, as I expected he would.

In stark contrast to Atherton's strength of mind was the September meanderings of the first-class counties as they formally voted on the ECB's blueprint for change, Raising The Standard, a document full of worthy intentions to close the damagingly large gap between Test cricket and the recreational game.

The aim of Lord MacLaurin of Knebworth, the chairman of the ECB and the main proponent of change, was also to encourage the ultra-conservative first-class counties to reform. But from the moment he floated the obvious remedy of a two-divisional championship, with promotion and relegation, he was met by predictable intransigence.

During a summer tour of the counties, his Lordship became so disheartened by the entrenched opposition to two divisions that he backed alternative proposals for the introduction of an American-style system of three conferences, an idea so awful that almost overnight it managed to unite the radical and traditional camps in condemnation. In less than a year, a man billed as one of Britain's most decisive, clear-minded businessmen was trading in woolly-headed compromise. That is what English cricket does to people.

The conference solution, which also carried an increase in one-day domestic cricket, was a non-starter. But MacLaurin had always trumpeted that English cricket was outdated and that 'no change was not an option,' so a week before the vote, the ECB offered two further alternatives.

Firstly, there was a proposal for a two-division championship, with promotion and relegation, which MacLaurin interrupted a holiday in Spain to confirm that (along with 75 per cent of players, and at least as many supporters) he had supported all along. Secondly, there was something dubbed the 'radical status quo' with the top eight in an unchanged *four-day* championship rewarded by a televised *one-day* knockout competition the following season. The counties voted 12–7 to adopt the latter.

His Lordship stoutly suggested that 'English cricket has moved a long way forward.' By the standards of my ricked knee, perhaps it has. But I reckon I know what 'radical' means and I understand 'status quo,' and only one of those words is a true description of what took place. But then are *you* prepared to trust a journalist?

AUTUMN 1996

2
Setting The Trend

SOMETHING disconcerting has happened. I've woken up today to find that I suddenly live in the trendiest city in Britain. I wish someone had warned me, I would have dressed for the part. It's not every day that the media are united in the belief that Leeds is now the place to be. Does this mean that I'm finally 'it', whatever 'it' might be? And if it does, will I be offered a weekly column by the *Sunday Times*?

This reassessment of Leeds' charms has been reached on the flimsy grounds that Harvey Nichols, often identified with London chic, has opened a department store in Briggate, alongside what we are misleadingly informed is a collection of pawn shops and discount toiletry stores. Underlying all the pieces poking fun at gauche Northerners trying on expensive hats is a vaulting assumption of London superiority.

I happen to be very fond of Leeds, but for it suddenly to gain the mock approval of a few self-appointed London style experts just because it can now offer another outlet for expensive designer handbags leaves me thoroughly underwhelmed. What London thinks of Harvey Nicks opening in Leeds is largely irrelevant; what Leeds thinks matters a good deal more. That is something our national newspapers, in their ceaseless obsession with the capital, persistently overlook. Anyway, if the North has to be caricatured, we had rather do it ourselves. And where better to examine caricature, in a watershed year for English cricket, than at Headingley?

The columnists will soon tire of Yorkshire's supposed love affair with Harvey Nicks, but Headingley cricket ground has satisfied the need to caricature large swathes of the North for almost a hundred years. Not that much exaggeration has been needed. It has long been English cricket's most dilapidated Test venue, and racist outbursts on the Western

Terrace during the recent Pakistan Test have again lowered the reputation of its inhabitants to Neanderthal proportions.

Trouble most frequently occurs at Headingley on Test match Saturday, when the terraces are full of replica football shirts of Newcastle, Sunderland and Leeds United, and local cricketers are otherwise occupied in league cricket, often in successfully integrated teams. But Yorkshire is conveniently adopted as a hotbed of racism to appease liberal guilt elsewhere when, in truth, the scenes at Headingley are merely another manifestation of a national problem: Britain, a multi-racial country which still prefers to depict itself as white Anglo-Saxon.

The drunk lashing out at Headingley, the chief executive in the City who makes appointments on the basis of background rather than ability, MPs of all parties obsessed with the votes of Middle England, the armed forces' failure to eradicate racial prejudice, or the Hertfordshire golf club which strives to maintain a membership that is exclusively white and middle-class: all are equally culpable. It is England's traditional vision of itself, not just the boorish and unacceptable antics of a few Northern loudmouths, which still bedevils our society and our cricket. There is no more wasted talent in the past generation than Mark Ramprakash (Hertfordshire-born, of Guyanese and Irish parents) and how much of that is to do with his sub-conscious uncertainty about his identity?

For an example of English cricket's misplaced priorities, try this: with racist chants breaking from the Headingley terraces, stewards ejected a pantomime cow from the ground because it was disturbing people's concentration. As far as could be ascertained, the cow had not once foul-mouthed the Asian supporters, which made it a higher form of life than dozens of the spectators whose view it was supposedly impeding. No prizes for guessing who wins the mad cow award in this case (clue: it isn't the cow).

Headingley's authorities have announced an investigation, but already we know the findings will have little substance.

As always, they will blame media hype and excess alcohol, and play down the whole thing. They will also fail to widen their investigation to include Asian or West Indian community groups, or the Hit Racism For Six campaign.

If English cricket is to secure its future as a broadly based sport, its image must be modernized, and funding from the national lottery offers an opportunity. Even Yorkshire is striving to reinvent itself as a land where the flat cap is replaced by the mobile phone. I have just arrived at Headingley, where the county is unveiling plans to move to a new £32 million state-of-the-art stadium on the outskirts of Wakefield. The artist's impression promises everything – or nearly everything, the overwhelming need for a Harvey Nichols store at the rear of the main stand having been strangely overlooked. That rules out the enticing sight of Yorkshire pensioners binning their faithful anoraks and exploring the world of designer casuals.

'But Grace, luv, this il nivver be any good. There's just not enough room for mi flask and sarnies in t'outside pockets. And wheer am a goin' t'put mi Wisden? 'As t'dustman come yet? Get mi old cooat out agin, luv. I saw 'Utton mek an 'undred in this, tha knows.'

An all-seater stadium (which seems to have a changeable capacity ranging from 20-30,000) boasts its own marina, to ensure that the River Calder does not flood the outfield on the offchance that Yorkshire's drought ever breaks; a cricket museum in which Fred Trueman should be exhibited immediately, so warning us all against the perils of prejudice; a cricketing academy, to produce the next generation of players so Fred can slag them off and get their names wrong; and any number of community sports facilities, largely because they are necessary to win approval for the lottery grant.

The thought of Yorkshire abandoning Headingley is a cause for celebration, especially as it would offer an escape from the cups of tea slopped out by the caterers, Gilpins, so stewed that they leave a ring round the rim reminiscent of a student bathroom. One day I expect to see a hairy piece of Imperial Leather pop to the surface – you know, the leftover bit with the label on that seems to last for ever.

Anticipating that the lottery will meet £28 million of costs totalling £50 million seems a trifle optimistic. Sure enough, twenty-four hours later unattributed hints begin to emerge from Sports Council grandees of opposition ahead. For the six months to the end of September, about £600 million was raised by the lottery towards what is termed, ever so tweely, Good Causes. To spend as much as £28 million on a cricket stadium that will only be full for, perhaps, one five-day Test and a limited-overs international per year does not strike everybody as a good idea.

But Yorkshire's aspirations perfectly fit the model of the new England and Wales Cricket Board – the vision of a great partnership between schools, clubs and the professional game. More than twenty per cent of all cricket in England takes place in Yorkshire. Say that again: more than twenty per cent of all cricket in England. That being so, it sorely needs an efficient and inspirational administrative centre. Developed properly, Wakefield has the potential to become the driving force for all cricket in Yorkshire in a way that Headingley never has been. Or at least jolt Headingley's owners into a redevelopment programme that is years overdue.

During the depths of Yorkshire's decline, in the early 1980s, the only links between the county and its public occurred whenever the late Joe Lister, a secretary of the old school, harangued the hoi-polloi over the loudspeaker system. 'As you may know, or may not know, play is about to resume, so stop your promenading and return to your seats. Thank you!' And with his crowd-control duties satisfactorily dealt with, he would stroll around the back of the main stand in time to reach the Ladbrokes tent for a flutter on the 2.30.

What Joe Lister cared about marketing could be written on the back of a betting slip, but he cared deeply about cricket. He would have welcomed the idea of a great cricketing family

– but only if it never invited itself for Christmas, communicated occasionally by letter rather than inconvenience him by telephone, and never once bothered him at the office.

A new stadium also offers Yorkshire the opportunity to escape from the damaging images of the past. The Western Terrace has become a distorted symbol of Yorkshire cricket. I can no longer draw pride from the traditional picture of a cloth-capped old-timer glowering his prejudices at the world on a wind-torn terrace, when I am appalled by his intolerance. I can no longer smile indulgently at their clumsiness when Brian Close refers to 'bloody Pakis', Fred Trueman mispronounces another Asian name with an air of indifference, or Raymond Illingworth shows a failure of man-management in his treatment of Devon Malcolm on England's tour of South Africa. And these guys were my childhood heroes.

Sight of the White Rose Stadium plans, with its showy community facilities, reminds me of my own village club's application for grant aid during our pavilion appeal a few years before. Thorner Mexborough Cricket Club's application to the Foundation for Sports and the Arts was more modest – a £7,000 grant to fund a £21,000 development – but the principles were the same.

Soon after we had drawn up the plans, I happened across an official from the Yorkshire & Humberside Sports Council, who informed me grandly that the Sports Council had designated 1992 'the year of table tennis.' Without stopping to enquire what a year of table tennis would actually achieve, I conveyed this information to our club draughtsman. It was a simple task for him to add a small black rectangle to our plans, in the centre of a modestly-sized tea room. An arrow left no one in any doubt as to our intentions. 'Table tennis table,' it said grandly. We received £6,500 and I reckon we didn't waste a penny. Can't say, though, that we have much advanced the cause of table tennis.

Yorkshire has not had the opportunity to glory in success

for thirty years – the county last won the championship in 1968 – so, predictably, the press conference about the new stadium has an unmistakably self-congratulatory air. With characteristic humility, the proposed ground is extolled as 'the finest on the planet' – which is clearly bunkum, as its proposed capacity is about one-third that of Calcutta and Melbourne, while Lord's has the advantage of more than 200 years of history. Personally, I quite like Thorner too, even if one half of the outfield slopes rather too steeply down to Bottoms Wood.

We all sit attentively in the Rhodes and Hirst suite while Sir Lawrence Byford, Yorkshire's president, praises Wakefield City Council, and the leader of the council, Colin Croxall, praises Sir Lawrence. Then, having enjoyed the experience so much, they do it all again. The plans do not immediately reveal exactly where their statues will one day be erected, but if this comes off, it seems a fair bet that they will be.

Sir Lawrence has presided over a period of great change in Yorkshire cricket, much of it long overdue: the abandonement of the outdated reliance solely on players born within the old county boundaries, the acceptance of overseas professionals, the success of the Park Avenue academy in nurturing young players, and the introduction of some commercial nous. Now he promises Yorkshire a spanking new ground, 'and it won't cost us a single penny!' Oddly enough, with such an appealing manifesto to hand, he chooses to ramble on about his time as chief constable of Lincolnshire. More than once, he utters the phrase: 'When I built the Lincolnshire police headquarters...' which makes it sound as if he has done it single-handedly, and invites the question as to how he ever found time for any crime prevention when he was spending eight hours a day mixing cement.

Then, as he bemoans the racist element in Headingley's crowds, his mind wanders back to crowd-control measures at Leeds United Football Club in the 1970s, when hooliganism was at its peak. 'When I used to escort all those loutish fans from the station to Elland Road...' he begins. I was often among those crowds, forced to walk where I didn't want to go and assumed to be loutish just because I was a teenager and hadn't arrived in a jacket and tie. I am also convinced that we were normally escorted by more than one policeman. If Sir Lawrence had been doing it on his own, surely I would have managed to sneak down a side-street, probably while he was up ahead, relating the story of how he built the Lincolnshire police headquarters? As the press conference shows signs of fatigue, I sneak out of the door instead and return home to write a piece of unadulterated optimism. Yorkshire deserves nothing less.

The phrase 'subject to satisfactory grant aid' keeps coming to mind, however. Yorkshire cricket lives permanently in crisis, and a month later Headingley has a new owner, a millionaire property developer (are there any others?) by the name of Paul Caddick. Caddick's negotiating style is, shall we say, a little aggressive.

'The daggers are now drawn,' he thunders. 'For the next three years, we will not be doing anything to fund Yorkshire cricket, not even a coat of paint around the ground.' These are inadvisable tactics – for one thing, it is doubtful that anyone will notice.

The safest conclusion is that it will all end in tears. Perhaps those Southern caricatures are perfectly fair after all. I make a mental note to move to London and spend the rest of my life writing piss-taking pieces about Harvey Nichols moving to West Yorkshire.

3

Foot Of The Pyramid

IT is the week of the Wetherby League dinner and Thorner Mexborough Cricket Club is anxious to begin its team-strengthening plans in earnest. What better way for a village club on the north-eastern fringes of Leeds to advertise its special appeal than an evening consisting of 200 drunken blokes swilling down copious amounts of beer and red wine until memories are obliterated and legs collapse beneath them? Oh, OK then, there are thousands of better ways. But we don't have a yacht moored in St Lucia, or access to a hospitality box at Elland Road, and none of us are personal friends of Claudia Schiffer. At least, no one is letting on. About the only alternative to a welcoming night at the league dinner is a complimentary seat in the front row for the Christmas raffle draw and, as the first prize is provisionally a bottle of Blue Nun (well, you have to get rid of them somehow), that does not seem a good idea.

So it is that Tom Jordan, erstwhile Edinburgh University student, followed by several years dossing around in a bookshop, and now identified as the most intellectual solution yet to our middle-order collapses, finds himself listening to Arnie Sidebottom as he retells old Yorkshire cricket stories with considerable gusto, and occasionally trying to hold intelligent conversations with drunks to whom he has barely been introduced. There is little chance that Tom will remember their names; they can barely remember their own.

For someone embarking upon an MA at Leeds University, and who has spent much of the week immersed in a study of Darwin's effect on nineteenth-century English literature, the entire experience proves immensely valuable. He only has to watch Chris Walker slopping his after-eight mint into his coffee with an inaccuracy which brings to mind his more wayward spells of seam bowling to be more convinced than ever that Darwin's theory of natural selection is a total myth.

As it happened, Tom's willingness to attend such an august gathering had caused certain sartorial difficulties.

'I haven't got a suit,' he revealed, uncertainly, twenty-four hours before the dinner.

'Well, we're not proud, wear a jacket and trousers.'

'Yeah, well, I'm not sure that...'

'Ho ho, no jacket? Student life! Those were the days, eh? A lifetime of beer, sex and the chance to sleep through 9.15 lectures. *(cue boring old memories)*... Just put a tie on, it'll be warm in there.'

'It's not as simple as that. It's just that when I passed the interview, none of this sort of stuff seemed worth keeping any more.'

Several minutes later, it transpired that Tommy's wardrobe consisted of several pairs of jeans, a leather jacket and a pair of Doc Martens. That and several thousand books and a collection of tie-ups for what will be the longest pony-tail ever witnessed in the Wetherby League (apart from those attached to the real pony which grazes alongside our boundary fence and which could develop a dangerous attraction to him). The first thought was to wonder if he wanted to swap lifestyles, at least until I had safely negotiated a gathering mid-life crisis. The second was the realization that the only solution was to arrange a loan of a suit for the evening. As our captain Phil Ralli could happily restock several branches of Next without noticing the difference, he seemed the ideal man to address the problem.

Fifteen minutes later, on the way to a football match at Huddersfield, my clapped-out Oki mobile rang. That was surprise enough. Even more freakishly, the reception was good enough for a normal conversation. Well, fairly normal.

'This is another of your bloody signings, Hopps,' the captain railed. 'He doesn't even know his waist size! How can you get into your mid-twenties without knowing your waist size? He says that the shops he buys his jeans in sell them in small, medium and large. He just keeps trying them on until he finds a pair that fit! *And* he doesn't know what size his chest is! I said to him, "How can a man your age not know the size of his chest? Everybody knows the size of their chest." And do you know what he said? You won't believe it. He said that he wasn't interested in that sort of thing!'

The following evening, wondering whether to feign laughter at an unappealing Yorkshire comedian who manages to intertwine sexism and racism with rare dexterity, Tom is favouring a brown tweed suit which he presumably wore in his days as Dr Who's assistant. Clearly not a Phil Ralli cast-off. His father, Tim, a good friend and former playing colleague in village cricket at Great Bentley in Essex, had reminded him of its existence, languishing as it had for many years at the bottom of a cardboard box. Many prospective team-mates good-humouredly welcome Tom to the club by ridiculing his beige floral tie, which leaves him mildly aggrieved. 'I don't know why they've picked on the tie,' he mutters. 'That's the only bit I chose specially.'

Players who fail the Ridicule Test tend not to last too long in our First XI. Invariably, the most challenging delivery is not the little outswinger from the opposition's rotund medium-pacer, but the facetious comment from the corner of your own dressing-room. Quirks of character (real or imagined) are mercilessly exposed. Pretentiousness or arrogance cannot survive. It is amateur sport perfectly fulfilling its role as an antidote to real life, where the life-threatening and mind-numbing rules of social convention are abandoned in favour of a friendly and supportive verbal free-for-all. After seventeen years of Conservative government, it is about the nearest thing left to community, even if it is a touch more aggressive than an older generation might remember it.

As for the Wetherby League's choice of main dinner speaker, that is best forgotten. He exists on our table only as 'Mike Kelly Is Indisposed', because just as the chairman announced who was taking his place, the microphone feedback drowned out his name. It is just as well that, for us at least, he remained anonymous. Cricket dinners have changed tone over the past twenty years; audiences that once wanted to listen to gentle cricket talk now demand strident, stand-up comedy. It is difficult enough to persuade a village cricketer to think seriously about his game on a Saturday afternoon; only a fool would attempt to do so on a Friday evening with the beer in full flow.

That has spawned some marvellously funny and original speakers on the after-dinner circuit. It has also enabled a fortunate group of England Test players, past and present, to supplement their incomes throughout the winter by telling old gags about their team-mates: Dermot Reeve, Mark Nicholas, Geoff Miller, Fred Trueman, Dickie Bird... many of them could conceivably earn more talking about the game than they ever did playing it. Leagues, and clubs, throughout the country are reliant for their survival upon the profits that a well-run annual dinner can provide. In nurturing the English cricket 'family', a booming dinner-circuit has a vital role to play.

Unfortunately, it also provides a life-support system for ignorant and prejudiced comedians who make Bernard Manning seem a model of good taste. Working for *The Guardian,* I would say that, wouldn't I? And certainly, for the first fifteen minutes of 'Mike Kelly Is Indisposed' I am left in the slightly ridiculous situation of analysing whether a joke is acceptable enough before deciding whether to laugh. This often leaves me several jokes behind, and laughing uproariously in entirely the wrong place.

For the last half-hour, though, things are simplified as a general air of boredom descends. Phil Ralli, assumed by all around him to be totally inebriated, proves himself to be of perfectly sound mind by repeatedly calling for the speaker to 'Sit Down!' Chris Maycock accuses some of us of being the 'worst audience in the world', and perhaps he is right. No wonder we always get the table hidden around the corner right at the back of the room. If they ever stage the Wetherby League dinner at a venue where everybody has a clear view of the stage, someone will undoubtedly build a pillar, specifically to hide us behind. But the wine slips down well enough, the bus turns up on time and everybody wakes up the following morning. At do's like this, that is all you can ask, really.

*   *   *

A PUBLIC relations officer, agricultural consultant, psychiatrist, accountant, nursemaid and diplomat. Such was Doug Insole's assessment of the responsibilities of a county captain. In village cricket, you can immediately add: pavilion unlocker, shower cleaner, rubbish emptier, lawn-mower repairer, mole catcher, result phoner, averages checker, subs collector, ego massager, ball searcher, pad repairer, ego massager again and umpire payer. On a good day, you might even preserve some energy to shuffle the batting order or change the field. On an excellent day (and these come along very rarely), you might even shuffle or change things roughly in the right direction. Once a year, you might even hit a boundary, or take a wicket. It is an entirely thankless task.

So, Janice enquires with wifely common sense as I make a sheepish return home after the annual meeting, why on earth have I agreed to captain Thorner again? Point taken. It was a big enough disaster the first time. Well, I suggest, it might be good for the book. And anyway, no one else was mug enough to do it.

If Michael Atherton refers to the pressures of captaincy any time from now until next September, how should I best respond now that I am restored as a fellow representative of the breed? Should I scoff impatiently in the background, as if to convey the message: 'If you think that's pressure, sonny, you should try some real hardship in the second division of the Wetherby League.' Or perhaps the most attractive option is to nod sympathetically, in the guise of a fellow sufferer battling courageously against the stresses and strains of the modern game. Clearly, a policy decision is required.

What is clear to me, if not to Athers, is that there could be endless advantages in an unofficial captaincy alliance: the exchange of vital information between Test side and village club, all part of English cricket's much-heralded new spirit of family togetherness. Thorner could borrow England's motivational tape, which was introduced to the dressing-room upon David Lloyd's appointment as coach and which included, among other things, speeches by Winston Churchill, bursts of 'Land of Hope and Glory' and, just to bring it up to date, a few bars of 'Search For The Hero Inside Yourself' by M People. 'Great song that,' says Lloyd. 'Great song. How can't you get turned on to that?'

Andy Peebles, the Radio Manchester DJ, and Lancashire obsessive, who put the tape together, repeatedly promised me last summer that the tape was in the post, which was his way of saying that 'Bumble is a very good friend of mine and, much as I'd like to send it to you, I daren't in case everybody writes about it in the paper.' Everybody already had and I reckon his failure to deliver its secrets probably led to our collapse on a dog of a pitch at Amaranth in September. In return, our committee might consider lending England Thorner's dressing-room duty rota, as long as they study it in the strictest confidence. The secret is to make sure that the person responsible for turning off the hot water waits until the last person is out of the showers. It's simple really, and I'm sure that they would find it very useful.

An exchange of information between the committees of Thorner and the England Cricket Board could also be beneficial. We have not had to ban anyone for testing positive for cocaine, as has been the case with the Sussex fast bowler Ed Giddins, although twenty years ago, minutes before a vital promotion game, Rats Scriven was found lying drunkenly on a bench with a half-empty bottle of whisky by his side. We lost the match and fined him by nicking what was left in the bottle.

Like the administrators of the first-class game, we are also adept at forming working parties whenever we are presented with a difficult decision, in the hope that it will eventually go away. I think about proposing an emergency working party at the AGM when Phil Ralli resigns as captain, but I am too late; the dirty deed is quickly done. Phil ceremoniously hands over to me the captain's cardboard box containing some old scorebooks, an apple core and a poster advertising the 1994 Midsummer Barbeque, and smiles the smile of a relieved man.

Phil had threatened to resign in mid-season when we were hurtling down the table and one or two players' egos were in inverse proportion to their willingness to do some work on behalf of the club. The impending crisis brought an immediate excuse for a few of us to quaff a pint or two at the Mexborough Arms, during which time he was persuaded instead to go and see the chairman and strengthen his position with what would be an automatic vote of confidence. The plan seemed perfectly simple. Phil duly arrived in Aberford, home of the chairman Fred Wake, and explained his problems. 'Fine,' said Fred, sympathetically. 'If that's how you feel, we'd better call an emergency committee meeting right away to sort out a replacement.'

So much for Plan A. Plan B, which amounted to drawing up a working party charged with forgetting all about it, was hastily put into operation. During some lighthearted end-of-season fines, Phil was docked £1 for approaching the chairman for a vote of confidence and failing to get one. 'Hey, that's unfair!' protested Fred from the back of the room. 'I didn't know he wanted a vote of confidence. If he'd said, he could have had one!'

Fred also resigns as chairman at the AGM after steering the club through one of the dodgiest periods in its history – namely, the building of the new pavilion. I know from painful experience that it has been four years of hassle and, for someone entering his sixties, he has done magnificently to put up with it for so long. That is roughly what I meant when I mistakenly referred to him at the end-of-season buffet as 'our veneered' chairman, which was a confused amalgamation of venerable and revered. Still, veneered will have to do. Give him another coat or two this winter and he can play through a few more rain-affected seasons. Suitably, his parting speech is made in a torrential downpour which rattles so loudly on the Mexborough Arms' conservatory roof that his words are completely inaudible.

As he draws to a close, the chairman is given a rousing 'three cheers', led by the club's secretary Andy Laycock, a Leeds solicitor, who has been newly appointed as a director of Leeds Cricket, Football & Athletic Company, the owners of Headingley. That undoubtedly means that, being a journalist, I will ply him with alcohol all summer in search of stories and, being a solicitor, he will drink his port and tell me absolutely nothing.

Andy's 'three cheers for Fred' causes much mirth, as in Yorkshire we generally don't do that sort of thing, not even in the posher parts like Thorner, which seems to house the North's entire collection of doctors, lawyers and gynaecologists. Hereabouts, a slap on the back is traditionally regarded as an excessive show of affection. Instead of 'three cheers' we would have felt more comfortable with 'one yup', a mumbled expression of gratitude which is best done in a deep and embarrassed voice, with face pointed stoically to the floor. Eye contact must always be avoided. Andy, though, risks the fallout that could occur from a great clashing of cultures. As the laughter dies down, he informs us: 'That's the benefit of a proper private education, you miserable lot.' It probably is, although it is the only one I have ever discovered.

Financially, as usual, we are under pressure. We have roughly broken even on the year and are heading towards 1997 with a few hundred pounds to our name. Subscriptions and match fees bring in about £2,000 a year, and we need £5,000 to operate the club comfortably. We would love to take our modest place in the English cricket pyramid seriously by developing our young players to their full potential, but how can we ever afford to do it? Even at our lowly level, commercial activity is vital just so we can hang on from one year to the next.

The treasurer repeats this annual plea of poverty, and then he also resigns. As he is also the groundsman, at least this spares him a guilty conscience next year every time he has to buy some more grass seed. We respond by appointing Dawn, our tea lady, as our new treasurer in the hope that the requirement to impose a regime of sensible housekeeping will at least cause her to peg the price of the teas at £1.30.

It is consoling to think that we are not the only village club in turmoil. In *The Archers*, Sid Perks has resigned as captain of Ambridge CC in protest at members' apathy, David Archer is refusing to take the job on because of pressures of work and Jack Woolley is fretting about the annual dinner – the usual story.

Thorner's statement of accounts makes more interesting reading than might be first imagined. Umpires' fees have risen by nearly £200, a direct result of the First XI being promoted to Division Two, where there are more of them. Take this disincentive to its logical conclusion and if we are too successful we could go bankrupt. No wonder we are so good at losing. One second-teamer even proposes that first-team match fees should be higher, to take into account that our umpires are costing the club so much money. That does not quite seem to be what English cricket's pyramid of achievement is all about. Fortunately, the idea does not catch on.

The minutes of the 1995 meeting also include the following gem. Under 'Minutes of Last Meeting', item 1.3 reads: *'Although the match fees had been increased to £3.50, it was noted that in fact only the sum of £3 had been collected during the year.'*

It had obviously not been noted well enough – we have also managed to collect only £3 in 1996. The same minute would have to be included again next year.

As if embarrassed by the oversight, the meeting immediately votes to whack match fees up to £4, presumably to guarantee that we actually collect £3.50. This is done with much good humour, but they will all be moaning about the expense come next April.

Phil Ralli, meanwhile, accepts the new role of vice-chairman. No one is quite sure what it entails. 'I suppose now I'm in charge of vice, I should ring up Ed Giddins and offer him a contract,' he muses. 'At least he would put us within a sniff of promotion.' Such breezy word-play so late in the evening is looked upon with wonder. Since testing positive for cocaine, though, Giddins has heard it all. 'Do you want a snort leg for this guy?', 'Keep a tight line, Ed' and 'That's a snorting delivery' rank among the more memorable offerings.

As we are leaving, Chris Maycock offers his new captain a piece of advice. Typically, he offers this at 9.30pm, after several pints, long after the match has finished. 'You should build the team around David Hartley,' he presses. 'He's a young lad with a lot of talent. We're all getting too old for this.'

I heartily agree, and I'm just considering implementing a Thorner Push For Youth policy when our budding young Botham phones up to tell me that he is joining Scarcroft. For those of you unaware of the social niceties of village life on Leeds' northern outskirts, it is akin to an Arsenal player throwing in his lot with Spurs. I should have suspected that something was afoot the previous day when I dropped in some Christmas raffle tickets to find his father, Ken, bearing one of his most morbid expressions. As Ken is the local undertaker and was brushing the hearse out at the time, I have to admit that I failed to take the hint, merely presuming that he was acting professionally.

David has a lot of mates at Scarcroft, so his change of clubs is predictable. But I suspect that all last season's jokes about his flat-footed fielding haven't exactly helped matters. He is also one of those fast bowlers who does not always appreciate that to expect twenty-three overs to 'find his rhythm' in a forty-five-over match is occasionally asking a little bit too much. We will all desperately miss the sniggering in the slips at the fact that Phil's urge to take David off always coincided with Ken's arrival at the field to watch his son bowl a few overs.

'I'm going to take Hartley off,' Phil would conclude with an I-shall-not-budge air while half the side hunted for a ball lost in the bog by Bottoms Wood.

'You can't do that,' he'd be told. 'Ken's just arrived to watch him bowl. He's the junior sponsor. We can't afford to upset *him*.' At which point Phil would invariably agree to give Dave one more over, Dave would immediately take a wicket, more often than not with a rank long-hop, and announce, with his chest puffed out with pride, that he was just beginning to find his rhythm.

Dave was never going to see eye to eye with Phil's captaincy anyway, holding to that distinctive Yorkshire viewpoint that anybody not born and raised within the county should be grateful to bat at number eleven, never bowl, and hold no official position within any village club for his entire natural life. Phil has Greek ancestry somewhere along the line *and* he emigrated from High Wycombe, which is even worse, so he never had a chance. There are parts of Yorkshire where closer ties with the rest of Europe are not so much the issue as whether to call a truce with the rest of England.

But Dave is on the phone, politely making his resignation speech, so I stump up the energy for one last attempt to persuade him to stay. I point out, in my matiest Leeds accent, that we have had a change of captaincy, and wonder, well, whether that might make a bit of a difference. 'Well, it made me wonder for a second or two,' he says. 'But then I decided to go anyway.'

Perhaps the high point of my captaincy has already passed – for that second or two, when Dave was wondering whether to stay put, the club was in total unity. But the disturbing fact is that I'm going to Zimbabwe next week, and the team has a big hole in it. At least Atherton knows that Dominic Cork isn't about to ring him up and tell him he's joining Australia. It's mid-November, and everything is already going horribly wrong.

4
Packing

Twelve reasons why it's time to leave England for another cricket tour:

1. The Christmas lights have gone up in Wetherby in a desperate attempt to cheer everyone up and drum up some trade... and it's still only mid November.

2. The car windscreen is obscured by the first heavy frost and although I know that we own at least five ice-scrapers and dozens of cans of de-icer, I can't find any of them.

3. No matter how religiously I throw them straight in the dustbin, every time I walk past the doormat there is always another pile of Christmas catalogues lying on the mat.

4. I constantly trail around the house trying to turn on more lights, only to find that they were all turned on hours ago, and it still seems dark.

5. Someone asks me what I want for Christmas and I can never think of anything interesting.

6. I keep searching CricInfo on the Internet for cricket news I might have missed and, several hours later, find that I have been sidetracked and am surfing something totally unconnected about a plague of crop-eating insects in Czechoslovakia.

7. Brian Moore booms some old-fashioned prejudice on ITV about cynical Italian footballers.

8. The weather map turns blue and yellow.

9. Depression sets in so badly that I start listening to David Mellor on *Six-O-Six* when I'm driving back from football matches.

10. People only stop in the street to mutter about how it's not normally as cold as this at this time of year.

11. My mum and dad talk about hibernating for the winter.

12. The BBC's autumn schedule consists almost entirely of costume dramas.

It's best to concentrate on the reasons to leave England when you know you will be out of the country until the end of February. That way you build up the resolve to leave your real life behind for months on end. Reflecting on how I can possibly justify leaving my wife and children behind for what amounts, this year at least, to virtually the whole winter just invites me to be morbid. There is no justification on family grounds. The fact is that touring is like a drug you can't give up and, secretly, don't even want to.

Everybody assumes that this winter will be a breeze for England, and so it should be. Successive Test series against the two weakest Test nations in the world, Zimbabwe and New Zealand, offer an opportunity to build confidence and stability before next summer's series against Australia. In some ways, for England's players it is a no-win winter: lose and they will be pilloried; win and everyone will say, so what? The best solution to that is to win, and win well. Winning overseas would also be a novel experience. In ten years of overseas tours, England have won only one series, claiming victory in five of thirty-eight Tests, losing seventeen and drawing sixteen. It is an appalling record which illustrates the depths to which English cricket has sunk.

As an obsessive village cricketer, I'm equally concerned about leaving Thorner CC in limbo for nearly three months. Before leaving for Zimbabwe, I have sent round a circular enquiring if any players have any input about next season: you know, new signings, redecorating of the tea room, the shortage of prizes for the Christmas raffle, all the usual stuff. True to form, no one has drawn enough energy together to reply, which I shall assume means everyone is entirely satisfied. Everyone, that is, but the winner of the second prize in the raffle, who could well end up with a bottle of Liebfraumilch. The people who brought that to dinner haven't been invited since.

Then there is the need to exterminate our ever-increasing mole population before it entirely destroys the outfield. There are enough secret tunnels under our outfield to house the Ministry of Defence's entire underground war effort in the event of nuclear attack. We are already so short of players that the danger that midwicket might suddenly disappear into a gaping hole, never to reappear, is too awful to contemplate. Mole smokes have also proved ineffective, apart from the fact that the creatures now emerge from the ground in dark glasses and coloured beads singing Bob Marley songs. But it has to be conceded, even as I fret over where the replacement for David Hartley will come from, that Michael Atherton has rather more reason to regard his own winter as something of a watershed.

Every England captain is packaged by the media, sooner or later. Douglas Jardine will be regarded throughout history as the man with the iron will, Mike Brearley is the well-spoken type with the very big brain, Ian Botham is the huge natural personality who couldn't sit down long enough to hack it. Raymond Illingworth is both shrewd and pigheaded, Tony Greig forever abrupt and aggressive, and Ted Dexter lives in a dream world. Eventually, these assumptions expand so much that they are made to fit every situation. The truth, of course, is that individuals are not always as consistent as that – even Illy must have screwed up sometimes – but as journalists we are always searching for simple truths.

So what of Atherton? How is he perceived as he prepares for a cricketing year that might just conclude (although only the wildest patriots really believe it) with the winning of the Ashes? On a positive note, he is widely regarded as possessing commitment, fortitude, common sense and a determination to do England proud. The downside is that he can be seen to be moody and uninspirational. Illingworth ranted upon his departure as chairman of selectors that without a strong and responsible overseer (the sort of role that Raymond himself fulfilled, natch), Atherton's dictatorial qualities would make Saddam Hussein seem like a pussy cat. It wouldn't even be true for Nasser Hussain. It is all getting out of proportion.

Atherton goes to Zimbabwe knowing that during next summer's Ashes series, barring unforeseen disasters, he should surpass Peter May's record of skippering England in forty-one Tests. But while his dignity and unflappability has won widespread respect, the nation has never entirely warmed to him. The New Lad culture demands something a little less earnest than his discreet, slightly detached outlook.

Richard Littlejohn, in the *Daily Mail*, has accused Atherton of being 'the kind of earnest young man that believes what he reads in the *Guardian*.' If only... A week later, Athers bumps into Littlejohn in a London restaurant and complains that he has never been a *Guardian* reader in his life. I then bump into Atherton and complain that Littlejohn has now written that Atherton has insisted that he is not a *Guardian* reader. All that is needed now to complete the circle is for Littlejohn to bump into me and complain that Atherton has complained to him that I complained that he wrote that Atherton had complained that he was never a *Guardian* reader. It's high-powered conversations like these that make journalism so appealing.

Since Illingworth's departure, Atherton has finally won true influence over the direction of English cricket. This is very much his winter. Illingworth gives the impression that he believes the duty of all players under thirty should be to listen to advice wisely offered from people twice their age who are running the show. Apart from that, their sole responsibility is to be in the peak of physical condition, so allowing youngsters to dream of emulating them and older men to recall those glorious days before their own deterioration began to set in. It is a cricketing version of knowing your place, respecting your elders, awaiting your turn. The mood is so entrenched that, rather than encouraging a two-way dialogue in which young people can learn, it produces a hostile reaction in which the generations remain divided. It explains why Will Carling, when he was England's rugby union captain, frustratedly referred to the Old Farts.

The new mood of consensus sought by Atherton and England's coach David Lloyd is a far healthier state of affairs. Lloyd can still claim to be in tune with modern players; unlike Illy, he does not think that Kula Shaker is an ice bucket for making cocktails.

Atherton has already imposed his authority by prohibiting the traditional Christmas influx of wives, girlfriends, children and nannies. England's tour of South Africa the previous winter fell apart, with Atherton's exasperation rumoured to have reached its height when he was asked to draw up a baby-sitting rota just before he went out to bat in the Christmas Test at Port Elizabeth, and returned later to find several soiled nappies in his kit bag. OK, I just made that up. But 'hellish' was how he described it and, nearly a year later, he called a team meeting in Portugal to air his views.

Such rulings do not court popularity and, with England not due to return to London until the first week of March, it is a strained atmosphere when the party leaves Gatwick on 25 November. Graham Thorpe is given permission to leave a week late because his wife has just given birth to their first child, Henry James. Thorpey denies that the choice of names has any literary relevance. It would have been more likely had they christened the lad Stephen King.

From a cricketing perspective, Atherton has made a logical response to an unsatisfactory situation. If it is unnatural to remove players from their loved ones and pack them into twin rooms for more than fourteen weeks, then those who devised the itinerary in the first place are responsible. England could have toured Zimbabwe in November and returned home for a month off at Christmas before flying to New Zealand early in the New Year.

As a single man, though, Atherton might not entirely appreciate the risk he has taken. He is a self-contained individual who adjusts readily to a solitary and transient touring lifestyle. He actively enjoys the organisation that a hotel existence inflicts upon him: beds are made, pots are washed, books can be read. He calculates that high team spirits will enable his players to survive the absence of their loved ones.

But what about the wives? Their survival at home is much more fraught with problems. Friends who phone regularly when the family is intact can suddenly go AWOL when your husband is on another overseas tour. Children of a certain age begin to miss Daddy and their insecurity reveals itself in all manner of ways. Winter begins to bite, and with its descent come the endless head colds, the plumbing problems and all the things that you promised to sort out before you went, but never quite found the time. The long-distance phone calls become more and more agitated. The emptiness and frustration once the receiver is replaced become more and more evident.

The arrival of the family at Christmas is a convenient oasis – a twelve-week separation becomes five weeks apart followed by the bribe of a fortnight's holiday in the sun. By the time the tan fades, the family is about to be reunited. Without it, all manner of family irritations may occur that Atherton never remotely hears about. I write in support of Atherton's wives-and-family ban, and then arrange to escape from the Zimbabwe tour a few days early to meet Janice and the kids in Sydney. It is uncomfortably close to double standards, and I soon wonder whether I've got it all wrong.

There is another absentee in Zimbabwe. Dominic Cork will join the party after New Year in New Zealand, which will give him time to sort out the complications of a failed marriage.

These days there are more divorces over the course of a year in England than weddings. Few of us can travel away from home for such long periods without a quiet prayer that our relationships back home can survive the strain.

English first-class cricketers are the most overloaded in the world. One statistic doing the rounds shows that Australia's chief strike-bowler, Glenn McGrath, played one hundred fewer days' cricket than Cork in the past year, which says it all. In an attempt to regain freshness, England's preparatory week in the Algarve has concentrated on fitness to the exclusion of cricket practice, under the guidance of Dean Riddle, a fitness instructor seconded from Leeds rugby league team.

'I don't care if no one picks up a bat or a ball until we get to Zimbabwe,' says Atherton. Our Test players play so much that their love for the game pales, with many of our young fast bowlers collecting their first stress fracture of the back before their first girlfriends. Until that problem is addressed, our chances of success at international level remain scant.

I toy briefly with imposing a ban on wives and girlfriends at Thorner next summer. As the last thing most of them want to do is watch a bunch of sporting inadequates making fools of themselves, it might prove a highly popular move. But eventually I decide against it. Janice might assume that encouraging her own absence is the first step towards spending my Saturday afternoons with the family, which would be unfortunate as I aim to struggle on for a few more years yet. Then it must not be forgotten that Carol Wharton breezes in occasionally to bully 200 Club debts out of our most reluctant contributors, and if she withdraws her labour it would put us £1,200 a year down straight away. And the ex-captain is starry-eyed and in love, so in April he will no doubt be in emotional need of an affectionate tea-time delivery of freshly warmed socks. Most importantly, we might also be forced to ban Dawn, who makes the teas. This would be unfortunate now that her chocolate sponge cake has begun to rise so reliably. More reliably than the team, anyway.

It is with such idle thoughts passing through my mind that

I board a train at York station, with ample time to catch the 21.25 British Airways flight from Gatwick. An hour later I awake with considerable discontent as the train clatters across the Tyne Bridge into Newcastle station, some eighty miles further north. It has not been a propitious start.

5
Taxi!

You're cutting it a bit fine aren't you to get to Gatwick for a flight at twenty past nine we won't get to Victoria till gone eight the traffic these days you just can't move whatever the time of day is although I suppose Sunday mornings normally aren't too bad it's these ramps they're putting down all over London to slow down the traffic I ask you why aren't they trying to quicken up the traffic that's what they should be doing it stands to reason so where are you going then oh Zimbabwe so are you going to be with the England cricket team...

    'Ehhm, yes, I...'

...Oh really that must be a good job but they are a shower aren't they I mean I just don't know what's gone wrong with our sport these days we're losing everything even against all these darkie nations and we always used to give those a good hiding as a matter of course you could always depend on it people say they're getting better but I don't know it's not as if they have the sort of food or schools that we do so do you think we'll do well out there then this Atherton is he a nice bloke he always seems so miserable on the telly that's what people think I reckon he looks like he needs a good night out that's what he needs that's what they all need come to think of it although I suppose you press boys wouldn't be too happy if they stayed out drinking all night not that people drink like they used to I mean with the breathalyser and whatsit you just can't take the risk specially with Christmas coming up you can't move for cops stopping people around here the traffic just comes to a halt not that I've had a night out for nearly three weeks what with driving this cab around all the time I was up at five this morning and I don't reckon I'll finish until two this morning the wife says she never sees me not that I think that bothers her too much harrgh harrgh and Christmas won't be too much fun will it with Atherton banning all the wives and kids some people reckon it's a bit queer but you can't concentrate if you have the kids hanging around I reckon anyway I mean what would people think if I had my lads hanging around in the back of the cab whenever I had a fare not that they would want to now they've grown up there wouldn't be much room in the back they're both big lads harrgh harrgh it's all that boxing they did when they were growing up people seem to be against it these days but I reckon a bit of pain doesn't do any harm if it teaches you to respect authority...

'It depends really, if...'

...and they've never been in a bit of trouble either of 'em apart from a spot of bother at that pub in the East End a few years ago but the eldest says he wasn't involved and I believe him five times a week he used to box when he was a youngster all the kids did down on the marshes the Hackney marshes aye you had to because it was a hard upbringing and the schools they all used to encourage it then he had a teacher called Mr Greaves or something who didn't have another subject he couldn't have taught anything else to save his life but he could teach my lads how to box yes and cricket and football too but now he'd need to teach maths or chemistry or something not that any of them can be bothered to spend their Saturday mornings taking school sport anymore you had to be a good player even to get into the Hackney third team and enthusiastic nobody was more enthusiastic than me although I was never very good to be truthful it'll be about five past eight I reckon guv'nor if we can just get through this bit it's always busy what with the theatres although most of it seems to be going down Shaftesbury Avenue so we should be alright and then you'll probably catch the ten past if you're lucky then about forty minutes to Gatwick course you'll have to take the transit to the north terminal lemme see that will make it ten forty fifty ten to nine that is a bit tight innit you'll catch it you'll catch it don't you worry...

'I hope...'

...not that you've missed much they've lost a match already haven't they they're just not good enough that's what people think I mean you should know the answers what with your job like I said it's the schools what are to blame I mean your Labour government tried to ban competitive sport and wanted lads like mine to go ballroom dancing and stuff like that just imagine it the size of 'em and then when the Tories got in and you thought everything would get better they went and sold off all the playing fields a crime that was you can't produce top sportsmen if you don't teach 'em how to play when they're kids it stands to reason although Mr Major seems to like his sport he does and he's bidding for the World Cup football isn't he so he seems on the right lines do you think we'll get that then I don't know I reckon we'll have to watch out for the Germans but it's always like that with the bloody Germans harrgh harrgh and OK you got the fat boys who hated the cross-country running down at Hackney when I was at school but we all hated the lessons I mean we never passed any exams so when it came to football or cricket not that our cricket square was any good really it was a chance to get our own back and it wasn't long before the fat boy ended up in the mud not that he minded not that he had to mind come to think of it harrgh harrgh but they enjoyed it or at least some of 'em did if I'm being honest now Colin Milburn he was a fatty wasn't he and he did alright at cricket although he's dead now poor bloke like a lot of 'em are I suppose that's what you find as you get older but all this fitness training can be taken so far if you ask me it's all sit-ups and weight training these days all that aerobic stuff or something I don't pretend to know much about that we never had that down on the marshes when I was a lad although it was bloody cold with that wind sweeping across the football pitch especially in winter although you'll be missing most of that I suppose well here we are then there's no point going round the front cos we'll just get snarled up in traffic but if you just nip down through that doorway and turn right you might just catch it if you're lucky so that'll be twelve quid then I've got some change somewhere I can never find it quickly when I need to and I'll have to have a dig around for a receipt what's that then oh thanks very much sir you make sure you have a good trip sir.

WINTER 1996–7

WINTER 1986-7

6
The Forgotten Art

LIFE becomes more emotional on tour, and if I mention this to people halfway down their third bottle of Shiraz, they concede it's a widely shared sensation. All that in-bred English self-control dissipates and the world takes on strange and heightened sensations. This explains why most days I want to tour for ever and other days I never want to tour again.

When I slap the CD player on and Kula Shaker sing about 'a long lonely road', it is easy to fall prey to lurking homesickness, even though, more often than not, I know I'm thoroughly enjoying myself. Often, it can be readily explained, such as the times I phone the family late at night (or at least late at night for me, they might be just having breakfast) and Janice puts the kids on the line and Richard tells me with innocent excitement which Thomas the Tank Engine figures have been revealed on the advent calendar over the past few days, or Jennifer just giggles away with excitement. Then there are the bad days – the betrayal days – when they refuse to talk at all.

On tour the weather always seems warmer, the colours stronger, the people more immediately congenial; summer seems to last for ever. Imagination runs free. Cricket, by its very nature, provides contemplative days, and the moment you retreat from the bars and the restaurants, it tacks on contemplative evenings. There are no bills to pay, often no TV of any consequence to watch, no comforting routine.

Many tour experiences are ephemeral. You do meet a lot of bores, most of whom ask questions such as 'Do you know the players?' and 'Is Atherton really as miserable as he sounds?' But diverting people also continually flit through your life, their entrance and exit largely unannounced, with the likelihood you will never see most of them again.

On tour most of us invariably drink too much and stay up

too late. Welcome to the roller-coaster. The easiest state in which to face up to an empty hotel bedroom is one of complete exhaustion, or preferably inebriation. Guilt then persuades you to counter this by going for a queasy jog down the road in the heat of the day while still severely dehydrated. Flies hanging around a jogging sports journalist invariably become alcoholics.

The England caravan is away for four months this winter and for the players, the emotions can run even deeper. Their every move is monitored and analysed. England cricket tours are a perpetual soap opera, where the characters do the most outrageous things and careers – lives even – can be changed over a matter of weeks.

Michael Atherton is made keenly aware of this early in the tour as England lose in three days to Mashonaland. His chronic back problem has returned and as he waits for another bout of injections to work their miracle, he walks around in the stiff, upright manner of an African balancing a jug of water on his head. He is not yet thirty and the next few weeks could well decide whether he skippers England against the Australians next summer or begins to wonder what the hell to do with the rest of his life. He is also in considerable discomfort. And people take him to task for not always looking idyllically happy!

Tours also offer a constant reminder of the passage of time: is it really six years since England 'A' toured Zimbabwe, or a year since Jack Russell's monumental batting resistance alongside Atherton in Johannesburg, or even a fortnight since England waved goodbye to wives, partners and children at Gatwick, tightening expressions and then seat belts before taking off for another winter's examination? Things are rushing on too quickly for my liking. I ring Janice and ask her to arrange a party to celebrate Labour's likely spring election victory and suggest inviting about two hundred people. The tour experience often makes me want to assemble much of my life in one room. Janice quietly suggests that half-a-dozen people round for dinner might be a better idea.

Most revealing on tour are the experiences born of a different culture. New places, like people, are discovered then half-forgotten with no certainty that they will ever be seen again. Escape the artificial restrictions of the luxury chain hotels, and anything can befall you.

Winston Bynorth – a freelance photographer better known as 'Mutley', after the grinning dog in *Wacky Races* – joins me in trying to summon a late-night taxi in the centre of Harare. Things are soon out of control as half-a-dozen 'runners' take it upon themselves to lend assistance, careering up and down the street in exchange for a tip. To add to the confusion, a Rixi taxi (with doors as creaking and dubiously hinged as Atherton's back) conveniently draws up alongside us. This causes the two most eagle-eyed of our cab hunters sprint back in panic, insist that the taxi has arrived through *their* exertions, and clamour for payment. My suggestion to Mutley that he pay one and I pay another goes awry when inadvertently we both tip the same bloke. I will no longer scoff critically when a Great Britain relay squad screws up on the baton handover.

The overtipped runner immediately scarpers with his riches, pursued by his scrawnier rival who is soon outpaced (largely because his shoes have no laces), doubles back to the car and clings to the passenger door to demand his rightful payment. The cabbie panics and, as we thrust some more money the runner's way, we slew around a corner and he falls into the dust. He rises with a waved fist, but not before checking that the currency is legal. This escapade proves so all-consuming that we barely notice the figure clinging to the other passenger window, hawking drugs. I am beginning to wonder if I have already had some.

It is precisely because touring can inflate the senses so much that those running English cricket should give more urgent consideration to the psychology of touring. Players away from their friends and families for so long must be taught how to combat homesickness and retain fresh and active minds. Rest periods are essential in professional sport.

When the opportunity presents itself, players must be encouraged to escape the grind of hotel-room-to-cricket-ground. It is plainly ridiculous when England waver for weeks before deciding that they can, after all, cram in a visit to Victoria Falls.

Cricket's administrators must also give serious consideration to enlightening their tourists about the country they are about to visit. They cannot expect a junior player to travel confidently around Zimbabwe on the back of a GCSE grade C in geography, a tour booklet full of hotel telephone numbers and a vague memory of a couple of ITV news stories about how a drought in Zimbabwe a couple of years ago was killing all the animals. We are entirely failing to educate our young sportsmen about how to travel with open, optimistic and inquisitive minds.

However grandly England's educated elite might regard itself, however much pride we might draw from our history of exploration, we have rarely been more insular in our attitudes. Package tourists flock to Majorca in search of fish and chips and Tetley bitter and look askance when they cannot buy Weetabix at the hotel supermarket. The country, egged on by irresponsible media, lapses into xenophobia given the slightest mention of the European Community. Why are they wasting so much money? Why are they so unfair to British beef ? Why do they want to take the bend out of the banana? Now we have stopped trying to conquer the rest of the world, it is high time that someone taught us how to enjoy it in a new light.

The widespread collapse of cricket in the comprehensive sector is an obvious and direct source of England's problems. But when it comes to explaining England's lousy record overseas (remember: one series win in ten years), why stop there? Blame can also be placed on the failure of the education system, our political leaders and our mass media to produce a more positive and imaginative outlook. As a nation, we have become increasingly suspicious, self-seeking, cynical and introverted.

David Lloyd is trying his utmost. He managed an England Under-19 squad in Zimbabwe last winter and he has advised the players for an hour or so about what they might expect. He has also issued an Australian-produced booklet about dealing with the media, all about turning negatives into positives. It is all admirable stuff, although an hour's advice is not enough, especially for young adults whose talent at cricket has meant they have had little chance to experience any wider form of life since their mid teens. To educate England's players about Zimbabwe should take a couple of days.

For instance, just look at the difficulties experienced by Phil Tufnell over the years. His overseas trips have been eventful, to say the least. The Middlesex left-arm spinner has only just been forgiven for some traumatic outbursts in Australia two years ago. The cause of his agitation was the split from his girlfriend Jane McEvoy and a violent dispute over visiting rights to their daughter Ellie. The previous English summer, he had admitted two charges of causing actual bodily harm and had been fined a total of £1,050, including £250 compensation. He was also threatened with having his spinning finger broken - although, in this case, not by the judge.

By the time England left for Australia, Tufnell had married the new woman in his life, Lisa, a former British Airways stewardess, but his personal problems remained highly volatile. Eventually, the stress of trying to combat it all from 12,000 miles away proved too much and he flew into a rage. Barely a week had elapsed when, in his own words: 'I was sitting there in the hospital with some bloke shining a light in my eyes and saying, "Tell me about your childhood," and I just thought to myself, "What the hell am I doing here? This is pathetic."'

Only Tufnell's pleading for leniency (plus the management's ingrained fear of bad publicity – the story did not break until after the tour) persuaded England not to send him home. They fined him £1,000 instead and washed their hands of him the moment he returned to England. It seemed that his international career was over.

At the pre-tour camp in Portugal, Tufnell had faced up to the intensive physical training with the determination of a man not wanting to give it away again. For someone whose idea of physical exertion is to roll *two* fags before breakfast, his bonhomie was stretched to the limit. 'Hello, Tuffers,' said one journalist cheerily as he completed another set of sit-ups. 'And you can fuck off,' was Tuffers' matey response. When he had regained his breath, his mood changed. 'Sorry, mate, it's all this training,' he said. Two extreme moods, within half an hour, both equally honest. With Tufnell, what you see is what you get.

Three years ago, in India, Tufnell uttered one sentence that became infamous. 'Done the elephants, done the poverty, might as well go home, mate,' he said. Many commentators in England pounced on that one line to pontificate about English cricket's collapsing morals. Now, I'm as critical of England's touring attitudes as anybody, but Tufnell did not deserve to become the fall guy. He made that comment in a press box in Delhi, and when I mentioned it in the *Guardian* some days later to illustrate his unsettled mood, I was at pains to put it into context, to stress that I had egged him on a bit and he had responded by joshing in kind.

Back in London, the context mattered not a jot. Tufnell's one line had empowered a chain of thought, offered a convenient theory, and they were going to milk it as much as they could. Four years on, people still do. Golden rule in journalism: always suspect the feature writer who wasn't there.

I actually wrote a paper on 'The Art of Touring' last year for the Acfield Report, an eminently forgettable investigation into English cricket's ills, which came up with some fairly wishy-washy conclusions, along the lines of 'twenty-four per cent of respondents think that selection committees should drink red wine and sit in a horseshoe formation, but sixty-two per cent prefer old-fashioned whisky and oak tables, with the rest undecided.' These conclusions were immediately resisted as dangerous radicalism by the representatives of the first-class counties.

On reflection, to suggest that I wrote a paper might be putting it too strongly. I bet Acfield never knew. After enduring a rather peevish ear-bashing at Old Trafford one morning (the M62 traffic had been horrendous), Lancashire's chairman Bob Bennett had invited me to contribute my views on a more formal basis. As Bennett would habitually adopt a knowing smile even if about to face a terrorist firing squad, it was impossible to decide if he was being serious without plugging him into a lie-detector test. The fact that the Acfield Report was concerned specifically with the management and selection of the English team suggested he might not be, but he was on the Acfield committee and insisted that he was being genuine. So I wrote it all the same. So far, in Zimbabwe, England are doing precisely the opposite of what I advocated. The paper to this day is probably providing excellent scrap paper for shopping lists in the Bennetts' Isle of Man tax retreat.

Perhaps God can help England's players to tour more successfully. He is represented in Zimbabwe, for ten days at least, by Andrew Wingfield-Digby, a director of the Christians in Sport movement. Even if Wingers-Diggers is undoubtedly the silliest nickname ever invented on the cricket field (and there have been more than enough), I am prepared to overlook this on the grounds that he is a decent and positive chap.

Wingfield-Digby possesses an honest faith that he has been called by God to reach the world of professional sport for Christ, which does not entirely delight the less God-fearing members of the English media, one of whom sarcastically remarks how fortunate it is that God came up with the suggestion of watching world-class sport rather than a lifetime providing succour for the poor in Rwanda.

His role as England chaplain has always been unofficial, but he was sacked all the same, eighteen months ago, when

Raymond Illingworth, flexing his muscles as chairman of selectors, banned God and mobile phones on the same day. Now Illingworth has gone, Wingfield-Digby is available to dispense spiritual comfort again and, for those players more obsessed with man-made communications, Zimbabwe are just about to launch a cellular network. Judging by the rest of Zimbabwe's communications industry, it is to be hoped that lines to God prove rather more reliable. Wingfield-Digby's philosophy of touring should be imprinted on the brain of every member of the England Cricket Board ever involved in the drawing-up of an overseas tour itinerary. 'Professional sport has to be seen in the context of a person's whole life,' he says. 'There needs to be a balance in their lives, taking into account their physical, mental and spiritual health. If you are playing, or practising, every day and otherwise remain cooped up in a hotel room, it must be hard to remain sharp.' Amen to that.

Meanwhile, in the Winston Churchill lounge at Gatwick Airport, Ian Botham gives a press conference before joining England as Team Motivator. 'The lads need to get out at night and have a few beers,' he says. It strikes me that, in their own way, Botham and Wingfield-Digby are saying largely the same thing.

7

Masters Of Disaster

IT is the eve of the first Test in Bulawayo, and England are already in crisis. Three defeats, offset only by a token victory against Matabeleland, have caused consternation. We have been here little more than three weeks and already Michael Atherton's prospects of leading England in next summer's Ashes series are being openly questioned. The Weakest Test Nation in the World vs The Side that Cannot Tour: it all has the makings of an uplifting contest.

England have prepared for the first Test by losing their opening one-day match against a President's XI (we agree to put that down to acclimatisation), by becoming the first touring side to lose a first-class match to Mashonaland (acclimatisation excuses that one as well), and by batting so appallingly in Bulawayo that Zimbabwe won their first one-day international for ten matches (acclimatisation again, obviously). By now England are acclimatised to losing, if nothing else. For England this is a no-win tour, but no one expected them to take that so literally.

All this talk of acclimatisation is strangely reminiscent of England's defeat in the Calcutta Test on the 1993 tour of India when Ted Dexter, then the chairman of the England committee, suggested in mitigation that the players were finding it difficult to breathe because of all the pollution, and announced an immediate investigation into smog levels at Test venues around the world. Nearly four years later, you will not be surprised to learn, the findings have yet to be announced. I think we need to know. I reckon the Dexter Smog Table is lying underneath my paper on The Art of Touring on the Bennett kitchen table.

If there is any consolation for some of the leftover British colonials watching England collapse against Mashonaland from the upstairs bar of the Harare Sports Club, it is that they clearly have little idea what is happening. The first alcoholic drink arrives soon after breakfast and then they probably imagine they are watching Cowdrey and Dexter putting the colony to the sword, not England's vaunted top six being embarrassed by James Kirtley, who has played only a dozen games for Sussex.

Many of them still speak whenever possible of Rhodesia, and prefer to imagine that Robert Mugabe does not exist, even though his residence is just across the road and his motorcade roars past, lights flashing and sirens blaring, every time he needs to pop out for a pint of milk. Mention how wonderfully relaxed Zimbabwe is and there is a fair chance that one of them will breathe: 'Ah, but you don't know the half of it. The blacks can be difficult...' Best not to give them the opportunity.

Among the many innovations that David Lloyd has introduced to try to rejuvenate English cricket – dressing-room maxims, Churchill speeches and fitness camps, to name but three – he has yet to turn to the power of prayer, but that seemed his best option after Mashonaland required only three rain-hit days to achieve a seven-wicket victory.

Kirtley is a fringe county player, but no fool, far from it. He made a favourable impression during his debut season for Sussex and is blessed with a consistent outswinger, as he proves while returning match figures of seven for 88. He is the son of the mayor of Eastbourne, and the grandson of a vicar, and is so polite that when I get this the wrong way round in the *Guardian*, he virtually apologizes to me for *my* mistake, an attitude that all those involved in sport should adopt immediately.

He imagined that his association with England this winter might amount to a spot of net bowling, a learning session or two in the bar, and the chance to relax in the sun and watch some Test cricket. Instead, he makes a key contribution to English cricket's latest embarrassment. England are bowled out for 197 and 180, twice losing their first four wickets before making 30. The first hour's batting in the Tests will be crucial.

Atherton takes England's defeat against Mashonaland badly. His chronic back problem has flared up again, which leads to predictable rumours that he has a screw loose. He must have, skippering this lot. He has sneaked away from the ground for two injections at a private clinic in Harare and prefers that the media know nothing about it. Predictably, it soon becomes common knowledge and, after the match, England's captain is interrogated about his fitness. Adopting his most stubborn expression, he keeps insisting that he is OK. The kindest intepretation is that his answers are misleading, but that the sham is preferable to sounding like a Whingeing Pom and so is acceptable in the circumstances. To sound as if he is making excuses after a humiliating defeat would not serve England's purpose. But to be evasive does not exactly help either.

While Atherton is at the clinic, a woman dies and a boy is brought in with horrific injuries after a road accident. This provides Atherton with a deeper perspective than that allowed to those of us charged with writing another thousand words about the state of his back.

'The losing of a cricket match was not enough to send me into a deep depression after that lot,' he states. 'My back is my problem, it is not a matter of national concern.' Unfortunately, it is. Atherton, as England captain, is viewed as public property, whether he likes it or not. (He doesn't like it, and never will.) Medical advice is that as much as possible he should stand in the field with his arms folded, but when he does everyone complains about his negative body language. Captaincy must seem an unendingly wearying business.

Atherton's unwillingness to glory in minor injuries reveals his serious lack of grounding in village cricket. Had life favoured him with such a background, he would have had no second thoughts about covering himself so thickly in Ralgex that the press would be able to smell his injury. Then he would have approached his inquisitors with a fake limp, a pained and rueful expression and a succession of put-upon sighs. Asked if he was OK, he would have grimaced and said:

'Well, you can pick me for next Saturday, but I'll have to ring you in the week when I see how it goes. I can feel it now, oowww, when I go like that.' He would then have braved the pub 'for half-an-hour', cheered up after six pints and finished the evening dancing on the table. A fortnight later, after another disheartening duck, he would suffer a temporary relapse and skip a weekend to take the family to Scarborough.

If Zimbabwe's entire pool of useful cricketers (plus partners) descended upon downtown Harare, they could not fill the dance floor at Sandros night club, and it is not a very big dance floor. Whatever the official title of the opposition, the same faces turn up time and time again. It is a rule of thumb in Zimbabwean cricket that whatever the question, the answer is always either Guy Whittall or Grant Flower. Amazingly, after all these years, nobody has yet realized that Eddo Brandes, the burly chicken farmer, is actually Dave Houghton in a straggly wig and with an extra pillow down his shirt. Henry Olonga plays an entire troupe of promising black fast bowlers. If England cannot win here, then the England Cricket Board's new national pyramid is clearly upside down.

It is a journalistic habit to mark such giant-killing occasions by recording what jobs the victors do for a living, and Mashonaland provides the usual list of tobacco farmers and big-game hunters. But a greater insight might have been offered by wondering what jobs *our* lot should be forced to take up should they continue to lose in such embarrassing circumstances.

Atherton might like to become a scientist, where he could develop something to prevent English cricketers becoming rusty after long lay-offs. The addition of a clipped moustache would enable Alec Stewart to consider an army commission, where he would rapidly rise to the rank of sergeant-major and spend the rest of his days barking out orders. Graham Thorpe could become the manager of a moderately successful non-league football team. Alan Mullally could become a guitar-strumming tour guide for an alternative travel company offering back-packing holidays in Nepal. Jack Russell would be a village postman, the sort who would always wake you up at 7am with an overly-cheerful whistle. Nick Knight would manage a health club. After a brief period of stardom, attempts to reinvent Darren Gough as a TV children's entertainer would prove unsuccessful.

This England squad has been conducting itself so professionally off the field that when Ian Botham arrives next week as motivator-in-chief, he will struggle to buy someone half a shandy. But when they lose to Mashonaland in only three days, they are shocked into a drink or two. To someone in England, enduring the daily office grind, the sight of an English cricket team singing and laughing in the bar of the Sheraton Hotel within hours of another national humiliation might sound disgraceful. But it is apt, because it pulls spirits together. Robert Croft does a spirited rendition of 'Great Balls Of Fire'; if only England could find some.

Ill-feeling still festers, though. The morning after the Mashonaland defeat, John Emburey, England's bowling coach, braves an interview with Garry Richardson on BBC Radio 4. 'Bad start, John, Simon Wilde in *Times* worst defeat in history,' is the gist of the question from Richardson, who prefers to broadcast without verbs and who could well be reduced to virtual silence if he ever falls out with nouns as well. Emburey is so stung by *The Times*'s assessment of the defeat that he accuses Wilde of being late for the match. This is a risible response – England might as well not have turned up at all – but *The Times*'s switchboard is jammed by retired colonels demanding an explanation. A power cut, jammed hotel lifts and Rixi cab-drivers who accept clients with no guarantee that they will ever be able to start the car are excuses enough.

This incident has a hilarious conclusion during England's one-day match against Matabeleland in Bulawayo. England have solved their transport problems by requisitioning a coach marked 'Bulawayo Girls High School,' but we are all answerable to the whims of Rixi Cabs. Four of us arrive eight overs late after a taxi takes us to the wrong ground. Hearing cheers as we cross the car park, we find with relief that England have in fact just lost their first wicket and happen to be sneaking past the visitors' dressing-room just as Atherton is stalking back. 'Nice of you lot to turn up on time,' he curses with the traditional bonhomie of a batsman who has just offered short-midwicket some catching practice. This causes suppressed chortles and, after suitable calming-down time, Atherton strolls along to the press marquee to share the joke. Wild Man, determined not to be caught out again, has been sitting there since about 6am...

Press marquees have their charm. Normally hermetically sealed from the action, they offer a more intimate view of the action: sights as well as sounds, which doubles the likelihood of staying awake. Not everyone likes such elemental exposure, however. For example:

David Norrie (News of the World): 'What's that bloody noise?'
Colleague: 'It's a bird, Norrers.'
Norrie (grunting): 'Oh, s'pose that's alright then.'

At least England manage to record a first-class victory by beating Matabeleland by 115 runs at Bulawayo Athletic Club, as Darren Gough takes advantage of a quickish pitch to record career-best bowling figures of 11 for 139. Gough is fired up by the sight of one Matabeleland player, Dash Vaghmaria, fielding in a Yorkshire capped sweater which was given to him by Richard Blakey during the county's pre-season tour of Zimbabwe. 'Look at 'im,' explodes Gough, pointing at an increasingly fidgety fielder. 'It took me four years to get capped. 'E's got 'is in two minutes.'

The next day Vaghmaria wisely opts to disguise himself by batting in shirt-sleeves, but Gough, brought back into the attack, has spotted his man. Surrender is his only option. Vaghmaria plays his first ball from square leg and has his stumps splayed with the next. You could almost imagine Fred Trueman looking on with satisfaction: 'Aye, not bad, lad, but ah'd av knocked 'is poles out wi't first 'un.'

It is good to see Goughie recapturing the pride and zest that was so refreshingly apparent when he broke into the England side. Since the stress fracture of his foot that cruelly cut short his tour of Australia in 1994-95, he has worn protective inner soles, but in Zimbabwe he has suffered blistered feet, so he has thrown the inner soles away. 'Ah don't need 'em,' he announces. On such discriminating medical grounds are career-threatening decisions taken. The only problem with Gough is that every time he bowls, the Barmy Army break into song again. He is the only Test bowler in the world who is best watched with a pair of foam earplugs.

The advent of the Barmy Army, a loose affiliation of England's more vociferous supporters, has not been welcomed by the traditional cricket spectator – or, indeed, the majority of the media – who prefer to regard cricket as an opportunity for peaceful contemplation. Others talk fondly of the 'longueurs' of the game, which, as the Concise Oxford Dictionary defines that as a 'tedious stretch of time', might not seem all that worth preserving. The Barmies, with their repetitive chants and their Union Jack shirts, are persistently dismissed as moronic, but fears that cricket is about to be swamped by soccer-style hooliganism still seem exaggerated. The Barmies also have the advantage of being both young and enthusiastic, and English cricket, if it is to survive, needs both of those qualities. When they turfed up in Australia on the 1994-95 tour, back-packing and burger-biting their way from place to place, they were widely praised in a country delighted by their lack of 'English reserve'. In Bendigo, the mayor even posed alongside them for the local newspaper. Most of the England players, preferring blind loyalty to critical analysis, love them for their simple and unaffected support.

During a rain break, as England move towards victory, Jack Russell lightens the collective mood by pencil sketching

Tufnell, a portrait that will become a collector's item if only because Tuffers is not smoking a fag.

'Cor, Jack, you ain't 'arf made me look miserable,' says Tuffers.

'You *are* miserable,' says Jack. He had better not follow up with a sketch of Atherton looking fed up, otherwise the *Sunday Times* will feel obliged to criticize his attitude again.

Graham Otway is the proud perpetrator of The First Piece That Has Pissed Off Our Brave Boys – an article in the *Sunday Times* which contends that Atherton is largely responsible for a bunch of miserable tourists – and he spends several days bracing himself for the inevitable confrontation. 'Where's the frog?' asks Atherton accusingly, which invites sniggers within the Bulawayo press marquee at a previously unheard nickname. The next time Otters strolls towards the tent, he is treated to a rendition of 'The Frog Chorus' by Paul McCartney. The song's refrain, We All Stand Together, is not altogether convincing when hummed by a bunch of journalists.

Press box gossip also concerns which Sky TV broadcaster will be persuaded to do a bungee jump at Victoria Falls. Charles Colvile is the popular choice, but he has eschewed the opportunity. Too expensive to insure, probably. It reminds me of those childhood hours watching Blue Peter when John Noakes always took on the dangerous jobs while Peter Purves cut Fairy liquid bottles into interesting shapes. Colvile has chosen the Purves route, which involves standing in front of colourfully ethnic fruit and vegetable stalls, and I can't say I blame him.

Instead, Sky's rumoured victim is now Brian Murgatroyd, whose talents as a cricketing memory man have become famous in an oddball magazine segment on Sky called 'Stump Murgers'. In this, Murgatroyd, wearing full batsman's regalia, fields all kinds of weird questions about 1920s batting partnerships with barely a pause for thought. He then hits an imaginary six, with a theatrical flourish at the top of his back-swing that suggests he should have gone into amateur dramatics; with that memory, he would never have needed a prompter. The whole thing is completely dotty. As I can barely remember England's side in the last Test, I never fail to be massively impressed.

Medical warnings that bungee jumping can adversely affect the central nervous system could make 'Stump Murgers' even more interesting in future. Imagine him being asked which Test ground has staged most centuries by Australian left-handers and replying, without delay, 'Three bags of chips and a tub of treacle, please.'

The one-day international is staged at Queen's Sports Club (or sometimes at Queens Sports Club, because no one seems to have a clue whether it has an apostrophe), the venue for the first Test. England stutter to 152 all out, and only get that far because Nasser Hussain digs in for 49 not out. The middle order falters against John Rennie, a bespectacled medium-pacer who is clearly more dangerous than he looks. How does he look? Well, you know the player who wanders up to your ground on a Saturday afternoon halfway through the season and says he might fancy a game, and although you have him in the back of your mind, you never quite get round to picking him because Rex is fit again after his prostate operation, and you then discover to your dismay at the start of the following season that he has joined a better league and has just taken six for 40? That's John Rennie.

When Zimbabwe collapse to 106 for seven in reply, England seem to have found an escape clause. But Zimbabwe's captain Alistair Campbell comes in at number seven with a scarred face and bruised hand (suffered in a collision with Guy Whittall in fielding practice) and knocks off the runs in no time. It is the first time that Zimbabwe have beaten a Test side in a one-day international by batting second. Campbell announces that they have never been more confident about winning a Test series.

Old Etonians are trained to find explanations for occasions of national disaster and Johnny Barclay, a tour manager awash with boyish enthusiasm, excels himself in vacuous words of encouragement. Imagine that it's like a play, he tells those he feels may lend a sympathetic ear. We've had a few little hiccups, but on the opening night everything will turn out fine. Now, it may be a tour manager's duty to promote a cheerful line, but the Barclay's 'It'll Be Alright On The Night' approach abandons all pretence at intellect. England have been colliding with the scenery and duffing their lines so badly that to feign a lack of concern is nonsensical.

Barclay's willingness to express such guff comes from the fact that he is privately appalled by what he regards as media cynicism, and so prefers to treat all-comers with contempt. The media, for its part, is increasingly unconvinced by his perpetual retreat into jolly, lightweight waffle and his inability to arrange the simplest press conference with any degree of professionalism. Better is expected from a man who is being so determinedly groomed for an influential role in English cricket for many years to come.

If there is a choice between interviewing Atherton in a quiet room with microphone facilities or in the middle of a field directly below a loudspeaker blaring out African dance music, then Barclay has displayed a wondrous knack for organising the latter. 'I'm not very experienced at this,' he suggests disarmingly. Getaway! England's retreat into such amateurism is mind-boggling. Supporters wander into official press conferences bearing cans of lager and ask questions like, 'I bet you'd fancy a pint of Boddies now, Athers?' I have an overpowering desire to find out where they work, drunkenly gatecrash *their* office on my return to England and try to mess up their afternoon.

Faced by such an atmosphere, Atherton reluctantly mumbles stock replies to stock questions, which nobody can hear anyway, except listeners to the BBC who complain that he sounds depressed and miserable. He has actually had the longest and loudest laugh in Zimbabwe since the day he arrived, but it does not come across that way. His refusal to accept that he needs to cultivate a positive media image might be regarded as an admirable display of honesty in an age of spin doctors, speech writers and advisers. But the need for the game to promote itself means that somebody should have insisted that he accepts his wider responsibilities. Atherton needs to elevate his mood on TV and radio, just as he recognizes the need to lift it for a team meeting. Not to do so is a strange shortcoming in such an intelligent man.

The most distressing aspect of England's losing start in Zimbabwe is that it fits the pattern of much of the past decade, that of a limited side playing well below its potential as it finds the art of touring a total mystery. Everybody has their gruesome favourite as England's worst performance in recent memory: defeat against a West Indies Board XI in Grenada three years ago immediately after the infamous 46 all out in the Trindad Test; the second of two defeats against the Australian Academy at North Sydney the following year; or the defeat against Zimbabwe in the 1992 World Cup at Albury when they were haunted by Eddo Brandes, the rotund chicken farmer. Those performances were confirmation of tours that were beyond repair. On the eve of the first Test in Bulawayo, this tour is not beyond redemption. But the time for improvement is now.

8
Balderdash

EVERY tour has a song. It is just that the one that will always remind me of Zimbabwe 1996 is so bloody irritating. Rarely an hour passes around this England team without somebody caterwauling 'Wonderwall'. If Oasis claimed copyright for every time it has tunelessly wafted from hotel windows, dressing-rooms and airport lounges, the Gallagher brothers could fall out for life and still have millions in the bank for their retirement.

Alan Mullally often seems to be humming it to himself in the outfield, or in the middle of a bowling spell, and it will be no surprise one day to find his guitar perched alongside the Gatorade at third man. Even in these days of tense media-player relations, most tourists manage to mumble some greeting in a hotel corridor. Mullally generally sings the line of a song instead. I've been trying to learn D-Ream's 'Things Can Only Get Better' so I can retaliate the next time we pass by.

Chief guitarist in this England troupe is Wayne Morton, a first-rate physiotherapist who, nevertheless, seems to gain as much kudos from teaching a player a new chord as he does from curing a back problem. Another of his odd jobs is to cut hair, and he receives a surprising amount of custom considering that he insists he has had no training whatsoever. The scissors he uses are the pair he normally employs to hack at the Elastoplast and clip the occasional critical press report. Ron Keeling, the nearest thing to an England travelling hairdresser (Ron has a barber's in Chorlton-cum-Hardy, a mile from Old Trafford, and first cut hair in the Lancashire dressing-room for Barry Wood nearly thirty years ago), is due in New Zealand and will have the opportunity to tidy up Wayne's most obvious errors.

Wayne also bowls in the nets, lots. This winter he has tried to add leg-spinners to a repertoire previously limited to peppery medium-pace. At Thorner it would be classified as 'fast', and as he lives about six miles away from the ground, I keep telling him that when he retires from his 'rubbing' he will make us a useful third seamer. 'Third seamer!' Wayne scoffs, deeply insulted, before striving for an extra yard of pace. Pity the England player batting against Wayne the day I suggest that he'd barely make the Thorner second team.

Other Wayne sightings logged by the press include 12th man duties, educating players in the art of fly-fishing (normally casting an imaginary line) and social secretary. Not that the job of social secretary has been too arduous in Zimbabwe. He could double up as tour manager to allow John Barclay to go home. He is held by some journalists to possess such an influence among the more impressionable members of the squad that one half expects him to be skippering by the time we arrive in New Zealand. Already, some of the players have dubbed this Wayne's Tour.

We have not been in Zimbabwe long before the usual wall of suspicion builds up between the press and the players. This is not as much a Wonderwall as a Whingeing Wall, with players taking umbrage at anything that might be intepreted as personal criticism and the press responding by grousing that most of them are overpaid, egotistical, cosseted nancy boys. It's nice to be back. The simplest way to pressurize a journalist is to invite him to share a drink at the bar and politely, though firmly, invite him to justify his opinions. Few in this England side have developed the self-possession to do this; they are desperately in need of a full-time media officer. Amazingly, respect and friendships between individuals survive all this nonsense and it is still possible for both sides to try to do a professional job in trying circumstances.

The response of the average journalist to arriving in a new town or city is obsessively to discover all its attractions in less than twenty-four hours. Good restaurants, late-night bars and companiable locals are all ticked off as proof that the England bandwagon has arrived and put down new roots.

Only then does the madness abate and it becomes acceptable to go to sleep for a few hours.

Many years ago, before TV coverage transformed them into sporting superstars, players used to tour like this as well. Now most of them prefer to order room-service and listen to 'Wonderwall'. Already Zimbabwe has been rejected as a duff country with nothing to commend it, a judgement based on little evidence and considerable prejudice. It did not help when A Man From The High Commission addressed the players at the start of the tour with a list of what they should not do: don't drink the water, don't go out at night, don't have sex, don't talk to strangers – and very few suggestions about what they might actually enjoy. By not attempting to embrace the country, they are asking for trouble. It does not augur well for results on the field. I am already regretting my support for Athers's policy of banning wives and girlfriends. The dangers of them being a distraction seem outweighed by the fact that their arrival might lighten everybody up a bit.

The media must take its share of the blame for the players' mood. It was in Ian Botham's heyday that touring attitudes began to change. England players until the early 1980s were eager to sample the wider attractions of touring (well, the bars and clubs, anyway), but tabloid newspapers despatched news reporters who filed lurid reports about Nights of Shame. Now the wheel has turned so much that players are under attack for hardly leaving their hotel rooms. Robert Croft, the spiky Glamorgan all-rounder, and the two Yorkies, Darren Gough and Chris Silverwood, do venture out from time to time – and their tour records are as good as anyone's.

Nick Knight and Jack Russell have also found time to do some painting, although whether this would have any positive effect on Russell's form is hard to gauge, as the best wicketkeeper in England is spending his time ferrying drinks. He does it with enormous enthusiasm and lots of comments about 'if a job's worth doing'. At least he is fortunate not to be twelfth-manning for himself. Players have been summoned onto the field to be reminded to soak his Weetabix in milk exactly eight minutes before the lunch interval. That's perfectionism.

These differing attitudes are undermining the relationship between the media and players, and as long as the mood remains so tense, England's prospects of winning overseas will be considerably diminished. Touring sides with a siege mentality rarely prosper as much as those who feel that they belong in the country. The press slag off the players for not recognising the wider aspect of touring, which involves socialising with the local people. The players claim that the press would exaggerate the slightest indiscretion and splash it over the front pages. Personally, I couldn't care less if half of them were discovered gang-banging the Bishop of Montevideo.

In Zimbabwe, England are playing a board game called 'Balderdash'. That is, they are playing 'Balderdash' when they are not singing 'Wonderwall'. Sometimes they do both together, which is promoted as being wonderful for team spirit and makes for a really exciting evening. David Lloyd, the team manager, is already resentful of the criticism this has received in the newspapers, especially when it is written by journalists who have spent half the day on the golf course. Understandably, he also takes umbrage at suggestions that he is operating some kind of unofficial curfew and confining players to their rooms; the fact is that most England players simply cannot imagine anywhere where they would like to go.

'It's disgusting personal criticism,' Lloyd says. 'We're professional sportsmen, we can't get drunk every night. We've had up to twelve of us playing Balderdash, laughing and joking for hours,' he says. 'We've had a grand time.'

You pays your money...

I make a mental note to ask Simon Mann, of BBC radio fame, to bring out Balderdash when he joins Thorner on our club tour to Sri Lanka in February. If we play Balderdash as much as England, it could yet be the making of us. And a squad containing sixteen batsmen, one wicketkeeper and a medium-paced dobber will need all the help it can get.

There are also more sombre stories: Steve Whiting arrives

to cover the tour for the *Sunday Mirror* and, while arranging his accreditation in central Harare, he is mugged in the street in broad daylight. The muggers have picked on a man suffering from multiple sclerosis, accompanied by his young daughter. Thankfully, they both seem none the worse for the experience. John Etheridge, *The Sun*'s man on tour, has Z$1000 (about £70) stolen from his golf bag in Harare 'somewhere on the back nine', and when the police arrive to shake a few caddies upside down some of the missing money tumbles out.

I lose the same amount in Bulawayo... and that disappeared from the hotel safe in the Holiday Inn. Nice to know that one of the world's most reputable hotel groups is making such a pig's ear of security.

Spitefully, I pin up a large notice in reception to warn all English visitors in the hotel that There Are Thieves About! The hotel management do not appreciate such an attempt at crime prevention and within an hour the notice is ripped down. It still seemed a satisfying way to get my own back.

I try to report the incident more formally.

Irate Cricket Writer: 'I've had some money stolen from the hotel safe. I'd like to formally file a complaint.'
Man On Reception: 'Yes.'
I.C.W: (many minutes later): 'About this complaint...'
M.O.R: (looking around evasively): 'Yes, sir.'
I.C.W: 'Is there a problem?'
M.O.R: 'No problem.'
I.C.W: 'I need to write down what has been stolen.'
M.O.R: 'One moment, sir.'
I.C.W: (several minutes later): 'I have a plane to catch in eight days' time. Do you think we can do it before then?'
M.O.R: (evasively): 'Have you filled in the form?'
I.C.W: 'No... I know I shouldn't ask, but do you have that form?'
M.O.R: 'I have no forms.'

I.C.W: 'I'm not surprised, there's probably been a run on them. I'd like to speak to the duty manager.'

M.O.R: 'He is not here this evening.'

I.C.W: 'Who is in charge?'

M.O.R: ' The duty manager.'

I.C.W: 'But he's not here.'

M.O.R. 'No, sir. One moment, sir. There are many people. Checking out, madam? Have you had anything from the mini bar?...'

9
Rising Sap

FREE days on tour (even unofficial ones) are a rare commodity, so four representatives of the English media pile into a taxi and head for the Matopos Hills, about half-an-hour's drive out of Bulawayo. Our driver is a sociable sort called More Blessings, though when he is turned back at the entrance to the game park – no taxis are allowed because of a tour operator's cartel, and the Zimbabwean official is resistant to our guiltily half-hearted hints about 'extra payments' – we conclude that Mixed Blessings would have been more appropriate. We return to Bulawayo with More Blessings looking a picture of despair in the rear-view mirror. He cheers up considerably when we promise that he will receive his full fare.

The journey is lightened by what the Essex scorer, Clem Driver, once scathingly dismissed as one of 'Pringle's handwritten tapes'. Derek Pringle, the former England all-rounder, is over here representing the *Independent* and has brought along some 1960s Kenyan music to put us in the mood, and most of the lyrics seem to concern what a wonderful man President Kenyatta is and how everybody should pay their taxes.

I wonder why this has never quite caught on in England. Imagine turning on Radio 1 and hearing these lyrics to a reggae beat: 'John Major, my friends, is really quite nice/ Don't pay your taxes once, but pay him them twice/ Mr John Major, he will wipe away all of your tears/ So vote him in for four more years.' On balance, I think I'll stick with Ocean Colour Scene. And even Tony Blair.

After much successful haggling, we return in an official tour minibus with a guide called Daniel whose knowledge of the sexual properties of the plant life of the Matopos is quite revealing. It is not the sort of thing you should discuss so far away from wife and family. There are so many oils and lotions on one hill in the middle of the Matopos that it is a miracle Anita Roddick has not opened up a branch of the Body Shop.

Sex life on the Matopos, in a bygone age, went something like this, or maybe not:

When man and woman become attracted, the most pressing need is that they both clean up a bit. So they wander along to the soap nettle bush and, by squeezing the bark, produce a liquid soap and splash around in a nearby river to their hearts' content.

Woman, though, is concerned that man might lose interest and turns to the assistance of the lavender cotton plant. By crushing the leaves in her fingers, she makes a perfume and applies it liberally in all the right areas.

Man is impressed. I've got to have her, and I've got to have her now, he tells his mates, but I'm not quite sure how to approach her. Get some liquor down your neck, they advise. So they all party around the base of the fig tree, where they convert the fig fruit into an intoxicating brew. Slurring Matabele war songs, man pronounces himself ready for action and, hitching up his shorts, sways off into the bush.

Man and woman get along famously and a bit of casual snogging is soon the order of the day. But friends have told them lurid stories of sexually transmitted diseases and both are wary. So they treat themselves to the healing properties of the fried egg tree. This is particularly versatile, its red sap providing dye for paintings and its wood making good furniture. But their priority is to boil the bark and roots of the tree and drink its essence. Combined with a suitable quantity of fresh meat, the STDs are successfully treated.

Man is so delighted at the way things are going that he spends another night carousing under the fig tree. But his alcohol intake has become so large that he would not manage an erection if seduced by an entire troupe of Bulawayo dancers. So he seeks the help of the sausage tree – sexual imagery clearly being as basic on the Matopos as everywhere else – and, to his relief, soon begins to throb with anticipation.

Everything is now going swimmingly: man and woman are washed clean and free of sexually transmitted diseases, woman smells delightfully, man is rarely sober, and the new furniture and abstract paintings have arrived just in time for the wedding day.

Nothing can go wrong, and for a time it doesn't. Man and woman make love and, after a short time, woman becomes pregnant. She cares for the developing embryo with various concoctions drawn from the large sour plant and settles down for a long and happy marriage. But man turns out to be dishonest and unreliable and within weeks of their wedding day is having drunken affairs on the side. Soon he deserts her. Woman is distraught and her friends advise her to abort the baby while there is still time. She accepts their urgings and swallows the poisonous long pods of the cassia bush. The village is briefly in mourning before the whole cycle begins again.

It has to be concluded that life on the Matopos was entirely obsessed with sex. Even the cave paintings are little more than early attempts at pornography. Many are indistinct and I am just admiring the thick thighs and comforting breasts of a young woman when I am informed that the breasts actually depict the buttocks of a man. 'And look at that,' says Daniel, pointing with his stick at what I had assumed to be thighs. 'That is big dick.'

It strikes me that you can interpret these worn-away scratches however you see fit. It is really a case of whatever takes your fancy.

'When you bring parties of elderly women on to these hills, do you also tell them about the big dick?' I ask Daniel.

'No,' he smiles. 'Normally they point it out to me.'

Later on, in the hills, we spot some clipspringers, which are noted for travelling around in threes: two females to every male. To a group of men thousands of miles from home, this immediately seems like a satisfying sexual arrangement . The clipspringers have not quite got it all right though, otherwise when they reached middle age they would concede the inevitable and switch to a threesome including two males and one female.

As well as Daniel, we are blessed with another expert guide. Derek Pringle spent the first eighteen years of his life in Kenya, which has given him quite an insight into the Do's and Don'ts of Africa. Wandering around a nearby dam, he explains in quick succession the ways to avoid death by lightning, being eaten alive by crocodiles or mauled by lions. As our only brush with death has been when I accidentally trod on a dung beetle, and its mate flapped its wings and flew mournfully away, his advice all seems a bit superfluous, but here goes anyway:

Lions, according to Pringle lore, are best countered by banging two sticks together, which tends to confuse them. The crocodile is more complicated. The trick here is to squeeze its mouth together, on the grounds that although it is skilled at slamming its jaws shut, it is not quite so handy at opening them. Eventually it will get bored and swim away. Good body hygiene is also an advantage. Crocs like to store a human body under the bank until the smell suggests that it has rotted to their satisfaction. Play dead, hold your breath for several hours (it has to be said there were slight flaws in the Pringle theory) and you can swim away to safety. Those with bad body odour might find themselves on the takeaway menu, which might put one or two of our lot at risk.

But it is Pringle's lightning position that causes most amusement. Zimbabwe has one of the highest lightning tolls in the world; since the start of the rains a couple of weeks ago, there have already been more than thirty deaths. The best way to ensure that the lightning does not pass through your heart or your brain is to crouch on the floor with your buttocks stuck high in the air. The worst you can expect, in this case, is a bad case of inflamed haemmorrhoids. Considering Cecil Rhodes's supposed sexual preferences, an approaching storm must have caused quite a stir among white settlers on the Matopos: 'Come on, boys, there's a storm brewing, everybody into the lightning position....'

We are not laughing in the press tent at Bulawayo Athletic Club a few days later when a violent storm stops play and forked lightning strikes a TV aerial only fifteen yards away. The sight of several distinguished and white-faced cricket writers adopting the lightning position with indelicate haste is a sight I had never anticipated I would witness. My view is partially obscured, however, by the fact that I have just dived under the nearest desk.

10

We Flippin' Murdered 'Em

First Test, Zimbabwe v England, Queen's Sports Club
Bulawayo, 18-22 December.
Zimbabwe 376 (A Flower 112, Campbell 84; Silverwood 3-63,
Croft 3-71) and 234 (G Whittall 56, Waller 50; Tufnell 4-61);
England 406 (Hussain 113, Crawley 112; P Strang 5-123) and
204-5 (Knight 96, Stewart 73).
Result: Match drawn with scores level.

ALONGSIDE the sightscreen, somewhere between the wooden shack housing the BBC's *Test Match Special* team and a life-sized plastic elephant's head, which reeks more authentically than it looks, David Lloyd paces up and down with growing apprehension. What has had the makings for the past two hours of a thrilling England Test victory, in search of 205 in 37 overs, is about to disappear in the wake of shamelessly negative bowling and dormant umpiring.

Thirteen runs are required from Heath Streak's final over, and thanks to Nick Knight thrashing his third ball over deep square-leg for six, England's hopes still flicker. Gough winks encouragingly at Lloyd from the middle of the pitch like a Northern ham actor. If England don't win the Test, Gough could well win the consolation of a walk-on part as one of the Joker's apprentices in the next Batman movie. Lloyd, meanwhile, is as hyperactive as The Riddler, and there are still many questions unresolved.

Three runs are required from the final ball, which Knight middles towards the cover boundary, but Bryan Strang intercepts and fires in a quick left-handed return to the wicketkeeper's end. The throw is slightly high, causing Andy Flower to stretch to collect it, but Gough has no chance and runs his condemned third run like a man wading in galoshes through thigh-deep waves. The batsmen are just about crossing when Flower completes the run out. If Gough is sploshing around, Lloyd is mentally drowning.

England have finished on 204 for five, the first time in history that a Test has finished 'Match Drawn With Scores Level'. Even allowing for the two tied Tests, no side has ever come nearer to winning without actually doing so. At the informal setting of Queen's Sports Club, an enticing ground shaded by mahogany and wild fig trees, there seems no end to the mockery of this England side.

How have England not won? Fifty-nine from the last ten overs with nine wickets left sounded a breeze. Knight and Stewart (73 off 76 balls) batted superbly, to no avail, although Knight struggled for a time against a leg-stump attack from Zimbabwe's part-time off-spinner Grant Flower.

England also missed a trick by not running a bye or two to the wicketkeeper. Andy Flower flung himself full-length, left and right, to gather Streak's wide deliveries. Only to concede two byes was a fine achievement.

Amid the disappointment, many fleetingly recognize that they have witnessed an outcome that might not be repeated for another hundred years. Even the Barmy Army, who have spent much of the last hour droning the usual inebriated stuff from the Last Night of the Proms, are silent, as if touched by a spiritual experience. The last two hours have not been the classiest Test cricket ever played, but they have been among the most compulsive.

Lloyd does not take it so calmly. He has become incensed as Zimbabwe have spent the final hour deliberately bowling wide of the stumps, with the tacit approval of the umpires. Only three wides have been given in the innings – Lloyd feels that there should have been another half-dozen. Nothing has infuriated him more than the failure of the Zimbabwean umpire, Ian Robinson, to call 'wide' from the fourth ball of Streak's last over, a decision which even brings boos from the press marquee (EW Swanton would have been appalled) when the full horrors of the decision are confirmed by the Sky TV replay. Lloyd is gunning for a fight. All the little irritations of the past month – unprepared nets, no towels for the showers, filthy dressing-rooms – thrash around his mind. Zimbabwe bowled wide on the Under-19 tour and they've bowled wide now. He is disgusted.

Some view Robinson's decision as incompetent; I settle for accusing him of one of the greatest abdications of responsibility in Test history. Zimbabwe's tactics arise from an understandably professional response – they might be Test novices, but never again will they be termed Test innocents – but the umpires' failure to limit such morally dubious methods is mind-boggling. Had Dickie Bird been standing, he would have become increasingly agitated, muttered something to the bowlers about there being limits, and, by calling maybe just one extra wide at the right time, would have made it clear to the bowlers concerned that they were obliged to mix up their tactics. Robinson (and, to a lesser extent, the neutral umpire, Steve Dunne from New Zealand) remain immovable.

As chief administrator of the Zimbabwe Cricket Union, Robinson is responsible in Zimbabwe for appointing the umpires and, as he openly classifies himself as one of the top three officials in the world, it should be no surprise that he regularly appoints himself. As chief administrator, he will also be the first person to receive the match report from England's captain Michael Atherton, and as Robinson has had a wretched game from start to finish, he would best be advised not to study his rating too closely.

Lloyd's prowlings encourage baiting from a few beer-swilling Zimbabweans. The most subtle Zimbabwean joke occurs when a bloke drops his trousers and points his backside at you; the verbal jokes are generally much coarser. Lloyd is a direct and emotional man, a Lancastrian who believes in frankness in every social situation. He flicks his barrackers a meaningful one-fingered salute, and knows they deserve it. As he stalks back to the dressing-room, he is met by a Mashonaland cricket official, Ian Goggin, who offers stock congratulations on an excellent and exciting match.

Lloyd rejects them with feeling, leaving Goggin in no doubt that England feel they have been cheated. Lloyd has overstepped the mark and it is not long before the match referee, Hanumant Singh, is made aware of the confrontation and calls the parties together. The referee will take no further action, but that night, Lloyd's behaviour is the talk of Bulawayo.

Lloyd is still flaming with anger in the England dressing-room, so much so that Ian Botham – 'that great hunk of beef,' in the words of his Sky co-commentator, Mark Nicholas – is advised not to go inside. Great Hunks of Beef are braver than that. In his capacity as technical adviser to the bowlers, Botham goes in anyway and tells Lloyd to 'stop it'. England's coach has achieved a remarkable feat, told to calm it by the greatest roisterer in the history of English cricket.

'Calm down? That's rich coming from you!' Lloyd explodes.

'I've mellowed,' Both replies.

After a cooling-off period by the Queen's Club swimming pool, Lloyd walks into the after-match press conference. He looks as distracted as Graham Taylor in his later period as England's football manager – and that's distracted. All that is needed to complete the picture is Phil Neal sitting alongside him repeating: 'That's right, boss,' but Johnny Barclay was unsuitable for the part. Lloyd describes the experience as the most depressing point in his England career.

Asked about Zimbabwe's negative tactics, he says pointedly: 'No observations,' slamming his mouth closed like a cage door before the red-white-and-blue lion escapes. He is told that Alistair Campbell, Zimbabwe's captain, is 'defending his tactics to the hilt' and that even Knight, man of the match for his 96 not out, has ventured that 'England would have done the same.' 'No observations,' Lloyd says again. Then he makes some. Just as there is always a tour song, there is always a tour interview. This is it.

'We murdered 'em,' says Lloyd, barely able to conceal his anger. 'We got on top and steamrollered 'em... we have flippin' hammered 'em...we murdered 'em and they know it... To work so hard and get so close, there is no praise too high... We have had some stick off you lads... We flippin' hammered 'em.'

This is about as passionate as it could get without Lloyd actually sobbing in front of us. He expects an English press conference automatically to share his anger and take his side. In his mind, this is no time for neutrality. The rest of the press conference is wrought with tension.

When Martin Johnson politely suggests to Lloyd that England would have employed the same tactics, Atherton tartly intervenes: 'Write it in the *Daily Telegraph* if that's what you believe.'

'I'm not going to write it anywhere else,' says Johnson.

There is a history to this, which basically involves the fact that Johnson's penetrating humour has ruffled dressing-room feathers. His particular sin has to been to ridicule England in the *Telegraph*, which habitually observes the cricket scene in a more temperate fashion.

Atherton and Johnson then become involved in a prolonged stare-out which ends with them both politely inviting each other not to take life so seriously. The silence probably lasted about four seconds, but I could swear that in the meantime the sun set and rose again at least twice.

To break the tension, I ask Barclay if England have run into any more trouble with the match referee. He responds that they are 'clean so far', which is not quite the case. At Eton, they probably call that being 'economical with the truth'. Others might have a different word for it.

The previous two tied Tests had been essentially joyous affairs with both sides able to celebrate an equal share of a special occasion, but here there is no comparable excitement, just England's excruciating recognition that success has eluded them. Asked about taking part in an historic Test, Atherton murmurs: 'It means nothing. It would have been nicer to win.' The pressure of not beating the weakest team in the world is palpable; England's overseas record now stands at five wins in their last thirty-nine games.

Time is pressing, stories have to be written, and the Rixi

cab (a collapsing Datsun 120Y) that we finally stumble across is arguably the oldest in town. A mile from the Holiday Inn, our driver, Samson, is signalled into the side of the road for an impromptu MOT check. A failure and he instantly loses his licence and we must look for alternative transport. Samson looks petrified and it is clear that we are in shtuck by the way he keeps muttering, 'No problem.' The policeman chews over the weight of evidence: a bald tyre; two doors that won't shut properly; two bare wires hanging from the dashboard to start the engine; a boot that allows air to pass through directly from the floor; and a steering wheel that must once have fitted another make of car very nicely. After much frowning, he approaches the window.

'OK, off you go,' he says.

'Thank you, sir, thank you, sir,' says Samson. He looks astounded. 'Passed!' he says. 'I passed! There, I told you there would be no problem.' We tell him to put his tip towards his next MOT test.

*   *   *

The first four and a half days of the Test rarely possess the same tension as that fateful final session. England's pace attack of Mullally, Gough and Silverwood bowls poorly during the first two sessions, and the aggression of Campbell takes Zimbabwe to 206 for three. Mullally, the troubadour left-armer, is particularly off-key, leading me to wonder whether on the days that he bowls badly, he also sings badly (forgetting the lyrics perhaps, or not quite hitting the high notes), or whether his two talents are mutually exclusive.

Thanks to a herculean effort by the off-spinner Croft, England peg Zimbabwe back to 256 for six by the close of the first day, but the bowlers begin the second day equally sluggishly and Andy Flower's watchful century takes Zimbabwe to 376 all out. Few Tests have been lost from there.

England's task, on a sound batting pitch, is to make 500, and to do that they have to conquer their misgivings about leg-spin: 'Keep the demons in the bottle,' as Lloyd puts it. England's bottle has long been uncorked. Anil Kumble, Shane Warne and Mushtaq Ahmed have all tormented them in recent seasons and Strang, although derided by Lloyd as a bowler whose Test wickets have cost him 65 runs each, has a career average that is tumbling by the month. Sure enough, Strang has Atherton leg-before on the second evening and follows up the next day by dismissing the Surrey pair, Stewart (outrageously adjudged leg-before as he sweeps at a leg-spinner curving past off-stump) and Thorpe.

The Test has reached its mid-point and, at 180 for four, England are not yet hammering and murdering. But salvation comes in the form of hundreds from Nasser Hussain and John Crawley, and a first innings lead of 30. Hussain's two comeback hundreds against India the previous summer were significant primarily as personal achievements, stressing the harder edge to his cricket that promises to sustain him at England level. On this occasion, his 113 serves as a rallying cry for a restless team.

Hussain is dropped first ball, at short leg, off Strang, and survives an lbw appeal next ball up as he fails to pick Strang's googly, but he then reveals the will and patience over six hours to bat England into a strong position. His dismissal on the fourth morning, hooking at Streak, is a freak, Bryan Strang sticking his right hand into the air at long leg like a school-crossing lady raising her lollipop at approaching traffic.

If Hussain plays Strang ably, Crawley plays him with conviction. He begins the fourth day on 51 not out and has to contend with the familar sight of a crumbling lower order, but protects it so skilfully that he is last out, having made 112, with England in credit.

Strang finishes with five for 123 in 58.4 overs, and a right shoulder sorely in need of a massage. This is partly due to the patriotic inclinations of some of the English press who the previous night helped to keep his girlfriend-cum-masseuse, Heather, talking and drinking tequila in a Bulawayo bar with friends until the early hours. We calculate that the longer Strang has to wait for a proper shoulder massage, the more likely it is that England's batsmen will set about him the following morning. The sacrifices we make for England, and do the players give us a shred of credit?

Strang is honoured in the public prints with the traditional stories about how the mysteries of leg-spin were revealed to him during a teach-in with Warne, involving the Australian's usual collection of flipped oranges, spinning lemons and games of pool. All that is left is for Warne to explain that his perfection of the flipper owes everything to the tidal patterns he discovered one glorious day while out surfing. Leg-spin has revelled in such mystery since the day that B T Bosanquet first invented the googly by spinning a billiard ball against a cushion and observing which way it returned. No other cricketing skill is so theatrical. Imagine Nick Knight suggesting that he had learned the secrets of the square cut while woodcutting with Brian Lara.

A lead of 30 sounds insubstantial, but Zimbabwe have been detained in the field for longer than they hoped and, psychologically, the lead is larger than it sounds. By the end of the fourth day, the spinners reduce them to 107 for five. The only discontent arises from a ticking-off by the match referee, Hanumant Singh, for some over-exuberant appealing.

With a lead of only 77, Zimbabwe look ripe for defeat, but Andy Waller, on his Test debut, and Guy Whittall counter-attack spiritedly and it is two o'clock before England's innings begins. Rather than murdering and steamrollering, they have taken four and a half days to wrest control. They return to Harare, venue for the second and final Test, with the series still level.

The excitement of the Test is not always captured in its essence by the *Bulawayo Chronicle*. The final-day photograph, showing Atherton fielding to Tufnell's bowling, is captioned: 'England's Kevin Ryan (left) and Tony Shuttleworth in action as NZ umpire Steve Dunne watches them closely at Queen's Sports Club yesterday.' This follows other unlikely headlines over the past fortnight: Woman Drowns Baby In Can Of Paint; Father Christmas Revealed As St Nicholas; and Woman (53) Steals Donkeys. Oh, yes, and the most unexpected of all: England Beat Matabeleland.

11
The Final Farce

CRISIS in Bulawayo. As the first Test builds towards its memorable climax, a handful of journalists join the English management in earnest huddles around the boundary edge of the Queen's Sports Club. Under the mahogany and wild fig trees, alongside the immobile biltong seller, and in the shadow of the ubiquitous Coca-Cola sunshade, grave expressions reveal a matter of national import has taken place: *England have refused to attend the media's Christmas Day panto.*

England have actually held a formal team-meeting to discuss whether to accept the media's traditional invitation for an hour's drinks late on Christmas morning. Instead of the usual, 'Yeah, I s'pose so, as long as it's not for too long,' there have been howls of protest and cries of, 'We're not drinking with that bloody lot... especially 'im and 'im.' Many individual relationships are holding up well, but not all. And when it comes down to group pressures, Players v Press is about as hostile a fixture as Celtic v Rangers.

Around the boundary, explananations are sought and offered. Atherton repeats that it's 'nothing personal', but always impatient with the ways of the tabloids, this time he is equally put out by the broadsheets. If he can explain how to convey a record of one overseas Test series victory in ten years more positively, we are yearning to know. Lloyd explains that it's not a management decision, but the players are incensed by 'the extent of the personal criticism... some of it has been disgusting.' Barclay, who acts as if he doesn't understand what all the fuss is about, joins together a collection of nice-sounding sentences that mean absolutely nothing at all. These days there is a desperate need for the England team manager to have a political mind; instead, Barclay forever takes refuge in the anodyne phrase. He is an amiable fellow, unmalicious, charming and with a nice line in self-deprecating humour, the sort of nice chap who is often described as totally harmless. But if he does not recognize the wide-ranging nature of his role, he is no longer harmless, but harmful.

Journalists spend their entire working lives trying to divorce professional criticism from personal relationships. This England side is more concerned with insisting that there is a limit to the amount and to the style of the criticism they are prepared to take. A squad that has lost to Mashonaland and has made a mess of the first one-day international might have expected to take a bit of flak, but the personal nature of some of the coverage has hurt. The response is presented as a show of support for the captain. If that is so, questioning their strategy is easier than questioning their decency.

Whether England attend a Christmas Day panto, amateurishly run by the travelling media, sounds like a supreme irrelevance. But it does have long-term implications. It is yet another example of a struggling side mistakenly retreating into itself and, by doing so, creating additional pressure. A siege mentality is easy to adopt in football, when even trips into Europe rarely last longer than forty-eight hours. The professional golf and tennis circuits exist in their own protective bubble, wherever they might be in the world. But cricket tours have always possessed a different mood. Over four months, they have to. The only sensible choice is to arrive in a new town or city, relax and get on with life.

Several of us have downed much South African Shiraz in Les Saisons restaurant to draw up a workable script, one with jokes that would survive the absence of props that never turn up, and the probability that half the cast would either forget their lines or deliver them in the wrong place. On this rare occasion, the most cutting lines were to be about ourselves: self-flagellation in the interest of maintaining harmonious relations.

Personally, though, I preferred the Yorkshire Nativity Play, which we presented during the 1994-5 tour of Australia, with

Raymond Illingworth as God (naturally) and Fred Trueman, Brian Close and Geoff Boycott as the grumbling Three Wise Men. Follow that star, the Wise Men are told.

'Call that a star!' says Fred (played by Christopher Martin-Jenkins in a rich Yorkshire brogue). 'In my day we had real stars. Our stars used to shine 365 days a year, 24 hours a day. They *were* bloody stars. I just dunno what's up with the stars of today. They don't know they're born, today's bloody stars.'

Two years on, we leave Les Saisons convinced again that we have written the funniest play in history, even if a gravely bearded restaurant owner does not seem convinced. Next morning, in a more sober light, we reckon it might still need touching-up here and there. Now it doesn't matter. The stage at Sandros nightclub in Harare will remain empty. Perhaps, as they just have for the late theatre critic Jack Tinker, they will dim the lights in London's West End theatres as a show of mourning.

Much of the credit for the organisation of our Christmas Day festivities goes to David Norrie, esteemed correspondent of the *News of the World*, and the snubbing of the panto briefly blackens his mood. Leaving a lift in the Sheraton Hotel in Harare, the following conversation revives memories of his dislike of birdsong in Bulawayo, only this time the irritation is caused by the choice of hotel Muzak.

Norrie: 'What's that bloody noise?'
Colleague: 'It's Christmas, Norrie.'
Norrie (grunting): 'Oh, I s'pose that's alright then.'

Journalists like nothing better than symbolic moments, and the snubbing of the 1996 panto will be taken to represent a further breakdown in relations between those involved in professional sport and the media. There is no future in such hostility, for either party. And that's enough about that.

12
The Scream

CRAIG White has arrived from Australia. The Yorkshireman has been called up as cover for Ronnie Irani, the Essex all-rounder, who has developed a back problem and who was not bowling well even before it started to hurt. Already, Irani has the makings of one of those tourists who is selected in a blaze of optimism in early September then somehow becomes surplus to requirements almost before the plane has taxied down the runway. Joey Benjamin, the Surrey seam bowler, must have wondered why on earth he was ever chosen for the tour of Australia then virtually overlooked, two years ago. England's selection policy remains inconsistent, with short-term speculation too often favoured ahead of long-term judgement.

While in Bulawayo, Irani is driven by car to Harare for an X-ray, an arduous five-hour drive in the heat of the day. If his back trouble is not serious when he sets off, who can imagine what state he will be in by the time he arrives? He has not had the best of tours and there are unkind suggestions that he should be sent by Rixi cab, one of those with no recognisable suspension and metal sticking through the seat covers: 'Come on Ronnie, let's go the pretty route.'

Irani returns relatively intact, and disturbing news soon follows that his bowling action will have to be redesigned. A year ago, in South Africa, Raymond Illingworth sought to remodel Devon Malcolm's action in the middle of a tour and the consequences of that raged in tabloid newspapers and TCCB disciplinary hearings for months, as what began as a technical disagreement, thanks to stubbornness on both sides, developed racial overtones. To imagine that England are about to embark again upon the same course is astonishing. After all, David Lloyd and Irani might both be Lancastrians, but one is from Accrington and the other is from Leigh. Folk can be so parochial in those parts that another race row could only be days away.

'Chalkie' White is the bearer of glad tidings, as a successful member of the England 'A' side that has just cut a swathe through Australia. Yes, Australia. Six months before the Ashes series, England's shadow squad has returned home victorious, with no lesser Australian than Rod Marsh, the stumpy, tinny-swilling, wicketkeeping scourge of past England sides, praising them as the happiest collection of Poms he has ever set eyes upon. Marsh, now in charge of the Australian Cricket Academy, gives credit for that to England's management team of Mike Gatting and David Graveney. Anybody not in Zimbabwe could almost believe that next summer we might win the Ashes.

Gatting and Graveney have developed an affirmative and relaxed managerial style. Players are treated like adults, encouraged to socialize off the field and enjoy their cricket. They do just that, and become the first English side to win respect in Australia since Gatting skippered England to the Ashes a decade earlier. 'A' tours are both shorter and have a smaller percentage of family men, which means homesickness is less likely to set in. They are also far less pressurised, with little fear of media intrusion, but it is tempting to draw comparisons with the suffocating caution of the senior side. As far as can be determined, Gatt has never suggested getting out the Balderdash. He does volunteer a marvellous quote, though, a final reminder, perhaps, of a prodigious appetite that has gained so much attention over the years.

Journalist: 'Would you be interested in the post of chairman of selectors?'

Gatt: 'Not really, not while I'm playing. I'd have too much on my plate.'

White has made a sound contribution too, both with stylish middle-order batting and fast-medium bowling which, although still a touch untutored, is blessed by the ability to occasionally summon a rapid change of pace. His chief shortcoming is a lack of self-belief. His Australian links don't help him gain acceptance, nor does a square-jawed expression that might have come straight out of the bush. But although his teenage years were spent in Victoria, he was born in Morley, in the heart of West Yorkshire, and all Yorkshire folk regard birthright as the ultimate qualification. Anyone who remembers stealing apples from a Pudsey churchyard as a nipper – the same churchyard frequented by Len Hutton, no less – and wearing a Union Jack T-shirt as a teenager at a Test match in Melbourne sounds English enough for me.

White's world is in a whirl. He had barely begun a family holiday in Australia – he emigrated in childhood – when he answered England's call. Three days after arriving in Zimbabwe, he walks out to bat in the second Test at Harare Sports Club with England's first innings in turmoil. He has come from harder, quicker Australian pitches, and had he thrashed a quick fifty, it would have made a mockery of all this talk about acclimatisation. He doesn't, making nine in an hour to the accompaniment of nearby thunder and lightning before a loose drive makes him another victim of a moribund pitch.

As White returns to the pavilion, a group of twenty-something England spectators rush alongside the press marquee to barrack him. One of them is carrying a dummy with a head based upon Edvard Munch's 'The Scream'. At first, it seems an acceptable and appropriate response to England's failings overseas. Over the years, we have all dabbled in turn in explanations, excuses, encouragement, sorrow, depression, frustration, anger, resentment, and finally ridicule. 'The Scream' sums up the prevailing mood perfectly. There is nothing else left to say. The next step is abandonment.

The dummy's head might be strikingly artistic, but the rest is less impressive; in fact, it is deeply unfair. The Scream dummy has been dressed in a T-shirt bearing the legend: 'White, You're Shit!' They could have at least bothered to make it rhyme. As the player passes by, one of them yells his slogan: *'White, you're shit!'* The shock is immediate.

In a football stadium, with 30,000 spectators yelling abuse, yet another verbal attack would have passed unnoticed, unless you possess the pride of Eric Cantona. On some cricket grounds – Melbourne, Calcutta, or even Headingley on its more raucous days – it might not have seemed exactly out of place. But this is Harare Sports Club, which possesses the genial, laid-back atmosphere of a small club ground. The cry inflames the air.

Throughout English cricket's history, the relationship between players and spectators has traditionally been supportive. Barracking has largely been regarded as tasteless, as 'Just not cricket, old boy.' But times are changing and the number of spectators who habitually show respect and patience whatever the provocation diminishes every year. Top-rated TV programmes such as *They Think It's All Over* are just one manifestation of professional sport as a vehicle for ridicule. Tabloid newspapers, lampooning our failed sports stars by turning them into vegetables, are another. English cricket is particularly vulnerable to the change of mood. Our persistent losing run overseas, aggravated perhaps by the gradual retreat of the modern Test cricketer into his own secluded world, is introducing a more hostile atmosphere. Patience is running out.

The gibe against White seems particularly cutting because its perpetrator is relatively sober, intelligent and just out for a bit of a laugh. White does not deserve to be picked out. I lose my temper and shout from the press marquee. 'You're in the *Guardian* tomorrow, mate. I just can't decide whether to call you a twat or a prat.'

This might have been the end of it, but I have inadvertently shouted at the wrong man. So amid some sniggering from fellow pressmen, I sidle out of the tent to make the point slightly more amicably. White has been here for three days – England have been screwing up for weeks. Surely there are more obvious targets?

It emerges that in the soap opera sub-plot, 'White, You're Shit,' I have made a guest appearance in episode three. This is a dispute that threatens to run and run. White first ran into his personal barracker at Lord's in 1994 and was provoked into a dismissive signal in return. Alright then, let's be honest: it is alleged by his assailants that he briefly gestured that they were all wankers, or at least that the one doing the shouting was. As the powers-that-be at Lord's will probably call a disciplinary hearing to press a charge of gross vulgarity, it should immediately be added at this point, m'lord, that such accusations are entirely untrue.

The second occasion arose a year ago after a three-day Test defeat in Cape Town. White was not even playing, having just arrived on tour as a replacement; again England had lost the series and there might have been rather bigger fish to fry. No matter, The Scream rediscovered its target. White has been unfortunate enough to be chosen as the scapegoat.

The justification is that The Scream doesn't think that White is good enough, and anyway it's all meant to be a bit of a laugh. In cricket, too, it is unwise to make misguided, class-ridden assumptions that his barrackers are, say, unemployed dockers, labourers or part-time storeroom assistants, all regarded as particularly vulnerable to the derisive society cultivated by our mass media. White's chief assailant actually turns out to be an official in the House of Commons, a civil servant who one day might be virtually running the country. There must be lots of sniggering from Monday to Friday behind the woolsack. David Lloyd wonders aloud in that night's press conference as to whether his mother knows he is there. Later, I ask his mates the same question. 'His mother doesn't know the half of it,' they reply.

From White's perspective, to be singled out for such persecution is unfair. For HOC Chap, it's just a sharp sense of humour getting a run out. HOC Chap is beckoned over to the nets by the player later that day and explains frankly that he just doesn't think he is good enough. OK, responds Chalkie, that's fair enough, but wear that T-shirt again and I'll deck you. As negotiations go, there is more chance of a peaceful settlement in the next Anglo-Irish talks. White is noticeably broader this winter, having done a lot of weights to strengthen his upper body for bowling. HOC Chap's most convenient way to take more exercise would be to use a heavier biro. The fight, if it ever takes place, is unlikely to go the distance.

What White doesn't realize, and what I stumble upon the following day, is that the 'White, You're Shit' campaign is logged with detail in the HOC Chap's tour diary, which is penned daily and then read out amid considerable mirth. Self-indulgent, admittedly, but the nature of this diary is well worth recording. The point is not to encourage the castigating of White, but to try to answer this question: what moves a bright and cheery group of spectators to taunt an England cricketer with such persistence and with what many would regard as malevolence? Neither is it intended to expose David Lloyd, whose allegedly tempestuous reaction to the incident makes his outburst at Bulawayo seem a peace offering by comparison. Lloyd is an immensely straightforward, loyal and emotional man, who believes in arguing his players' corner. Many other England coaches would have reacted in exactly the same manner.

I suspect that much of the breakdown in communication and support again lies in the modern approach to professional sport. The more England's cricketers withdraw from the social life surrounding the game, the less they will be regarded as real people and the easier it will become for journalists and spectators alike to caricature them. The mood is already shifting. What has happened to White could happen to anybody: Atherton, Irani, Mullally, Caddick, the lot. It should serve as a warning that cricket must strive to maintain its relationship with those who watch the game. It is just unfair on this occasion that White, who is about as easy-going and unpretentious an England cricketer as you could wish to meet, has borne the brunt of it.

Here then, from the angle of the spectators themselves, is the story of The Scream:

Wednesday 25 December:
We settled for a quiet meal at the hotel in preparation for a rather demanding next five days. As we sat in the hotel bar over a gentle beer, who should walk in? Only Craig White! There is a time and a place for everything, and the civilized surroundings of the Holiday Inn bar was probably not the place to launch into a standing chorus of 'White, You're Shit!' We managed to contain our glee and hoped that the beers he was drinking signified that he was playing tomorrow.

Thursday 26 December:
And he was! Oh, joy! Oh, happy day! What's more, confirmation of this fact came over the loudspeakers as we gathered around the boundary around a Sky TV interview with Ian Botham. The news prompted a little team jig of delight, much to the amusement of the watching David Gower. The great man struggled to stifle his titters as I hastily exchanged my tour T-shirt for the 'White You're Shit' number I had knocked up after Treats excitedly informed me of his call up for the injured Ronnie Irani.

Amazingly enough, this jocular T-shirt was to cause the England dressing-room more difficulty than the Zimbabwean bowling. Which was quite a lot of difficulty. Indeed, it got an earlier run-out than anticipated, as the England batting – on a slow but harmless pitch – capsized to 73 for five. The inflatable Scream changed into the White T-shirt and helped me to give the batsman appropriate encouragement from the boundary rope.

The Scream and I soon moved to a position near the pavilion, the better to commiserate with White on his impending dismissal. Got distracted by the nearby England net practice. Overseen by England's greatest all-rounder since W G Grace, it had all the energy and professionalism of a Chipping Sodbury 2nd X1 net on a wet Wednesday in September. So lacking in interest was it that I was distracted by the cricket – notably by White's dismissal for a painfully slow nine.

One of the press boys next door took a spot of umbrage at my flaunting the T-shirt at the outgoing White and came over to tell us so. After an amicable exchange of views, Sticks, Swamps and I almost managed to persuade David Hopps of the Guardian *that we may have had a point, if a little cruelly made. This hopefully rescued him from the dilemma of whether to call me a twat or a prat in his report, as he initially intended.*

Back at the nets, tempers were beginning to fray. Not with the 130 for eight scoreline, it appeared, but with my T-shirt. 'Oh, very clever that is, very funny,' fumed David Lloyd sarcastically as he marched over to confront me. 'It's not supposed to be funny, just true,' I told him. He stabbed a finger in my direction and drawled in thick Lancastrian: 'You're just a little smart arse, you, aren't you?'

I told him that I'd paid my money to watch England, was entitled to voice my opinion and that this performance was embarrassing. 'Well, fuck off home, then,' was his blunt reply. Then he offered me outside!

'Can you back it up?' he demanded. 'Let's see what you are made of. Holiday Inn tonight – just you and me. He won't be there, but I will. Can you back it up? Will you be there?'

Completely dumbfounded, I tried to point out that this wouldn't do a whole lot of good for English cricket and he might, as England coach, have something more constructive to offer. By this stage the poor man was verging on dementia. 'Can you back it up? CAN YOU BACK IT UP?' echoed in my ears as I beat a baffled retreat.

But the coach wasn't the only one to be unimpressed. Who should be bowling in the nets but the great all-rounder himself, Craig White? He beckoned me over. Slightly sheepishly, I trudged along to explain myself, still clutching The Scream. I told him as gently as I could that me and my chums didn't think he was quite up to it at Test level and, if he remembered, it was us at Lord's in 1994 and us at Cape Town last year. And when news came through of his call-up... well, I just had to knock up a T-shirt.

Yes, he did remember and no, he didn't find it very funny. So unfunny, in fact, that he threatened to punch my lights out if I wore it again! Better get myself down the gym – it was going to be a busy night.

Wednesday 1 January: [After White has been further provoked by barracking while fielding at deep square-leg during the final one-day international.]
...Wisely or unwisely, we'd decided that the best way to get rid of hangovers was to drink our way through it. So perhaps it was a good thing that the Keg and Sable was closed and we were forced to dine at The Sheraton, this time at the buffet restaurant. Halfway through our main course, who should stroll in and occupy a nearby table but our hero himself, accompanied by Alec Stewart and Robert Croft. Nothing was said until I ventured over to the dessert trolley. As I hovered indecisively between some rather chocolately profiteroles and a tempting cheesecake, I became aware of a presence at my elbow. It was White. He whispered with cold menace: 'It's OK shouting at me from twenty yards, but you tell it to my face.... White concluded with an 'I'll mess you up, boy' that John Wayne would have been proud of.

Accuse me of naïvety, but I cannot imagine the same scene taking place in Australian cricket, perhaps in any other Test nation in the world. In Australia, spectators might criticize their sports stars as loudly as anywhere when things go wrong, but they identify more with their successes and failures. It is not their style to set themselves apart and undermine through ridicule. And if they did, punches would definitely have been thrown. Australians would regard the response of Lloyd and White as fairly low-key. The Scream, indubitably, is another face of English cricket.

13

Bring 'em Home

Second Test, Zimbabwe v England, Harare Sports Club,
Harare, 26-30 December.
England 156 all out (Crawley 47 not out; G Whittall 4-18,
Streak 4-43) and 195-3 (Stewart 101 not out, Thorpe 50 not
out); Zimbabwe 215 all out (G Flower 73, P Strang 47 not out;
Gough 4-40, Croft 3-39).
Result: Match drawn.

SUSPICIONS are growing that Zimbabwe is not exactly enamoured of David Lloyd's 'We murdered 'em' speech in Bulawayo. It does not take an overly keen journalistic insight to reach such a conclusion. The banner spotted in the stand on a wander around the boundary on Boxing Day during the first day of the Harare Test seems to offer a clue:

Wanted
David Lloyd
For Murder of Zim Cricket Team
Last seen with his finger up his nose
talking complete bollocks
He knows it and we know it

It might not go into history with quite the same force as the famous *Sporting Times* 'Ashes' obituary when England lost the Ashes at The Oval in 1882, but it is fair to say that Zimbabwe's supporters have got their point of view across.

Frivolously, I yell out to the spectators concerned that they should try to provide another banner the following day, only this time about Atherton. Later, I learn that Mrs Atherton was in the crowd and, not surprisingly, was mildly put out.

This tiny *faux pas* does have the effect of encouraging a slight rethink about Lloyd's outburst against Ian Goggin, the

Mashonaland cricket official who happened to cross his path immediately after the Bulawayo draw. It was suggested by some that we should be particularly affronted because Lloyd's outburst happened to be heard by various high and mighty figures in the crowd. I can't remember who: the Queen's dressmaker, perhaps, or the wife of the match referee. I can't remember who because to suggest that Lloyd's rant was more sinful just because certain VIPs happened to be within earshot is the sort of nonsense that the Empire thrived upon.

English officialdom has proved itself incapable of restructuring the first-class game, but give it a petty row to investigate and it springs into action. The men at the head of the England Cricket Board, due to come into operation in a few days' time, on 1 January 1997, have arrived in Zimbabwe and have wasted no time in giving Lloyd something between a mild ticking-off and a fierce dressing-down. Lloyd suggests the former, but he is in a minority. Others whisper that any repeat of the incident will bring about his sacking. The ECB clearly has the aptitude of the soon-to-be-defunct Test and County Cricket Board for obfuscation, with neither its chief executive Tim Lamb nor its chairman, Lord MacLaurin, the departing chief executive of Tesco, willing to reveal what the punishment was.

The media judiciously settles for 'severely reprimanded', which covers most things and is thought to be pretty accurate. Personally, I think that when officialdom maintains such secrecy with no justification, the press should no longer feel obliged to make educated guesses, but regard itself as free to make up something totally irresponsible, such as: *'Lord MacLaurin, the new chairman of the England Cricket Board, mercilessly thrashed David Lloyd with a limp Tesco lettuce yesterday in a hard-line response to his controversial outburst at the end of the Bulawayo Test.'*

That would soon make them tell everybody what really happened.

The English press, though, has other priorities. It is busy organising a charitable appeal, which soon becomes known as the Heath Streak Appeal Fund. During the flight from Bulawayo to Harare, the Zimbabwe fast bowler at the centre of the 'wides scandal' described the umpiring in the Bulawayo Test as 'pretty lenient'. Such a simple and honest remark naturally incurs the wrath of the match referee, Hanumant Singh, who decides Streak needs his come-uppance and fines him a percentage of his match fee. After realising that this comes to about three and sixpence, the press dutifully organise a whip-round for Streak and shove the cash in an envelope along with a slightly pompous (if heartfelt) declaration about protecting free speech. The message comes back from the Zimbabwe dressing-room that they are all very grateful for the gesture, but in future would we all like to approach players through the proper channels...

The only problem with all of this is that the next England player to be fined his match fee for a comment in the newspapers will be round to the press box like a flash, insisting that we all cough up the best part of £3,000. He will be sadly disappointed.

Lord MacLaurin could hardly have made a more instructive start to his two-year contract as the ECB's chairman. While the second Test drags on, Lloyd is also obliged to smooth over relations with Ian Botham after an exclusive story in the *News of the World* suggesting that Botham is dissatisfied with the vagueness of his role as technical adviser to England's bowlers. Furthermore, it all goes under the headline of: 'Make Me The Boss!'

Botham has had dinner with David Norrie, the *News of the World* correspondent, and has been quoted as saying: 'I need to know where I stand. I am not prepared to let my name and reputation be dragged down by this team if I have no real input. I would be guilty by association.'

Lloyd and Botham arrange a public display of unity during a tea interval on Sky TV, for whom Botham is working as a commentator. Botham insists that they have laughed about the story and that his comments were taken out of context, but he never quite denies everything, so we can assume that most of it is true. Lloyd says that the arrangement with Botham is in its infancy and that he is a legend. 'We are thrilled with what he is doing,' he says.

Botham can hardly complain about the shortcomings of an informal coaching arrangement that has been designed to suit his other responsibilities. But such loose arrangements are fraught with dangers, especially if and when a famous ex-player wishes to distance himself from a struggling side. England's players would be hurt to suspect that Botham could be so carelessly disparaging of their talents. They idolise him so much that on the night after the drawn first Test in Bulawayo, they spent much of the time singing that there was only one of him. If only there were still one of him on the field.

England's depressed state of mind is summed up, notoriously in the eyes of many, in John Crawley's tour diary in the *Sunday Telegraph*. The many millions stuck in mind-numbingly boring nine-to-five jobs are adamant that England sportsmen travelling the world should count their blessings. Crawley has a different perspective on modern-day touring: 'Bulawayo is the film *Groundhog Day*. Absolutely nothing to do. I go to my room and work out Take That's 'Back For Good' on the guitar and after realising I'm getting sad, I go to bed at 10.15.'

Better might have been expected from a Cambridge history graduate, even if crowded modern itineraries allow limited scope for non-cricketing activities.

* * *

The off-the-field shenanigans are more diverting than the Test, which for the most part is deadly dull. Zimbabwe have produced another wicket that England loathe: soft and springy, lacking the pace to encourage shot-making, but for batsmen willing to reduce their ambitions, dead enough to enable them to survive for long periods.

Lloyd's 'We murdered 'em' eruption keeps springing back to mind on the first day, if only because England are hell-bent upon murdering themselves. Their conviction that they were robbed of victory in Bulawayo makes them impatient to dominate the Harare Test from the outset. But a side convinced of its superiority against the weakest Test nation in the world is not prepared to work hard to prove it. On a pitch demanding patience and application, they manage neither and early on the second morning they are bowled out for 156, with only Crawley's unbeaten 47 bringing any consolation.

From his Spanish poolside, Raymond Illingworth slaps on some more factor 15 and complains in the *Daily Express* of 'soft cricket and soft cricketers'. The implication once again is that England have been betrayed by the system. What is even more striking, though, is that from the moment he stood down as chairman of selectors, Illingworth has made money by pillorying those who, only a few months before, were asked to place their trust in him. He is free to express his opinions, but the switch has been uncomfortably swift.

Guy Whittall, a sparky all-rounder who, if he was English, would probably have been a useful but unsung county cricketer, causes such havoc with his gentle medium-pace that he finishes with four for 18 in sixteen overs. Dave Houghton, Zimbabwe's coach, extols him as a 'partnership breaker', in which case it is amazing that he takes any wickets at all: England's largest amounts to 34.

Atherton blows another chance to graft himself back into form with an innings of self-denial. In one-and-a-half hours he reaches 13, including a hooked six off Brandes, but has never looked remotely capable in Zimbabwe of the sort of herculean efforts that saved the Johannesburg Test a year earlier. His rigid drive at Whittall's trifling outswinger falls to Campbell at first slip and sets an unwelcome trend for England's entire innings.

Lloyd describes it as the most depressing point in his England career.

Zimbabwe do have a batsman of infinite patience: Grant Flower is clearly a robot, programmed not to recognise boredom. Summoning up the discipline that England lacked, he bats nearly six hours for 73 before he drives Gough to short midwicket. For those able to stay awake, it provides a valuable insight into the concept of eternity. He is fortunate not to be adjudged caught down the leg-side off Croft when 29, but umpire Tiffin is presumably dreaming of the tea break and gives him not out. This is admirable, mind-numbing commitment during which the changing cloud formations over Harare Sports Club become dramatic by comparison. At lunchtime on the second day, one cloud divides very slowly and peacefully, looking something like a wellington kicking a dog, and it is quite the most exciting part of the day.

Flower played a monumental role in Zimbabwe's only Test victory, 201 against Pakistan on the same ground two years ago, which engineered a Zimbabwe victory, by an innings and 64 runs, amid allegations of match-rigging levelled at Pakistan's captain Salim Malik. If there is one asset that Flower possesses at the crease it is honesty – honesty of stroke and honesty of approach. He has a puritanical look that suggests one day he will knock on your front door on behalf of a little-known religious sect. When he does stride down the pitch to lift Tufnell one bounce into the long-off advertising hoardings, the ball falls near a spectator in a John Major mask, who pronounces the whole thing as extremely interesting. At least, it looked like a mask. By then it was hard to tell. Trevor Bailey, the holder of the slowest Test half-century, virtually six hours in Brisbane in 1958–59, is on the ground to witness Flower's innings. As well as doing some expert summarising for *Test Match Special*, Bailey is acting as tour host, and there could be no more appropriate person to have to keep the punters happy.

Flower's innings brings Zimbabwe a first-innings lead of 59. England, flirting with danger at 89 for three soon after lunch on the fourth day, recover to 195 for three by the close. Stewart's century, allied to a scratchy half-century from Thorpe, gives them a lead of 136, but torrential overnight rain prevents play on the final day. The Test, and the two-match series, is drawn. Flower is made Man of the Match and makes an acceptance speech even duller than his innings.

The press conference proves livelier. Zimbabwe's captain Alistair Campbell, irritated by England's claims that they have dominated both Test matches, accuses them of 'a superiority complex'. If England have adopted a superiority complex, it is only to make up for the inferiority complex that they have had against everybody else for years. And it is also a superiority built on sand; England are talking a good game in a calculated attempt to dispel their feelings of insecurity. But Campbell has a point. Watching some Mashonaland players practise in the nets at Harare Sports Club, three England tourists disrespectfully dismiss them as 'bloody clubbies'. This hardly seems to fit in with AC Smith's vision of a grand new alliance in England between schools, clubs and the first-class game.

Although England officially praise Zimbabwe's playing abilities, in truth they have little respect for them at all. Their history and traditions tell them that they should have won, even if they were never entirely sure that they would. Result: deep down, they have been petrified of failure. Instead of employing a fitness adviser, they would have been better with a sports psychologist.

Campbell's reasons for complaining of a superiority complex are slightly different. Yes, it's that old Lloyd quote again, come back to haunt us.

'When they say, "We murdered you and you know it," they are clutching at thin air,' he says. 'It gets under my skin. I think England will get better in New Zealand and do well there, but they should abandon their superiority complex and accept that both sides played well.' Campbell then assesses England, Zimbabwe and New Zealand as roughly on a par.

Wisden's unofficial Test league table suggests otherwise, still placing England seventh, ahead of Zimbabwe and New Zealand, but in media terms that is just unnecessary detail. For the first time in Test history, an international captain, as near as dammit, has judged England to be the worst side in the world. Australia, meanwhile, are the best side in the world. And the Ashes series is only five months away.

* * *

A New Year brings a new opportunity for change. But those still resistant to the belief that 1997 has to usher in a radical shake-up of our domestic game have even less justification for their resistance as the tourists mark the advent of the England Cricket Board by losing the last two one-day internationals, both at Harare Sports Club, and granting Zimbabwe a 3-0 clean sweep in the series. England have now suffered twelve successive overseas defeats in limited-overs matches. Endless changes of personnel, whether players, coaches or chairmen of selectors, have proved incapable of arresting the downward trend.

England lose the first game on run-rate, allowing Zimbabwe to reach 200 after reducing them to 38 for four and 126 for seven, then falling five runs short of their rain-revised target of 184 in 42 overs. *The Times* accuses them of 'frailty of temperament, technique and intelligence'. Alan Lee, fulminating in front of his telly back in Cheltenham, writes: 'England's cricketers battle through about twenty-five limited-overs games a summer for their counties and learn precious little from them. Their sheer volume and monotony breed an air of going through the motions and discourage anything dynamic or inventive.'

Lloyd calls for England's players to prove their spirit and professionalism in the final match, but they have clearly had their fill of Africa. They respond to the coach's clarion call by losing by 131 runs, collapsing to 118 all out against Eddo Brandes, the burly chicken farmer, who bowls superbly to take five for 28, including a hat-trick made up of Knight, Crawley and Hussain.

Lloyd describes the defeat as the most depressing point of his England career.

This depression lasts about five minutes before he is vowing to 'regroup, re-plan and come again with confidence.' He could depict the end of the world as a good thing:

'It'll be a good test of our lads' mettle, the end of the world. We know it'll be tough, no one needs to tell us that. The end of the world will be saying, right, now let's get among 'em. What we'll be saying is that the end of the world's not the end of the world, well, I suppose in some ways it is, but it'll also be a chance to have a look at some of the younger lads. The spirit's still as good as ever. We had nine lads playing Balderdash while the world was ending, loving it they were. They'll come through this alright, they'll have to, that's why they're here.'

Atherton, asked about his future as captain, insists: 'I have been appointed until the end of the winter and I have a job to do.'

All this seems a fair response, certainly when compared to some of the other nonsense doing the rounds. Barclay, England's ever-so-optimistic boy-man, piffles: 'I know what people are thinking back home – I think they are a little disappointed.' It would be interesting to know what, in Barclay's opinion, would constitute an English cricket crisis. Others display more anger. Terry Dicks, a rent-a-quote Tory MP, calls for the England team to return home in disgrace, a worthless contribution which makes one despair for our parliamentary system. The *Sun*, meanwhile, turns the heads of Lloyd and Atherton into sheep, and interviews W G Grace from beyond the grave about what can be done about it. You've got to laugh. The Good Doctor is pretty much lost for words. He is not the only one.

14

Pyramid Selling

CONSIDERING that England's greatest sporting obsession in the Nineties is supermarket trolley-pushing, the choice of Ian MacLaurin as chairman of the newly constituted England and Wales Cricket Board could not be more appropriate. Britain, once described as a nation of shopkeepers, has become a nation of shoppers. And as chief executive of Tesco, MacLaurin is credited as one of the most influential figures in that revolution.

These days he has risen to the rank of Lord MacLaurin of Knebworth, which will go down marvellously well with cricket's status-conscious administrators, and might even mean that they vote in favour of the radical changes that he is determined to implement in English cricket during his two-year term of office. These will not be revealed until mid summer, with the Ashes tour in full swing, but presumably they will amount to more than widening the aisles at Test grounds and offering every spectator a Loyalty Card which will entitle them to a free bunch of bananas for every £10 spent. Ian Charter, Baron MacLaurin of Knebworth, born fifty-nine years ago in Blackheath, is a doughtier leader than that. He has won a reputation as tough but fair, single-minded, a winner, a team man, determined and ethical.

Not that all that necessarily makes him a winner in English cricket. The ECB does not officially come into being until 1 January, still a few days hence, and already Raymond Illingworth has predicted that MacLaurin will resign in frustration within months.

MacLaurin, with the England Cricket Board's chief executive Tim Lamb in harness, has arrived in Harare to witness the conclusion of England's tour – the second Test, followed by the shameful one-day climax – and he also plans another ten days in Wellington, accompanied by various ECB handmaidens, in February. He still seems to possess more energy than some men twenty years younger. I know; I am twenty years younger.

MacLaurin addresses the English media in the cosy environment of the Harare Sports Club bowls pavilion, and the supportive tone is set when John Etheridge, the *Sun*'s cricket correspondent, asks him if he realises that he is seen as the Last Chance Saviour of English Cricket. This title has been held by many, latterly Illingworth himself, but there will come a time when someone really is the Last Chance and that time might not be as far off as some people think. MacLaurin demurs at the suggestion, but with a steely Scottish expression that suggests he does not entirely dislike the image, and looks slightly reminiscent of James Bond on the occasion that somebody suggests: 'You do realise, 007, that you are the only man capable of saving the world.'

MacLaurin's businesslike attitudes will be severely tested by the staid and outdated attitudes of the English counties, but he is already talking a courageous game. What is more, he talks it as if the words are not platitudes but the harbinger of firm policy statements. When he talks of 'a blank piece of paper', you just know it will not be blank for very much longer. Cling to MacLaurin's words and, unlike some other English cricket administrators, you will not be suffocated in candy-floss. This is quite an unnerving experience in a sport where tinkering is regarded as preferable to progress. MacLaurin, suitably for someone who has made his mark in retailing, is now involved in Pyramid Selling. The introduction of a pyramid structure in English cricket, installing a clear and efficient chain of achievement from the smallest schoolboy right through to the Test arena, is the most vital element of the ECB's vision. Most radical (and not yet addressed to any great degree) would be the introduction of movement between leagues, as has operated successfully in non-league football for many years. Clubs possessing the drive and ambition to improve their squares and facilities, attract good players and invest in youth development would be offered the rise in status that their efforts deserved. Clubs putrefying in an endless time-warp, with no commitment to improvement, would gradually decline, as indeed they must.

Predictably, in a sport that epitomizes Britain's tendency to look back rather than forward, the idea of implementing premier club leagues in all regions of the country, and introducing a system where achievement rather than tradition is paramount in determining in what leagues clubs play, is already meeting stubborn resistance from certain local officials whose own little empires are under threat.

'People have to realize that the England side is the top priority,' MacLaurin says. 'Everything flows from them. The ECB is working to introduce a national pyramid from schoolchildren to club cricket to first-class cricket to Test cricket. We have to have an England side that is competing at the highest level internationally. You cannot look at the recent performances of England sides and say that this is just cyclical. There are some fundamental things which need to be put right.

'There have been a lot of sacred cows in this game, and there should be no sacred cows anymore. Cricket has had its halcyon days. There is a lot of money in other games. County cricket has not had to perform too well because the clubs knew they were pretty secure, because of the revenue brought in by Test cricket. But in this day and age, no one is secure. There will only be guarantees if England are among the best two or three teams in the world. Our domestic cricket is pretty uninteresting – counties can be out of every competition by mid July – and we have to recognise this. Maybe promotion and relegation, maybe a two-tier Sunday League, all these things are on our agenda.'

The mood in the press conference is quite striking. When MacLaurin is not briefing the media, the tone of the questions carries the implication that the media is anxious to brief him. There is a kind of pally, nice-to-see-you-sir-and-jolly-good-luck-but-we-think-we-should-really-warn-you-how-awful-things-have-really-become approach to it all. This is understandable. Whenever anybody has talked of radical change in cricket, the approach of the first-class counties has been to concede the need for a working party, form a committee with minimal powers, and wait for the whole thing to be forgotten. Had the TCCB run Tesco for the past twenty-five years, they would still be investing in loss-making village stores, stressing their historical importance and announcing yet another working-party report into the pros and cons of introducing one or two larger out-of-town sites.

MacLaurin's sporting background is also designed to mollify cricket's traditionalists: ex-captain of Malvern College, Second XI cricket for Kent, football for Corinthian Casuals, before turning to business at the age of twenty-two. Now, as then, his love of cricket is unlikely to submerge his business instincts. He concludes with a warning to those who believe that the Board's proposals for change will be delayed in endless committee obfuscation.

'You can't take the view that committees are an excuse for no action,' he says. 'That is something that we must avoid at all costs. We will put forward by mid-year a very strong plan for the game. I have a completely open mind, but when I get the strategy, I won't be open minded any longer.'

This uncompromising stance is branded on his mind when he and Lamb watch England capitulate in the final one-day international. Both regard the Zimbabwean experience as 'a shambles' and resolve that it must never happen again. MacLaurin assures the players of his full support, addresses them about their rights and responsibilities, and talks of 'drawing a line'. And if he is doing that, so shall we. Who knows, it might just work.

15

An Australian Crisis

ENGLAND view their arrival in New Zealand as a Return to Civilisation. Listening to them, one would think they had spent the past seven weeks back-packing in the Amazon jungle. They munch takeaway pizzas and exclaim how nice it is to be back in civilisation. They peer in shop windows and exclaim how nice it is to be back in civilisation. They even wander around some of the shabbier New Zealand towns, which at their worst resemble film sets for a low-budget Western, and exclaim how nice it is to be back in civilisation. They should win the series: not only are they comfortably the more talented side, whatever the horrors of Zimbabwe might have suggested, but they feel safe.

Civilisation, NZ style, also offers the sort of evenly paced, seaming pitches that England's players relish, and even more civilised opponents, a NZ Selection XI in Palmerston North, and Northern Districts in Hamilton, who in four-day matches allow England to administer a thoroughly good hiding. The build-up to the first Test in Auckland goes so smoothly that it supports the contention that if England played all their Test cricket in New Zealand, they would be regarded as one of the top four sides in the world.

The country is changing, though; long regarded as like England in the Fifties, it now seems to have skipped to 1972, most of the Sixties having been far too dangerous to contemplate. In Palmerston North, it is virtually impossible to eat more than two mouthfuls in any restaurant without having to listen to The Eagles. What odds Alan Mullally singing a few bars from 'One of These Nights' before the end of the Test series? Considering the way things have gone so far this winter, One Of These Days might be more appropriate.

Lloyd strives valiantly to explain England's sense of well-being. 'The observation that we are more comfortable here is valid,' he says. 'Everything we see – the pitches, the food, the people, the climate – is more conducive to us.'

The reference to preferring the people is a bit naughty, and sounds just the sort of thing to cause further offence in Zimbabwe. Another few hours and some huge, red-faced bloke will be slapping his Castle lager down on the bar at Morgans and swaying off to check the flight times from Bulawayo to Auckland.

But Atherton is not the only Test captain held to be in crisis; in Australia, Mark Taylor is suffering similar hardship. After the horrors of Zimbabwe, it might be stretching credulity to the limit to suggest it, but any inkling that the Ashes series might not be the one-sided affair we have come to fear seems worth examining, so I wave farewell to England's restless, uptight world and hop on a flight to Melbourne.

The story is gruesomely familiar. Taylor's ambition to lead his country in the Ashes series is also threatened by a combination of abysmal results in one-day cricket and the worst batting form of his life. The captain awaits the fourth Test against the West Indies in Adelaide with only one first-class fifty in twenty-two successive knocks, and a top score this season in one-day cricket of 29.

Taylor's feet are leaden; so are Atherton's. Taylor's trademark shots, the cover drive and the tuck of his hips, have virtually disappeared; when did Atherton last square-drive with authority? Taylor's technical deficiencies are illustrated by an open-faced bat which causes him to slice to slip or drag the ball onto his stumps; Atherton has repeatedly edged into the slips or fallen prey to a break-back delivery that has him lbw, creasebound. Taylor is also deemed to be weighed down by excess responsibility; similarly, is it not Atherton, to Raymond Illingworth's mind, who should concentrate on his own game and leave the wider picture to others?

Eager to test the depth of Australian depression, I attempt

a spot of impromptu market research. The farewell T-shirt produced by England's sponsors Tetley, who have stoically spent years being identified with an unsuccessful product, bears the message: *'England Cricket Team Tour of New Zealand 1997 – Don't Wind Me Up.'* It sounds suspiciously like a scornful goodbye, but the England lads, who by now are used to far worse, seem oblivious to it. Give them a T-shirt declaring 'England Cricket Team: Pile of Crap in Zimbabwe', and as long as it had a designer logo somewhere, one or two would wear it without delay.

Pausing only to scrawl 'press corps' in black felt-pen on the back, it is time to don the T-shirt and risk the derision of Melbourne's meanest streets. The feeling that I will not return alive is encouraged when staff at the Rockmans Regency Hotel enquire whether I might like to settle my bill before I go. But in a full hour, there is only one disparaging holler, and I didn't spend *all* of the time hiding away in that restful little coffee bar just off Collins Street; you know, the one with the wonderful chicken and asparagus foccacia. Even that solitary cry went: 'You're just as bad as us, mate.' Australia, for once, is feeling vulnerable. It has to be worth staying a little longer. And anyway, in January there are few more uplifting places.

The combination of a one-day slump plus defeat over Christmas in the Melbourne Test has encouraged Australia's taciturn new coach, Geoff Marsh, to theorize that too many of his players are losing concentration on the job in hand because they are already dreaming of the Ashes series six months hence. This causes consternation for at least one sports writer of considerable repute. Mike Coward, writing in *The Australian*, wonders why his country should be so obsessed by the approach of a piddling Test series against one of the worst sides in the world. He describes an Ashes tour as a 'gravy train' and contends that the series is virtually irrelevant when compared to the tougher challenges presented on tours to the West Indies, South Africa, India and Pakistan.

'English cricket is an irrelevance on and off the ground,' he thunders. 'And this is not the ramblings of an Anglophobe. It is a statement of fact. No longer does the cricket world look to Lord's for direction and inspiration... England is a soft touch; a snack, a snaffle for every professional team with ability, energy, imagination and fight.'

Coward's anxiety for Australia to break free from its British heritage, and act like the republic it is clearly destined to become, is understandable. He does overplay it a tad – it might be an oxymoron, but England v Australia remains a local derby between two countries 12,000 miles apart. All the same, his assessment might make us realize that there is a limit to how long we can fail. Traditions, however valuable, cannot support us for ever.

The creeping importance attached to one-day cricket is a central cause of Atherton and Taylor's diminishing status. They are both reliable, resourceful and of high calibre, but arguably not adaptable enough to be worth a place in the one-day side. Taylor's predecessor Allan Border famously commented that he could hardly remember anything about his one-day career. But Australia's run of eleven defeats in fourteen limited-overs internationals, and their failure for the first time to qualify for the final of the World Series, has caused reverberations.

Taylor, like Atherton in Zimbabwe, asserts that Test cricket remains the priority (and Australia still lead that series 2-1), but such logic is drowned out in the general frenzy. For the first time, one-day failures threaten to cause the sacking of an England or Australian captain. For those of us who respect the true challenge of Test cricket, that beggars belief. But the public cannot be assailed by the limited-overs hype one minute and then told it is all completely irrelevant the next. They are not that gullible.

The Sheffield Shield competition is also being subjected to as much flak as our poor, discredited county championship. The Shield, contested by only six teams, has long been assumed in England to possess a quality and intensity that our historic hotchpotch of eighteen first-class counties cannot match. Not any longer, say Australians. The Shield has been devalued by the perpetual absence of Test players because of international calls. Ian Healy, the Australian wicketkeeper, has played in thirty-five Shield matches, eighty-five Tests and more one-day internationals than he would care to remember. No one is sure about the identity of the top six batsmen in the country: Michael Slater and Ricky Ponting have both been dropped, to be replaced by the likes of Justin Langer and Matthew Hayden, who are heavy run-scorers in the Shield but whose aptitude for Test cricket remains questionable. The Australian media, supported by past Test players of repute, is warning its administrators to 'beware of the English county cricket syndrome'. There is no more dire pronouncement than that.

Adelaide, though, subdues the fears. Well before lunch on the fourth day, Australia beat the West Indies by an innings and 217 runs to take an unbeatable 3-1 lead in the five-Test series and retain the Frank Worrell Trophy. When it comes to fashioning a sporting crisis, they clearly aren't a patch on us. Curtly Ambrose, whose fast bowling on an uneven pitch had overpowered Australia in Melbourne, is injured and instead the Test is settled by wrist spin. Not Shane Warne either, but Michael Bevan, a batsman-who-bowls-a-bit whose match analysis of 10 for 113 represents the best return by a left-arm wrist spinner in Test history. This is the same Michael Bevan who barely bowled at all for Yorkshire in last summer's county championship. Even when they are purportedly concentrating on beating the West Indies, Australia are still taking the mickey out of the English.

Bevan is a most un-Australian cricketer. He is introverted, complicated, moody, and prone to such anguished self-analysis that he makes Mark Ramprakash look like a free spirit. On at least one occasion, he has responded to a dismissal by standing speechless in a shower for the best part of half an hour with all his clothes on. His batting is still riddled with tension, as an unbeaten 85 in five and a half hours in Australia's first innings testifies. But he is a physically impressive man who bowls his wrist-spinners with great strength. It is just that at the moment, he does not seem to know whether he is a fast batsman batting slowly or a slow bowler bowling quickly.

Taylor speculates that the Test is a watershed – confirming, once and for all, the demise of the aggressive and antagonistic all-pace attack. The battery of four fast bowlers, with which the West Indies have enjoyed supremacy in Test cricket for the best part of thirty years, is now deemed to be outmoded, replaced by a return to the more romantic notion of a bowling attack of variety which has wrist spin at its heart.

Courtney Walsh, the West Indies captain and one of the senior members of the Fast Bowlers' Union, clearly regards the theory as piffle but is too polite to say so. But wrist spin's rise from obsolescence is startling: Australia possess Shane Warne and Michael Bevan; in Zimbabwe, Paul Strang is making rapid progress; Pakistan take pride in Mushtaq Ahmed, India in Anil Kumble; and South Africa delight in Paul Adams. Bevan remains the odd man out – he is the only one of them not to have bowled out England. Not yet, anyhow.

For England, the whole debate is meaningless. We have no true fast bowlers and, the disappointing Ian Salisbury apart, no leg-spinners either. All we can do is wonder whether, over the next few years, we are going to be blasted out or spun out. In an era of covered pitches, no one, as yet, has seen fit to predict the glorious revival of the medium-paced dobber.

A decade and more ago, Find A Fast Bowler competitions became a trendy solution, with the winner normally turning out to be a schoolboy javelin-thrower who was promised expert coaching – normally with the assistance of a publicity-conscious soft-drink sponsor – and was then never heard of again. Now there are calls for youthful leg-spinners to be rounded up throughout the nation – presumably David Lloyd will have to nip down to the fancy dress shop to hire a pied piper uniform – and transformed overnight into Test bowlers by expert tuition from Australian coaches. These fanciful notions arise because of one consistently damning fact: the failure of our school and club cricket system naturally to produce players of variety and worth.

It is a popular assumption in Australia that the Ashes series could most accurately be marketed as 'The Walkover', especially so as England have failed to win the opening Test in Auckland in the most extraordinary circumstances. Danny Morrison, New Zealand's number eleven and the holder of the record number of ducks in Test cricket, manages to hang on for nearly three hours in an unbroken stand of 106 with the century-maker Nathan Astle. When Morrison joins Astle, New Zealand lead by 11 and England wait for him to miss one or slog one up in the air. It never happens, and Paul Weaver in the *Guardian* records that afterwards 'reporters filed silently past Atherton's grey features as if he was lying in state'. Lloyd touches his captain's collar sympathetically and the 'we murdered 'em' style of Bulawayo is replaced by generosity and sportsmanship. 'Epic,' he says, and those present find it hard to disagree.

In New Zealand, they are marketing the Danny Morrison Duck Caller, which spectators are encouraged to blow every time he comes in to bat. It clearly doesn't work, and England's bowlers should demand their money back.

England are contriving to draw winnable Test matches in the most extraordinary circumstances. This time at least most of the nation slept through it, going to bed with New Zealand eight wickets down at lunch and still twenty-six runs away from avoiding an innings defeat. What we would have given for a leg-spinner! What we would also give for a first-class system that bred harder cricketers. Only in 1996 were points for a draw reintroduced in the championship. Bloody-minded resistance from tail-enders has been virtually unheard of. For all England's first-class cricket overload, here they were faced by a situation they rarely encounter.

Far worse than all this, however, the bloody Aussies have undermined Thorner Mexborough's possibilities of sweeping all before them next summer. While in Adelaide, I receive a fax from Adrian Wake, our vice-captain, leading batsman (apart from his incurable addiction to cutting length-balls) and hostile fast bowler (on the days at least when he manages to hit the cut bit, or a racing heartbeat does not force him to abandon his spell and relax at third man for a while). Adrian has decided to chuck in his job and go to Australia for a year. 'Just imagine what a better player I'll be in 1998,' he faxes, even joking about 'tipping the first division title in Thorner's direction.' This must have been a typographical error. Clearly, he meant 'third division title'. The way we are haemorrhaging players at the moment, relegation is a distinct possibility.

Anyway, vice-captains are not meant to have the ambition and imagination to travel 12,000 miles in search of self-fulfilment; they are designed to plod a couple of miles on a Friday evening to roll pitches and mark the white line around the boundary. Instead of checking whether he has the appropriate working visa, the vice-captain's role is to check whether there are enough new balls in the box. Rather than stocking up on travel adaptors and the *Rough Guide to Australia*, his priorities should stretch no further than finding a new head for the shower that doesn't work and burrowing in second-hand bookshops for the *Rough Guide to Mole Catching*.

As his captain, I ring him up to tell him this.

He laughs, and doesn't change his mind.

The peculiar thing about Adrian's year off is that we all sensed this would probably happen in November when we unanimously re-elected him vice-captain without a moment's thought. No one wanted *his* job, either. And anyway, we were following one of village cricket's abiding principles: always ignore a problem until it smacks you in the face. Then refuse to get involved on the grounds that you have to finish a loft extension and leave it to someone else to sort out.

I loaf on a bed in a Melbourne hotel room and draw up two alternative Thorner First XIs. Side A is good enough to sweep aside all before it; Side B stares mockingly at me from the page. Side A only needs about six huge strokes of luck and it will all stitch together by the spring; Side B is what we will probably end up with. It is too early to resign, but whether I can outlast Michael Atherton is dubious, and we haven't played a match yet.

*   *   *

Australia's West Indies series finishes in Perth, the world's remotest city, where even fellow Australians are greeted as visitors from another country. Perth is clean, fresh and modern, but lacks the substance and excitement of Australia's other major centres. Some Australians put this down to it being so full of English. The Perth Test, though, is often much more stimulating.

Assertions that the great era of West Indies fast bowling has come to an end are best not followed by a Test in Perth, and certainly not one on a pitch which by the end of the third day has a dozen cracks, as much as eight feet long and up to two inches wide, snaking from end to end. By then, the West Indies have demolished Australia's batting twice and won by ten wickets, with their fast-bowling trio of Walsh, Bishop and Ambrose taking eighteen wickets between them. Tony Greig should have abandoned his humidity counter and offered a reading on the Richter Scale.

When you are out of form, luck often deserts you – and Taylor's woes persist. In the first innings, he is run out for two, beaten by Chanderpaul's brilliant diving save and return from cover. Second time around, he scrapes a single and then does well to edge an excellent delivery from Ambrose. He prepares for South Africa with only a fifty-fifty chance of retaining the captaincy for the Ashes series.

For The Best Side in the World, Australia have problems. Add a single Test in India and they have lost three of the last six they have played, and the only specialist batsman to have made a century in that time is Matthew Hayden, who is supposedly too technically flawed for Test cricket.

Taylor has put Australia's selectors in a quandary. He is an imaginative and intuitive captain, a marvellous ambassador and a man who, in his three years in charge, has rounded their image without reducing their effectiveness. Under his captaincy, the non-stop sledging that was a feature of Australian sides under Allan Border's captaincy has regained a sense of proportion. When tempers become inflamed on the field, it is clear from the outer that he responds immediately to control the situation. But his lack of runs has begun to impair his authority and the Perth Test finishes in a hot-tempered atmosphere.

On the second evening, Brian Lara, after making his only Test century of the series, complains bitterly of excessive Australian sledging, particularly against the young opening batsman Robert Samuels. Lara alleges that the abuse has been non-stop, and in particular that Samuels has been called 'a loser' by Glenn McGrath, which, if true, is pretty objectionable stuff.

On the third morning, Lara emerges as a runner for the West Indies captain Courtney Walsh, an unusual gesture from such a senior player which Walsh describes as 'touching' and Taylor regards as 'provocative'. While running for Walsh, Lara tumbles to the floor under an accidental collision with Hayden. As he complains, more than one Australian fielder testily advises him to get up and shut up. Later, the umpires summon both captains before the match referee, Raman Subba Row, who tells them to cut out the nonsense.

In England, war with the media would immediately be declared. Sandbags would be piled high, machine-guns trained. The whole episode would become a matter for evasion and half-truths, with the public-relations officer turning off his mobile phone, England Cricket Board officials announcing that the matter was now closed, and the captain grumpily refusing to express an honest opinion, partly through a perpetual fear of being misrepresented, partly because he failed to recognize that it was his responsibility to do so. Journalists would complain that the matter had been mishandled, officialdom that it had been 'blown up out of all

THE RECUPERATION

Jack Russell's non-cricketing interests helped him to survive an inactive and dispiriting tour of Zimbabwe. As well as endless walks around the boundary, (top) he also found time in Bulawayo for painting (bottom) and to visit some of the most famous sites of the Zulu uprising. *(Graham Morris)*

THE OUTBURST

Weak umpiring in the Bulawayo Test frustrated England's victory bid. Alec Stewart (top left) practices in front of the stuffed head of an African elephant, while England's coach, David Lloyd, (top right) will never forget the outcry at his post-match outburst. The scoreboard (bottom) confirms that England have missed victory by the smallest possible margin, the first time that a Test has finished 'match drawn with scores level.' *(Graham Morris)*

THE EXPLANATIONS

Michael Atherton offers a defence of England's performances in Zimbabwe, or as much of a defence as he cares to, to the English press corps (top) and (bottom), the hierarchy of the England and Wales Cricket Board: Lord MacLaurin and (extreme right) Tim Lamb. *(Graham Morris)*

THE REFUELLING

Shane Warne explores the MCG kitchens during the Melbourne Test between Australia and the West Indies.
(Mark Ray)

THE CONTEMPLATION

Michael Atherton strolls around the boundary at Fitzherbert Park after
being dismissed cheaply during England's tour match against a New
Zealand Selection XI in Palmerston North. *(Graham Morris)*

THE TOUR

Thorner Mexborough CC's tour of Sri Lanka brought a series of defeats, the first (top) against a St Thomas' College XI. There was also time for beach cricket and a lark with the locals when the coach broke down. *(David Hopps)*

THE VILLAGE

Thorner Mexborough CC 1997: Back row l-r: Andy Laycock, Richard Chapman, Alan Davies, Paul Foster, Rod Johnstone, Ed Day. Front row l-r: Jon Eagle, Phil Ralli, Chris Walker, the author (allegedly), Phil Warren, David Wharton. *(David Hopps)*

THE CLASH

Rising tension as Thorner take on the might of the Australian media on the eve of the Headingley Test. Australia won that one, too, despite the best efforts of Thorner's close-catching cordon. *(Mark Ray)*

proportion'. Resentment, dishonesty and distrust would be the order of the day. The public would trust their prejudices. In this, like so many other areas, English cricket is operating unsuccessfully.

By contrast, Taylor's assessment of the situation is strikingly intelligent and honest. Probing press-conference questions receive detailed, thoughtful answers, which are conscientiously recorded in the following morning's newspapers. An inflammatory issue provides both good headlines and the examination it deserves. Taylor has had his say, the media has had a good story, and the public have been informed.

This is far more than just another 'row' story, or even just the latest episode in the troubled and talented career of Brian Lara, truly great batsman one minute, irritating pest the next. The most important implication of Lara's accusations is that Taylor's authority as Australian captain might be weakening, an inevitable consequence, perhaps, of his own poor form. No matter how impressive a captain he might be – and Taylor is among the best – it is far easier to lay down the law after scoring a century than it is when trapped in such a miserable run of batting failures. Subconsciously, his team-mates are more likely to respect his words when he is playing well.

Taylor, for the sake of his own future, needs to address the issue. He sums up Lara's behaviour like this: 'I think he is an antagonist, there is no doubt about it. He looks for things out there, for things to happen. It gets him going and it gets other people away from their game. I think he plays it well, along the lines of Ranatunga [the Sri Lankan captain, whose gamesmanship had so irritated the Australians the previous winter]. He works on the same sorts of theories and looks to put other players off. I've great respect for Brian, he's a very good player. I don't believe our sledging has got worse. If he has got a problem with me or my players, I'd like him to come to me and tell me.'

Taylor shrewdly reminds the media of Australia's

unblemished disciplinary record during his captaincy. When he did miss a short tour of Sri Lanka, two Australian players did run foul of the authorities – Steve Waugh and Ian Healy, who just happen to be the two likeliest men to succeed Taylor should he lose the captaincy. He has deflected criticism of his team and he has subtly bolstered his own position. It has been another masterly and enlightened media performance of the kind that Atherton has rarely been taught, able or willing to produce.

16

Old Country, Young Country

AS luck would have it, the Adelaide Test coincides with Australia Day, which gives a nation not overly given to soul-searching an opportunity to indulge in an examination of its national psyche. Australia is adjusting to life as a multi-cultural society and, although that brings its attendant problems anywhere in the world, it is doing so in a comparatively tolerant and relaxed fashion.

Australia remains strangely reluctant to formally break its ties with Britain by becoming a republic, and the election of a Liberal Government threatens to delay the process still further. But times are changing. Australian schoolchildren no longer learn the loyal affirmation of allegiance – 'I am an Australian. I love my country. I honour her Queen. I promise to obey her laws' – and the nation is struggling to re-identify itself.

As English cricket searches for a way out of its depression, Australia offers a powerful message as to the way forward. The Australian national identity arises naturally from its perception of itself as a young and changing country. As a young country, it yearns to look forward, and to define itself not by what it has achieved in the past but by its present well-being, and by its ambitions for the future.

It is a mood, crucially, which appeals to a younger generation. Achievement in sport therefore naturally becomes a vital element of the nation's sense of worth. When Mark Waugh scores a Test century for Australia, or Kieren Perkins swims to a gold medal in the Olympic freestyle, the nation shares their pride in the most unaffected, unabashed manner imaginable.

On Australia Day, a succession of prominent citizens are wheeled out to express this feeling. Les Murray, the poet, praises a burgeoning 'celebration of inter-marriage and the unlikely ethnic mixtures that exist in the ancestry of most Australians.' The Aborigines apart, of course – they have recently been subjected to an attack by Pauline Hanson, an oddball right-wing independent who disturbingly has won election as an MP in a redneck area of Western Queensland. As representative for Oxley, she has become known as the Oxleymoron.

Those given licence to extol Australia's virtues take pride in the country's positive outlook, their hopes for the future, and their optimistic and easy-going attitude to life. Such a message was powerful enough for Tony Blair, after studying the Australian experience at first hand, to adopt the theme of 'Young Country' for his set-piece speech at the 1995 Labour Party conference, one which received media acclaim across the political spectrum. Not enough has been heard of it lately.

During the European Football Championships in 1996, we, too, briefly captured that vibrant, youthful mood as the combination of England's progress to the semi-finals and some wonderful summer sunshine encouraged an atmosphere of simple, unbridled joy.

Even then, the *Daily Mirror*, in a crass and cynical contribution, sought to twist such happiness into a series of cheap racist jokes about England's quarter-final opponents, Spain. Equally uneasy was a percentage of the intellectual elite which resented such a rare sense of unity arising from something as 'base' as football. Broadsheet newspapers and Radio 4 carried their pathetic complaints about sport's presence as a lead news item when there were supposedly far more important things to consider. 'Should we join the ERM, day 842,' perhaps? This hostility often seems to arise from the fact that the poor, psychologically threatened darlings all hated having to go on a cross-country run when they were at school. Presumably all the kids who hated maths can call for a ban on economic news?

The show of unity that surrounded Euro 96 occurs rarely in England, far too rarely. Most of the media might tell you that a royal wedding pulls the nation together, but it only unites two groups – those who revel in the country's traditions and those who live sad, vicarious lives through a succession of soap operas, of which The Royals is by far the most expensive to produce, on the grounds of having more extravagant sets.

There is much to be proud of in England today: our sense of irony, our comedy, our literature, the best of our TV and newspapers, the depth of our friendships, our landscape, our eccentricity, our beef (no, sorry, not our beef), our national health service (or what's left of it), our culture, our inventors, our reinvigorated music scene. With more investment, our cinema. With more encouragement, a returning sense of community.

But for the most part, England is a country that still defines itself by its past greatness, even though that sense of greatness is deemed to have ended with the end of the Second World War more than fifty years ago. The majority of the country is excluded from this by age; millions more by ethnic background. That brings great social pressures: apathy at best, dislocation at worst.

It goes some way to explaining why too often in recent years, it has been trendy to be miserable and uncommitted. Under-achievement has become the fashionable response to a stifling society whose benchmarks are perceived to be outdated. Those who do retain a sense of fun often combine it with a determined irresponsibility. Studies also suggest that our young people are the most unfit in Western Europe.

For all the talk of opportunity, many still see only privilege. The class system might have weakened, but it remains intact. Our great ancient buildings are constant proof of past achievements, many of our shabby modern designs a reminder of our faltering ambitions. Our history weighs heavily upon us. It is much easier to become a hero in England when you have been dead a very long time.

When England's tour of Zimbabwe was at its most calamitous, Jeffrey Archer, the former Tory vice-chairman and best-selling pulp novelist, wondered whether the players were embarrassed and inhibited by the achievements of the

British Empire, and advised them they had no need to be. Although he was looking at the problem from a more traditional perspective, he deserved some credit for at least being prepared to contemplate the problem.

John Major expressed his pride in England in a speech to Tory MPs on St George's Day in 1993. He extolled 'the long shadows falling across the county ground, the warm beer, the invincible green suburbs, dog lovers and pools fillers... old maids cycling to Holy Communion through the morning mist,' images which suggested not so much a modern vision of the land he had inherited as too many wasted hours reading second-rate English poets.

Before him, when Margaret Thatcher spoke of society, it was to dismiss the notion that it ever existed; how does that play in an England dressing-room trying to promote team spirit above individualism? At the Last Night of the Proms, Union Jacks are waved and the Empire faves – Land of Hope and Glory, Rule Britannia and the like – are chorused in a retreat into a world that no longer exists. What about the world that does? When Jack Russell tried to express his Englishness on Christmas Day in Harare by having his wife press the phone against the TV so he could listen to the Queen's Speech, his pride was undeniable but it only served to add to his eccentricity. There must be a more broadly based way of doing it.

Until recently, it was possible to advance the alternative argument: that England was bolstered by its history and drew confidence from it, whilst Australia's reliance upon its hopes for the future was intrinsically shallow. That argument is no longer persuasive – not in sport, anyway. Scores of young English cricketers are thrilled by their first sporting experience of Australia – by its vigour, its optimism, its drive – and are equally shocked when they return to the land they want to love and sense that pessimism, lack of ambition and the stifling morality of suburbia is more deeply entrenched than ever. They want to belong, but little gives them a sense of belonging.

Until England (or Britain, or the United Kingdom – even that confuses and perplexes us) redefines itself as an energetic, multi-cultural country striving to look forward, rather than a narrow-minded nation forever lapsing into nostalgia, sporting achievement will be so much harder to achieve. It is no fluke that many of our recent successes have been in individual sports, where the likes of Nigel Mansell, Nick Faldo and Linford Christie have all been fired by a cool and self-contained personal ambition. When it comes to team sports, the passion that Manchester United or Liverpool supporters feel for their club far outweighs their emotional commitment to England.

There is little doubt that the Australian cricket team feels a more powerful sense of national identity than its English counterpart, however much many England players might wish it otherwise. That is not the fault of the England players, but the system in which they have been raised.

The essence of that Australian pride is summed up in the concept of 'mateship'. No other single word sums up Australia's image of itself. It might be difficult for an Englishman to define, but the laconic, easy-going, outspoken, uncomplicated and sociable qualities of the country are all part of it. Its intention is to unite all ages, all backgrounds. In its simplest form, it is a basic expression of community.

When the England cricket team arrived in New Zealand, shaken by their experiences in Zimbabwe, Andrew Caddick explained to me his alternative theory of national pride. Caddick had been born and raised in New Zealand but, sensing that he was not being given a fair crack of the whip, emigrated to England in search of a fairer deal. A decade later, he felt badly served again, this time by being overlooked in the Tests and one-day internationals in Zimbabwe, and had a few things to get off his chest.

The Cad's theory of sporting pride was staggering in its promotion of individualism above collectivism. Wholly unabashed, he depicted his decision to play county cricket with Somerset and achieve residential qualification for

England as a straightforward career decision. His attempt to embrace a concept of what playing for England was about had not even begun; if Englishness is defined in the past, not the future, perhaps it never can.

'It's just like big business,' Caddick said. 'If the local man isn't up to it, a company might appoint someone from abroad to his job. It is as simple as that.'

The frustrations of those in England's dressing-room at their diluted sense of belonging were also evident during the final Test in Harare. Trevor Penney and Kevin Curran, two Zimbabweans, represent Warwickshire and Northamptonshire as English-qualified players but, when they were interviewed on Sky TV, both sheepishly avoided the issue of who they would prefer to win. Many England players were quick to take umbrage, believing that a commitment to the national side should be a pre-requisite for English qualification. 'Did you 'ear that?' asked Lloyd. 'Did you 'ear that? They wouldn't say it, wouldn't say it!' Yet Caddick's concept of playing for his country, which was based upon personal achievement and self-interest, did not seem to be much more worthwhile. With typically muddled thinking, England had felt obliged to recognize his good form for Somerset by selecting him for the winter tours, and then had lost faith in him almost before he had bowled a ball in anger.

England's extensive first-class system will always attract a number of refugees. Craig White might have been raised in Victoria, but who can fairly question his decision to return to his Yorkshire roots when there is photographic proof of his commitment to England in the form of him wearing a Union Jack T-shirt at an Australia v England Test at the MCG? Martin McCague, born in Northern Ireland, also has classic dual national status. For such players, national identity is not as straightforward as it is for many of us. All that can be demanded from those in their position is that they are honest about where their true loyalties lie.

One of the most unprincipled uses of English county cricket in recent seasons has been Andrew Symonds, who emigrated to Australia from Birmingham as a child, and drew attention to himself after scoring a century for Queensland against the 1994-95 England tourists in Toowomba. 'I'm a fair dinkum Aussie, mate,' he proclaimed, until he was offered a county contract by Gloucestershire, upon which he immediately clammed up about where his loyalties lay.

At the end of his first Gloucestershire season, Symonds turned down a place on the England 'A' tour to Pakistan. He was free to make what was an honest choice but, astonishingly, he still returned to Gloucestershire as an English-qualified player in 1996, even going as far as signing a formal declaration that he was available for selection by England if required.

Gloucestershire, out of blatant self-interest, colluded in the deception and accused the media of hounding him. The media was merely asking the obvious question: 'Does your declaration that you are available for England mean that you will play for England if picked: yes or no?' It seemed fair enough to wonder. The whole shoddy affair was brought to an end in Australia's summer of 1996-97 when Symonds was selected for Australia 'A', and jumped at the opportunity. By doing so, he abandoned his Gloucestershire contract without a second thought, but only after his cheating of the system had gained him two years' experience. Risibly, Gloucestershire held up their hands in mock surprise.

'I'm an Aussie and I always have been,' he said. 'It was not a very tough decision, mate. I know in my heart that I've always been an Aussie. I love living here, and the cricket and the lifestyle. I don't think playing for England was a temptation for me, mate. It would have been more of a soft option.'

It was a shame that he could not rise to such honesty in England. But then perhaps there was not enough national pride in England to shame him into it.

As long as England repeatedly fail at Test level, the call will still be heard for the return to an English XI exclusively born and raised in the country. That is not only futile in an increasingly mobile world, but dangerous when such a yearning can so easily be twisted into racism. Those who propose, with some twisted form of racial purity, that an English side must be drawn from English stock are suppressing the development of second-generation West Indian and Asian youngsters. They are repeating the old mistake of looking for a solution in the past.

Those who wish for a multi-cultural English side to be naturally drawn together and sustained by a shared vision of the future are seeking something far superior. Only when that vision is discovered will the English cricket team have an equal opportunity for success. It seems to me, with a general election a couple of months away, that Tony Blair should start dusting off the Young Country speech again. Even now, though, there is probably a spin doctor warning that to do so might have a damaging effect on the voting intentions of two OAPs in a marginal constituency somewhere in Leicestershire.

17

Flight From Sri Lanka

While England press in New Zealand for a rare Test series victory overseas, and one that will save Michael Atherton's captaincy career, Thorner CC abandon thoughts of winter afternoons by the sea at Scarborough and brace themselves for a fortnight's tour of Sri Lanka. If England have lost the art of touring, will a run-of-the-mill collection of club cricketers be any different? As defeat follows defeat, the group dub themselves 'Cricketers Anonymous'. By the time they return to England, they are anything but...

Sunday 9 February
While a two-man welcoming party sleeps soundly at the TransAsia in Colombo, oblivious to the fact that the coach driver has forgotten to convey them to the airport, the remaining twenty-four members of Thorner's tour party gaze wearily around the spartan arrivals hall at Katanayake airport for their dawn transport to the Mount Lavinia Hotel. Our coach driver and his junior have been afflicted by a sudden attack of shyness, parking about half a mile from the terminal and waiting for someone to find them. In a rough approximation to tour-group methods, Junior has a crumpled piece of paper on his person bearing the legend 'Mr Hoops'. Perhaps worried about his spelling, he chooses to hide this in his pocket, and then to hide himself. He is discovered by a search party after about an hour, just before their supplies of mineral water give out, and surrenders with some relief.

Our tour party is not exactly balanced; of the eighteen players, seventeen are batsmen. The only specialist bowler, Dave Wake, is the spit of W G Grace at fifty, except that W G's Achilles tendons were in better nick. Dave, though, is probably a better groundsman. We have four wicketkeepers, none of whom want to keep wicket in such heat and humidity, and about eight volunteer slow bowlers, only one of whom actually claims to spin it. But we do have an umpire and a scorer, which means that for once we won't have to do it ourselves. We have also brought Thorner's local builder. 'There's lots of work here,' mutters Grenville, who has been struck by a rare and sudden entrepeneurial zeal. He still goes to work on a pushbike, so Sri Lanka would suit him down to the ground.

Sri Lanka, for those seeing it for the first time, blasts the senses. The main road south is shared with contemplative cows, sleeping dogs, eating crows, and old men pushing handcarts. One bicycle is shared by two boys, with a pig resting across the handlebars. Three-wheeler trishaws jag in between fume-belching lorries and lopsided buses. The only obvious rule of the road is Might Is Right.

The tension and jet-lag soon disappear after a few hours by the pool. Our London contingent, led by Simon Mann of BBC Sport, relate with glee that they had frequently walked up the aisle of the Air Lanka flight looking for likely players. They had not managed to spot any. This does not fill us with immediate confidence... and the first game is tomorrow. Acclimatisation? That amounts to a splash of factor 15 and sampling the arrack, the local coconut-based firewater. It's great to be back.

Monday 10 February
Cricketers Anonymous 175–8, 45 overs. Old Thomians Swimming Club 179–4, 19 overs.
Result: Old Thomians SC win by 6 wickets.

England can take heart – another eleven club cricketers now realize the demands of playing overseas. We are so heavily outplayed on a steamily hot day that only some sterling drinking into the early hours secures the promise of a return fixture. 'You are welcome any time,' says Mohan, our rotund and genial host, 'but next time please bring some bowlers.' We present him with a calendar of famous Yorkshire walks, just in case he wakes up one morning and feels a bit spritely. *Walk no. 4: Nidd Beck: Arrive Katanayake Airport 0230, transfer 0535 from Heathrow to Leeds-Bradford airport, take no. 62 bus to Skipton....*

We *have* brought one fast(ish) bowler, but Adrian Wake has another heart flutter during his first over and ends up on the physio's bench even faster than did a dehydrated Tim Munton at the start of the England 'A' tour six years earlier. In the field, we run underneath skiers and dive over the top of drives. This contrasts vividly with the disciplined and enthusiastic St Thomas's College cricket practice on the boundary's edge. Their desire to learn can be sensed 100 yards away. After such a hapless effort, it is no surprise to us to be mistaken for England; autographs of such luminaries as Rolf Harris and Julie Andrews are soon well to the fore. Fake signatures are also evident on the bar bills; my triumph at intercepting a £20 bill I never signed for is tempered by the discovery of one for £40 that I obviously did sign, but cannot remember.

The tour party is gelling well. Gary Lonsdale has already been nicknamed 'The Cat' after surviving five catching chances in the first half-hour; add a few donkeys to do the bowling and we might yet improve a little. Cultural studies are also on the agenda:

'It's amazing,' says Adrian, 'these trishaw drivers offer you any kind of sex that you can think of.'

'Yes,' muses Simon Gilhooly, 'but why would you want to? I mean none of 'em are very good looking.'

By 2am, Dave Culloden is drunkenly wandering the streets of Mount Lavinia looking for his lost cricket bag. At 8am, he wanders the streets again, this time accompanied by a hangover. His kit has been in someone's room all the time.

Tuesday 11 February
Sumati, our coach driver, has mastered basic English. That is, he has mastered the one sentence, 'What time coach go in morning?' and just about comprehends the answer. His

'English-speaking guide' is still not revealing the full extent of his linguistic abilities, and we are beginning to wonder what his role is.

As my only knowledge of Sinhalese is Ehata Yanna ('Please go away'), many of our conversations are a complete mystery to both of us. Sample:

> *Hopps:* 'Sumati, you have passed the sports shop.'
> *Sumati:* 'About four and a half hours.'

Four and a half hours is, indeed, the estimated time to reach Mount Sigiriya, where we plan to climb a rock fortress that was once the home of a Kandyan king. But the delay at the sports shop, which Sumati has not passed at all but determinedly creeps towards at walking pace for most of the morning, is only dwarfed by the length of our delayed departure while Carol has emergency treatment for a mosquito bite on her ankle. Carol, as her sterling fund-raising efforts have proved, is not someone to cross lightly, not even if you are a mosquito. She looks so furious that any insect straying into her path will undoubtedly be splattered against the coach window. Her ankle looks even angrier.

We are proving particularly adept at losing luggage, or at least thinking that we have. After Culloden's moonlit kit-search, Simon Mann spends several hours fretting about a suitcase left behind in Mount Lavinia. Meanwhile in an adjacent room, at various intervals that evening, Phil Strongman and Sid Poole, our umpire, endlessly repeat the following conversation:

Phil: 'You sure that's not Simon's bag, Sid?'
Sid: 'No, that's not Simon's bag.'

Most of the party clamber up Mount Sigiriya just before sunset and as we gaze across the plains towards Kurunegala, venue for tomorrow's match, reality begins to dawn that it might be Simon's bag after all.

England, for once, also feel on top of the world. They have won the second Test in Wellington by an innings and 68 runs, an emphatic victory which promises to salvage Michael Atherton's captaincy for the Ashes series ahead. Roll of drums! Darren Gough takes nine wickets in the match and extols Atherton's strengths. 'Everyone respects Michael,' says the Dazzler. 'He gives us all confidence, he is a great captain.' More important for Atherton's survival is the ringing endorsement provided by Lord MacLaurin of Knebworth, who is back in New Zealand for his second bout of Test cricket this winter. 'Michael is a very strong character and a great captain,' says the Saviour of English Cricket. 'I am excited about going on working with him.' A change in fortune has come in the nick of time.

Wednesday 12 February
Cricketers Anonymous 204–7, 45 overs; Kurunegala Sports Club 207–5, 33 overs.
Result: Kurunegala SC win by five wickets.

A frenzied crowd several hundred strong fills the main stand at Welegadara Stadium as we do battle against the might of Kurunegala Youth Cricket Club. Any illusions we possess about our drawing power are shattered, however, when the real purpose of their presence becomes clear. The regional elections are in full swing and when the opposition campaign bus, bedecked in green, drives past, spectators dash excitedly out of the shade of the main stand to stone it. The order quickly goes around the team: Do Not Wear Anything Green! That even rules out our freebie tour caps emblazoned with the legend 'John Smith's Bitter'. Judging by the state of the election bus, he won't be the only one.

On a flat pitch and lightning-fast, bobbly outfield, with our lack of bowling we need about 270 to be competitive, but we fall away badly. Our plight is so serious that before going out to bowl, we adopt England's tried-and-trusted method and blare out 'Wonderwall' in the dressing-room. The Gilhooly brothers, who are guest captain and vice-captain for the day, also try to inspire the troops with a pin-up from *loaded* magazine. Fat lot of good either does. We concede 60 in the first six overs, although we do manage a few morale-lifting successes later in the day, most particularly a wicket for Paul Thackray, who bowls his leg-spinners so slowly that if he doesn't like them he can run after them and bring them back. Even so, we finish well beaten. Perhaps we should have played Balderdash instead.

In the hotel bar afterwards, Aranda, the opposing captain, pronounces that three things are important in life: 'Tolerance, honesty and prudence.' I add a fourth – taught by the Sri Lankans – a sense of humour. If I had to add a fifth, it would definitely be a bloody great big fast bowler.

As the sun goes down, Gareth Andrews takes a bottle of Carlsberg out to the coach, where Sumati is increasingly perplexed by our perpetual lateness. This is not what he had been given to understand about English punctuality. Gareth's gesture later seems inadvisable when Sumati drives the coach out of the hotel car park straight into a stationary Toyota. Mildly confused, he backs up and drives into it again before escaping retribution by driving two hundred yards down the wrong side of the road. As we twist into the hills towards Kandy, Gareth reflects: 'Perhaps I shouldn't have given him the arrack chaser.'

Thursday 13 February
Cricketers Anonymous 130 all out, 36.1 overs; Kandy Youth Cricket Club 134–5, 34.2 overs.
Result: Kandy YCC win by five wickets.

A heavy defeat at Kandy is our second of the day. The first setback occurs in the Topaz Hotel at about two o'clock in the morning when Gary Lonsdale, with alcoholic zeal, challenges the reception staff to a game of corridor cricket. 'You look good, I'll have to come off my full run,' announces one of Hunslet Nelson's finest. How he plans to negotiate the six downward steps lying in wait at the end of his run is not immediately apparent. He leaps into his delivery stride, smacks his head against an overhead beam and crashes with sickening force alongside the reception desk. Blood streams from a head wound.

For the night staff at reception, this could easily be a sacking offence. 'You were not here, you saw nothing,' they are told.

'Yes we were, we were standing right there,' they reply, with touching naïvety.

After half an hour with a bandage pressed to his head, the bleeding stops and Gary returns to his room with only a half-empty bottle of Carlsberg for company. The hotel doctor, back on duty at six o'clock, is booked for the purposes of applying two stitches, a tetanus injection and a funny little sticking plaster in the middle of his forehead. Clearly, The Cat has used up his nine lives.

The rest of the side do not look much healthier. There are many wonderful ways to see Sri Lanka, but groaning from a dressing-room floor is not one of them. The dressing-room is like a hospital unit, with heat exhaustion and a dodgy late-night buffet sharing the blame. Strongers rises briefly to bowl nine overs of off-spin, then collapses again. We are so short-handed that Paul fields for an hour in civvies. For once, the after-match socialising is forgotten.

In the evening, though, enough energy remains to debate the plight of English cricket: Gary tells of the Central Yorkshire League team who won promotion to the first division, barely survived in their first season, and so bought in a new team at large expense. Result of such short-termism: those who care about the club are forced out, the mercenaries finish in the same position and leave as well, and the club is left in a mess.

Phil Strongman has been moved by the desire of the young Sri Lankans to prove themselves through cricket, just as the same has struck him on previous visits to South Africa, Pakistan and Australia. What, he wonders, will inspire our own youngsters?

Dave Culloden bemoans the selfish and parochial attitudes in village cricket which cause small, unambitious clubs to try to hang onto their best young players instead of encouraging them to achieve their full potential at a higher level.

Chris Walker had spent much of the summer at Thorner reintroducing an under-13 side. Instead of offering assistance, most parents prefer to treat it as a baby-sitting service. Wakker remembers the inspirational mood in England during the 1996 European Football Championships. Why was that mood allowed to disappear as quickly as it had arrived?

Friday 14 February
Sumati is so perplexed by our continued lateness that he has taken to wildly overestimating journey times. When asked how long it will take to climb from Kandy to Nuwara Eliya, he rolls his eyes as if he expects several nights' camping by the side of the road. We breeze it in just over three hours, and stop at a tea factory en route.

At Nuwara Eliya golf course, all the caddies are four- or five-handicappers, so on one hole we caddy and they play. The Empire would not have approved, but the standard rises dramatically... they reach the green in two and we are much better at finding golf balls. Actually, they are also very skilled at finding golf balls, but only when they go back later in the day. They need to make a living as best they can. The lounge barman at the Grand Hotel earns Rs 1,250 a month (about £14) and on a good month will double this in tips. Servants' quarters amount to a bare room with a bed, and an outside tap for washing. Yet his clothing could not be cleaner, nor his manner more professional and polite. This explains the consternation the following morning when one of our number is tempted to souvenir an ash tray. If it is not returned, the cost of a replacement will be automatically docked from the room cleaner's wages. Once the implications are realised, the ash tray is speedily returned.

In traditional Englishman-abroad style, Denis Wharton has been overdoing the sunbathing and is glowing scarlet.

When there is a brief, late-night power cut, it is suggested that we should tie him to the roof of the bar and use him as a night light. Fortunately, power is restored before he can be found.

Saturday 15 February
After a dawn visit to World's End, a captivating viewpoint over Sri Lanka's hill country, a marathon coach journey is in prospect to the south coast. With traditional punctuality we depart an hour late, and after lunching amid the spectacular surroundings of Ella Gap Rest House, disaster strikes when the coach breaks down on the southern plains. While Sumati and his sidekick wash bits of the engine in a bucket of water (a solution that, after an hour, proves strangely effective), an impromptu game of rugby keeps both ourselves and the local villagers amused.

The characteristics of this tour party are becoming increasingly apparent. Paul Gilhooly actively welcomes the hardship. He is such a well-practised backpacker that he uses insect-*attractant* spray and regards the Lonely Planet guide as a cop-out for package tourists. By the end of the trip, he will undoubtedly be discovered at the river's edge, washing out his T-shirts with the locals. The two Londoners, Phil and Gareth, continue their ambitions to meet every Sri Lankan by the end of the fortnight.

We finally limp into Dickwella at eight o'clock, where the travel agent seems to have taken all this 'male bonding' too literally by booking rooms with double beds. The scenery, though, has been stunning and it has been a pleasure to sleep through it. In its fifteen-year existence, Dickwella beach resort had never sold more than 101 bottles of beer on a single night, so it is with some pride that we set a new record of 143. Who said this tour party are losers?

England still might be. Michael Atherton's captaincy is again hanging by a thread. In the final Test in Christchurch, he has carried his bat in England's first innings for 94, but England still trail by 118 with more than half the match remaining. A defeat here, and a drawn series, would make Atherton's survival for the Ashes summer untenable, however much we would like to think differently. And in Sri Lanka, we cannot see a ball of it.

Such gloomy news encourages Phil and Gareth to initiate the second state-of-English-cricket discussion of the tour. (Well, we have already covered the usual tour topics concerning relationships/parents/teenage angst/forgotten ambitions/bizarre sexual experiences/hopes and fears.) As good London club cricketers, village cricket is something of a mystery to them. Why don't Thorner practise? Why don't we suspend players who wander up ten minutes before the start of a match? Why don't we insist that club members must help with the junior set-up? Why don't we cut down on our drinking the night before a game? What sort of side is it that could reverse the batting and bowling order on the final game of the season and still win comfortably?

The sad and obvious answer is that too many village cricketers are not prepared to give the commitment necessary to achieve their maximum potential, and that we do not have enough resources to insist that they do otherwise.

Sunday 16 February
Today, we lost another cricket match – this time, a game of beach cricket against a group of Dickwella kids who wander up for a bit of a lark. They slog us into the sea and beyond the palm trees with uninhibited glee. We prod around, all the faults that have dogged us throughout our cricketing lives even revealing themselves in a tennis-ball hit-around on the beach. The tide is coming in, so when we bat the boundary is only ten yards away, but even this good fortune cannot save us. When the tide eventually rushes across the wicket, we complain about having to bat on an uncovered pitch. Our opponents wander off, chuckling. We retire to our rooms, to rub deep heat on aching hips, apply antiseptic cream to grazed knees and replaster blisters. You know you are getting old when your first-aid supplies take up more room than your cricket bag.

Monday 17 February
Cricketers Anonymous 149 all out, 44.1 overs; Galle CC 153–2, 34.3 overs.
Result: Galle CC win by eight wickets.

The old Dutch fortifications provide an imposing backdrop to the cricket ground at Galle and, accompanied only by a hawker who insists that a grubby pack of faded stamps will bring me a lifetime of happiness, I clamber to the top of them. The view might have changed, but the outcome hasn't. The first two deliveries that I witness from our flagging attack are smashed for four. We are heading towards another ignoble defeat.

Our bowling has always been useless; now our batting is heading the same way as we scrape 149 on another flat pitch. Only Gary holds out, batting forty-four overs for a stubborn half-century, and even he needs a runner after bruising a heel in the corridor-cricket escapade in Kandy. That runner happens to be me, and temperatures are in the thirties. The strange thing is that just standing out in the middle for three hours does wonders for my confidence. As I gaze around me, doing nothing more than running the odd single (and refusing many more), I'm increasingly deluded that I'm in brilliant batting nick.

Gareth is regarded as another of our batting 'bankers', but he is bowled swiping crudely to midwicket. 'If one of our batsmen had played a shot like that, we would have dropped him for three matches,' announces Malika, Galle's left-arm spinner. If we took such a view, we would never get an XI together.

Equipment in Sri Lanka is prohibitively expensive (a good quality cricket bat is the equivalent of three months' average wages) and we are in the habit of giving away the occasional cap, T-shirt and pair of batting gloves. When Bernie Chapman rues the fact that he had not thought to bring more unwanted equipment, this contrasts with the commercial attitude of some of England A's tourists to Zimbabwe in 1991 – as if proving themselves to be Thatcher's children, they tried to sell theirs.

Galle's outfield is shared with the local football club and it is notoriously worn and bumpy for football, never mind cricket. It is Galle FC's practice night and, after several post-match beers, we challenge them to a match in the half-hour before sunset. We win 2-1 thanks to an unapologetically robust, destructive game, allied to two pieces of goal-poaching by Nick Spencer. Perhaps England's national sport really is football after all?

In Christchurch, they must be wondering the same thing – New Zealand have set England 305 for victory. Virtually two days remain, but England have scored more than 300 to win only once before, in Melbourne sixty-eight years ago. Fortunately, if there is one thing you can rely upon from an England cricketer, it is that he will know absolutely nothing about the history of the game.

Tuesday 18 February

'What this tour really needs is a guitar player,' says Simon Bullough. 'A mate of mine carried a guitar around the world. He couldn't play it, but he met an awful lot of people.'

'Billy' Bullough is ruing the lack of music in a Bentota betting shop which, thanks to the six-hour time difference, is showing live TV coverage of English racing at nine o'clock at night. We resist the VIP section upstairs in favour of sampling some local colour, and Wakker's announcement that he went to school with Jamie Osborne, one of the jockeys who is competing at Market Rasen, causes him to be engulfed by Sri Lankans requesting tips. He magnanimously provides one, which fails hopelessly, and is relieved when he is not press-ganged into a refund.

On the wipe-clean board, someone has scrawled up the message, 'Carlisle Abandoned.' 'What?' asks Simon Gilhooly. 'For ever?'

England, meanwhile, have won the third Test in Christchurch, and thereby the series 2-0, thanks to another herculean effort by Atherton. England have triumphed by four wickets and it is Atherton who makes victory possible with 118 in more than six and a half hours. His dismissal, at 226 for three, predictably causes a sudden collapse, but his England team-mates have professed all along that they want to save him and, in the nick of time, they do just that as Cork and Crawley bat them home. Atherton had been on the field for all but the last three hours and it was those last three hours he hated most of all. New Zealand have hardly been the most testing of opponents, but it is a start. The alternative – beginning the Ashes series in chaos – was too awful to contemplate.

In the Bentota bookies, as a gesture of gratitude for Atherton's role in England's first overseas Test series win for five years, we put Rs100 on the 3.50 at Lingfield for him, but our selection finishes well-beaten. We toy with sending him a fax saying, 'You can't win 'em all.' Decide against it on the grounds that, after what he has been through, he already realises.

'We should go to New Zealand,' says Billy. 'Maybe even *we* could win a match there.'

Wednesday 19 February
News reaches Bentota that Phil Tufnell is on the back pages again, this time accused of smoking dope in the disabled toilets at a New Zealand restuarant. It is some time before this information is relayed to all the party, as by pure coincidence some of them happen to be on the beach, chatting to the local ganja man. I have even been promised a hash cake if I make 50 in the last match, which seems to cause everybody great amusement. Fortunately, as I have hardly middled a ball all tour, there is little chance of Scotland Yard taking an interest.

In the evening, we sample the delights of a variety show staged by the staff of the Serendib Hotel. It is their 364th show, and only the second time there has been audience participation. To general delight, Luci Bonnor and Billy Bullough provide their own version of a traditional Sri Lankan mime in which a drunken husband returns home to be lambasted by his furious wife. Both seem admirably cast for the roles. The Cat is inspired to perform his own tour stand-by... a spirited rendition of Don McLean's 'American Pie' in which the verses can variously appear more than once, in the wrong order, or not at all. As we are leaving, the discovery of a drinks receipt swimming in a bottle of Carlsberg causes brief consternation. The bottle is smashed (as is the culprit) and the receipt is dried out overnight so the hotel accountant can present it as evidence at breakfast the following morning. It is quickly paid, with apologies all round.

Thursday 20 February
Cricketers Anonymous 99–9, 25 overs; Mount Lavinia Hotel XI 103–8, 24.5 overs.
Result: Mount Lavinia Hotel XI win by two wickets.

Things are beginning to go wrong. Today, Moratuwa CC have failed to turn up, which robs us of the opportunity of a match on a Test ground, the Tyronne Fernando Stadium. The ground is a little damp, but eminently playable. The organiser is in Colombo 'on business', and when I telephone his wife she assures us that there is 'no problem,' which undoubtedly means that there is one, but no one wants to do anything about it.

Languishing by the hotel pool, our brave boys are taken aback to discover we have hastily cobbled together a 25-overs match against a hotel XI, who rush off for their kit with disturbing enthusiasm. They are even more surprised by the sight of the matting wicket at the nearby Irrigation Ground and promptly collapse to 99 for nine. This seems runs enough as Mount Lavinia's hotch-potch of bell-boys, waiters and receptionists hit 59 for eight, but visions of a first victory of the tour are shattered when a middle-aged batsman, name of Yabba, who has the frame of three average Sri Lankans, slogs them to victory with a ball to spare.

Passing time in the bar of a Malay restuarant while an evening tropical storm relents, I am about to pick up the tab for a round of beers when Upul, one of the hotel receptionists, is sick all over the floor, an outcome which owes less to the modest quantity of Lion Lager he has drunk than the three back-to-back, sixteen-hour shifts he has been asked to work at short notice. The Malay barman grabs the receipt and returns it a few minutes later along with a surcharge of Rs100. 'What's that for?' I ask him.

'Cleaning charge,' he replies.

Friday 21 February
Michael J De Zoysa XI 283 all out, 43.2 overs; Cricketers Anonymous 152 all out, 43.3 overs.
Result: Michael J De Zoysa XI win by 131 runs.

The toilet habits of the crows observing our performance from the roof of the main stand provide an apt commentary on our sixth successive defeat, although I am slightly relieved by my own failure, falling forty-six runs short of the threatened hash cake. Our final defeat at least takes place in the splendid setting of Colombo's finest Test ground, the Singhalese Sports Club, and we are rendered speechless when we discover that a first-class match has been put back twenty-four hours to allow us the privilege. What odds Lord's agreeing to delay a Middlesex match twenty-four hours so that a bunch of Sri Lankan tourists could play a friendly?

Wakker is mentally unhinged by such a grand occasion and runs in to bowl to his own eccentric running commentary, the highlight of which goes as follows: 'Walker, returning to the form that demolished Crossgates in his vintage 1991 season.' After bowling a leg-stump yorker, he then announces, 'And the best is yet to come,' a prediction not exactly supported by his next delivery, which is hauled over midwicket for six. Bernie also finishes the tour in style. At 3.10pm he runs himself out, first ball, and enters into a steaming silence. Six hours later, in the Cricket Café in Colombo, Phil Strongman gestures to Gary Sobers on the TV in the corner. 'He was a decent runner between the wickets, Bernie,' he says. It is the first time anyone has dared to broach the subject.

It's a Poya Day, a Buddhist religious festival linked to the full moon, which gives Sri Lanka the distinction of more Bank Holidays than any other country in the world. More pressingly, alcohol is forbidden, which ensures that our end-of-tour dinner at the Cricket Café is an unmitigated disaster. Normally, the waiters' perpetual confusion might even have been amusing; seen through glasses of Coca-Cola and mineral water, it becomes exasperating. Asked for the sixth time if they ordered crab, Denis and Carol Wharton understandably despair and walk out (they should have scuttled out sideways). Jokes are made about the first Sri Lankan McDonald's Drive-In: typical order, a Big Mac and five gallons of petrol to keep the engine ticking over. But any party mood has long since collapsed and thoughts of end-of-tour speeches, fines and presentations are all forgotten. This tour party has embraced the country in a manner that reminds you why people began to tour in the first place. But for the first time, we sound uncomfortably like Whingeing Poms. At least there is the Perahera (a vast religious carnival) to enjoy. And what's more, the bars open again at midnight.

Sumati, our coach driver, adds to the aggravation. We pass the hat round for a collection and are feeling proud of our generosity when Sumati reveals that his command of English has grown. 'Very small tip,' he complains. He receives little sympathy, and sulks descend all round. Gareth's London twang lightens the mood. 'It's those bloody mean Yorkie boys,' he says. 'Have another whip among the Yorkies.'

Saturday 22 February

Shortly after 7am, I peer around my bedroom door to discover that Dave Wake and Paul Thackray are responsible for the clamour that has awoken me. Their grave expressions cut through the haze of another late night.

'We think we've missed our flight, David, it left four hours ago,' says WG.

'No, impossible. I'm sure it's impossible. We can't have done that. No, it was Sunday, we haven't missed it. I'm sure we haven't.'

'Aye, well, you'd best check it out.'

Air Lanka offer no consolation. Our flight had, indeed, left at two o'clock that morning, twenty-four hours earlier than we had cause to believe. Sorry, sir, but they were at a loss to understand how I had been allowed to reconfirm our flight for *Sunday* when the computer had said Saturday all along. Sorry, sir, but Air Lanka flights to London were full until mid March. So full, in fact, that there were reports of up to thirty people failing to get on some flights despite holding valid tickets.

An emergency meeting, poolside, seeks an explanation. The tickets might say Saturday, but the confirmed tour itinerary we have all been using states Sunday. The travel company has changed the flights and omitted to tell me. Who would be a tour leader? When I ring London, the agent announces that he is about to leap on a flight to Bulgaria and there is nothing he can do. Thanks.

We take emergency refuge at the TransAsia in Colombo (I ask if we can cram twenty-six people in a family room, but eventually settle for cut-price triples) before I visit the Air Lanka offices in Colombo. They pass on the following helpful advice: it is not just that all Air Lanka flights to London are full until mid March, it is that all flights *to Europe* are full until mid March. We wait-list ourselves for nine flights.

There is only one consolation. If we must be stranded, there are few better places in the world for it to happen.

Sunday 23 February
Life left behind in England begins to take on overriding importance.

Example no 1:

Dave Wake: 'I've ordered an extra pint of milk for today.'

Paul Thackray: 'That's nothing. I've re-ordered my newspapers.'

Example no 2:

Andrea: 'I haven't paid my phone bill. You only get one reminder nowadays. I'll be cut off by the time I get back.'

Sunday is a Bank Holiday, and no one works on a Bank Holiday.

We pass the day drawing up a hit-list of potential lobbyists.

Monday 24 February

A crack-of-dawn phone call comes from Indika, whom I vaguely remember as being a senior official in Air Lanka. The good fortune awakens me instantly, and I long-windedly explain our problems.

'Air Lanka must do everything to help,' he responds. 'It is the duty of our country. You are our guests. We must come to your assistance.'

I congratulate him on his perspicuity for the best part of a quarter of an hour and am just about to ask him what time we are leaving when he says: 'Anyway, Mr Hopps, enough of this, are you still going to give me your broken cricket bat?'

Reality dawns. It is not Indika, a high-ranking Air Lanka official, returning refreshed and efficient from Bank Holiday, but Indika, a member of the Mount Lavinia cricket team, trying to solve his kit shortage. I vaguely promise to ring him back and stumble, groaning, to the bathroom, where I put my head under a cold shower.

Many hours later, Joe Rajaduria, British Airways' outstanding Colombo manager, unearths some planes with spare seats. The plan is this: Air Lanka will take us to Jeddah, from where BA will effect a 'rescue mission'. Air Lanka will want to take us to Jeddah just to get rid of us; BA will offer us discounted tickets on the basis of the publicity they will attract for saving a stranded English cricket team.

Late that night our escape route is plotted, but not before Air Lanka have inadvertently booked us on a flight to Kuwait and BA in London have hedged endlessly about the price. In the words of the Euro 96 anthem, We are Coming Home. At least, we think we are.

Tuesday 25 February

Cricketers Anonymous hardly seems an appropriate name as we return to England to surprising publicity, generated by an appearance on BBC Radio 5 Live intended to persuade BA to offer the flights for free (they don't). One tabloid bills us as a team from Mexborough, South Yorkshire, stranded in Sri Lanka until May. Colin, the barman at The Fox, our Thorner local, receives so many calls as to our whereabouts that he stops answering the phone.

It strikes me that my winter transport problems have at least brought a pleasing symmetry. It all began in early December when I inadvertently caught a train to Newcastle, it finished with flight confusion in Sri Lanka. Never mind, a few more weeks and I'll be criticising England for their cockups again. It's a much easier life.

SPRING 1997

18
Time For A Change

On the eve of the general election, Lord MacLaurin of Knebworth adds his signature to a letter to *The Times*, warning of the perils of a new Labour administration. Lord's Central has always been staunchly Conservative, but even by the standards of English cricket this seems a touch out of step with the public mood. Despite the entreaties of the chief executive of the England Cricket Board, the Labour Party are swept to power on 1 May with a national swing of more than 10 per cent. Panic queues are not immediately noticed outside Tesco supermarkets, although a rush is reported on sun-dried tomatoes.

Labour (44 per cent) wins 419 seats, the Conservatives (31 per cent) 165 and the Liberal Democrats (17 per cent) 46, the highest number of seats for a third party since 1929. There will be more people sitting on the Labour benches than spectators on a cold day at Grace Road. For the Conservatives, the result is a catastrophe. For cricket, struggling to remain in vogue, it also spells out a few warnings that it must respond to new imperatives.

After eighteen years, the assumption goes, the country has decided that it is time for a change. The Tories are widely perceived as expended, old-fashioned and mired in sleaze. The cult of individualism promoted so unequivocally by Margaret Thatcher in the Eighties has run its course, and although John Major has sought to soften it into his own vision of caring Conservatism, not enough people care nor know what that really is. Tony Blair, having argued persuasively that New Labour is worth trusting, enters Downing Street amid what two-thirds of the electorate, at least, perceive as a new mood of bouyancy and optimism.

On election night I find myself in Scotland, which fails to elect a single Tory MP. The excuse is the following day's

Benson & Hedges group tie alongside Forfar Loch between Scotland, who have just qualified for the World Cup, and Durham, who since becoming a first-class county have qualified largely for mockery. Over lunch, I bump into a bumptious old acquaintance called Mike Tremlett, whom coincidentally I last saw at University in 1979, in the final throes of the last Labour government. He is now a Scottish sports journalist and plans to cover the forthcoming Texaco one-day series. Even by journalism's standards, Mike is quite a talent at overstatement. He could not even contemplate a Labour majority of 179 without its becoming 300-plus by lunchtime.

Back across the border, Michael Atherton is asked whether this feeling of national unity will fuel England's attempt to regain the Ashes. Atherton routinely regards most questions by journalists as either shallow, boring, deceitful or manipulative, and works on the principle of 'the less said the better'. The England captain has little appetite for a detailed consideration of the relationship between a country's disposition and the performance of its national sports teams. As a *Times* reader, he has also probably read his Lordship's letter. He politely responds that the country clearly thought it was Time For A Change, and as far as the results of recent Ashes series are concerned, that is certainly the case. As England have been thrashed in the last four series, that much is clear.

Perhaps, in his more reflective moments, Atherton occasionally dares to consider things a little more deeply. Mark Waugh is one Australian cricketer who is not by nature outspoken, but his assessment of England in an Australian pre-tour magazine article is damning. 'England don't play as a team, they worry about themselves,' he says. 'When you're out there, you don't feel you've got eleven guys against you.' This is precisely the sort of reputation that Lloyd and Atherton are seeking to banish, and if they have any sense Waugh's judgement will be pinned on the dressing-room wall, next to a few yellowing cuttings from Zimbabwe.

It is dangerous to draw too many parallels between the temper of a nation and its sporting achievements, but Lloyd is striving to banish the self-centred reputation of a number of modern-day English cricketers. The obsession with 'what's in it for me' has, in its most extreme form, weakened the rapport with the supporters at large. Thatcher's children all, most England cricketers understand the creed of personal achievement. What they may not entirely appreciate, and what Blair's Labour government must begin to cultivate, is the importance of community. Without that, an absolute sense of team spirit, however well disposed they might feel to each other, must be lacking.

The 1997 *Wisden* underlines the fact that, like the Conservatives, cricket itself is undergoing a period of waning popularity. International crowds remain high and as many casual cricketers play as ever before, but underlying social trends are less encouraging. In his editor's notes, Matthew Engel comments: 'The blunt fact is that cricket in the UK has become unattractive to the overwhelming majority of the population. The game is widely perceived as elitist, exclusionist and dull.' Had Engel made such remarks in the *Guardian*, they would have been dismissed by traditionalists as pretty much what one would expect; to utter such criticisms in the pages of *Wisden* causes a minor outcry. As Martin Johnson discovered when his lampooning of English attitudes in Zimbabwe in the *Daily Telegraph* caused so much offence, it is not only what you say but where you say it.

Engel's analysis is convincing. Not since Botham's exploits against the 1981 Australians have cricket's claims to be the national game entirely convinced. As Engel goes on: 'The idea that there is any instant cure for England's habit of losing Test matches is nonsense. English cricket's deepest attitudes have to change. It has to make use of all the country's human resources. Britain has 35,000 schools and a hundred universities; cricket seems to work on the principle that the correct figures are a couple of dozen and two. Above all, it has to be ambitious for itself.'

The stumbling block is that rather than respond to the demands of a changing world, cricket in England, being intensely conservative, has long preferred to serve as an escape from it. The battle for control of the first-class game resembles a Tory party conflict: the traditionalists who want to preserve the county championship represent traditional Toryism; those, such as Ian MacLaurin, who seek to energise the system, and are suspected of implementing change for change's sake, are of a more modernising, business-oriented breed. MacLaurin's business record is impeccable, but only in English cricket could he be regarded as a dangerous radical.

The election over, John Major immediately announces his intention to resign as leader of the Conservative Party as soon as is practical, and pops off with his family to watch Surrey at the Oval. Nothing could be more symbolic of cricket's function as a retreat from a changing world. Major will be warmly greeted. Indeed, the *Telegraph*'s cricket correspondent, Christopher Martin-Jenkins, has recently written: 'Should he ever lose the stomach for the political fight, Mr Major would be an ideal chief executive of English cricket.' Perhaps Tim Lamb, who has been in the job for less than six months, should watch his back.

Major's inherent integrity and decency remains largely unquestioned, but his obsession with cricket is often used to caricature him as essentially dull and strait-laced. Blair, who has a keener eye for what passes as trendy, makes a habit instead of posing for pictures with the Manchester United manager Alex Ferguson.

In the *Guardian*, Will Buckley and Steve Caplin produce an amusing weekly computer-generated graphic entitled 'In A Perfect World'. 'In a perfect world,' they suppose, 'John Major would move on to the job he was born to do.' He is depicted in a new career as the Oval's scoreboard operator. 'That's Bicknell's fifth dot-ball,' he is saying. 'This could be very interesting.' The yawn of his youthful fellow operator could be taken to be the yawn of the nation. I immediately telephone Will and beg a print, which before the week is out becomes housed in the downstairs toilet.

One of the first acts of Labour's new sports minister, the loquacious non-conformist Tony Banks, is to receive Lord MacLaurin's resignation as chairman of the UK Sports Council. Banks, who had already indicated that MacLaurin's days were numbered, finds the resignation much to his convenience, and MacLaurin now has more time on his hands to supervise the restructuring of the domestic game.

Cricket seems out of step with the new political climate in other ways. There are around 120 women in the new parliament, about 100 of them Labour MPs, yet women are still barred from membership of the MCC. Formality is also on the wane in Labour Britain as the Government actively seeks to encourage a more relaxed, less stuffy lifestyle. The day that Gordon Brown chooses to speak at the Mansion House dinner in a lounge suit, so breaking with the dinner-jacket tradition, coincides with the launch of the England Players' Handbook, which seeks to lay down clearer guidelines on dress regulations.

The handbook has been drawn up by Bob Bennett, chairman of the ECB's management committee, a man whose career in officialdom was nearly destroyed by one unscrupulous photograph taken when he was managing the 1993 England tour to India. Dragging himself from his sickbed for a press conference, he was snapped modelling beach shorts, polo shirt and an expanding waistline. Even Gordon Brown would shy away from such informality.

Bennett's dress regulations turn out to be a sensible attempt to impose a sense of organisation. Few would defend the freedom of England players to wear coloured socks or bare their chests on dressing-room balconies. Neither will the world necessarily be worse off for the barring of baseball caps in dining-rooms, especially those being worn back to front. And if limits were not demanded on sponsors' logos, hardly an inch of some players would be left uncovered. The handbook even allows the wearing of 'smart jeans' in hotels and public rooms. Clearly, it is not seeking to be too rigorous.

More old-fashioned views, though, are never far from the

surface. As we prepare for the Ashes series, with our domestic structure in a state of crisis, the theme of cleanliness being next to godliness is much in vogue. The *Daily Mail* has proudly carried an exclusive: 'No More Spitting.' Australia will be petrified by our lads' hygienic habits.

According to the *Mail*, the Great Spitting Ban has been invoked by Gerard Elias, QC, chairman of the Board's disciplinary committee, in a letter written to county chairmen. Spitting has been deemed to upset sponsors and TV viewers. Fortunately, life is not so complicated at Thorner CC, where our occasional need to expectorate has, to my knowledge, not caused Fred and Jean at The Fox to consider pulling out of their club sponsorship. If we did it on the pub carpet, things might be different. Even less decorously, I have occasionally snorted from the nose while batting, my sinuses invariably over-reacting whenever I am lucky enough to reach double figures. Now, I know that I should slip off my gloves and stylishly pluck a pressed handkerchief from my pocket, but dammit all, most sides only bowl seventeen overs an hour as it is. Insist upon absolute decorum and we would never finish the match.

Allow ECB traditionalists to run Australian cricket and the first edict issued would be a ban on the Nasty Habit of Chewing Gum. Further meetings would eradicate The Unsavoury Practice of Perpetual Scowling and The Undecorous Consumption of Alcoholic Beverages From Tin Cans. Sledging would also be abolished, but only after Burping. Players could be forever trailed by cherubic spit-boys bearing convenient pewter tankards, and face-guards in case of a strong crosswind.

* * *

England's triumphant return from New Zealand is followed by several positive developments. The new chairman of selectors is David Graveney, who only retired from first-class cricket two years before. His co-selectors are Graham Gooch and Mike Gatting, who are not only salt-of-the-earth types but are actually still playing. This sudden fashion for appointing selectors in touch with the modern game is massively heartening. It is mildly sad to think, though, that no longer will selectors inadvertently bump into an England player and inquire 'Which one are you?' Conversations in lifts will never be the same.

England also adopt the Australian method of freeing the coach and captain from the selection committee. Curiously, Atherton's influence has receded the nearer he has approached Peter May's record of 41 Tests as England captain. He began with Ted Dexter, as chairman of selectors, promising him overwhelming influence upon his own side; remained as a selector during Illingworth's reign, but found it rather like turning up to a 10.15 lecture; and now has no official selectorial involvement at all.

The new selectorial trio affirm that the input of Lloyd and Atherton will still be valued. Unlike the days of Illingworth versus Atherton, England's selection meetings are more likely to be based on analysis, information and intelligent discussion. The Holy War school of chairmanship has thankfully been abandoned. The selectors immediately prove their eagerness for stability by reappointing Atherton for the entire series. There is simply no other sensible way to operate.

The leagues are showing less enthusiasm to be part of English cricket's Grand New Alliance. The ECB's clear-sighted promotion of a pyramid system for league cricket, so providing our most promising young players with a natural progression to the top, is meeting misguided resistance. Plans for a Lancashire premier league are the latest to collapse as bickering clubs and officials surrender to tradition and self-interest. Peter Westwell, chairman of the Lancashire League, a retired businessman who supervised Lloyd's early development at Accrington, is now among the resistance movement that is so frustrating the England coach.

'This is the Lancashire League, an historic league,' he

pronounces. 'We don't need a premier league. In the Lancashire League, we're planning for the year 200.'
Precisely.

Lloyd's faith in his England side remains as immoderate as a father doting on his young sons. The following conversation takes place in the Edgbaston press box as Teletext shows Australia two for nought in their opening match at Arundel.

Worried sceptic: 'Our batsmen are a bit short of runs, Bumble.'
Lloyd (passionately): Not as short as they are!'

When England arrive in Australia for an Ashes tour, the Australians promote the series. It goes without saying therefore that when Australia arrive in England in mid May to defend the Ashes... the Australians promote the series again. Quite what the ECB are doing, no one is quite sure, but within hours of their flight landing at Heathrow, the Australians are hosting their own opening press conference at the Westbury Hotel in London's West End.

The promotional video presented to the assembled media is blatant propaganda, although as Australia have won sixteen of the last twenty-two Tests between the countries, with England winning only two, to show an equivalent number of English triumphs would have entailed a further raid on black-and-white footage. The video, compiled from highlights of England's 1994–95 tour of Australia, begins with Shane Warne bowling Michael Atherton and continues in much the same vein. There are a few positive shots of Darren Gough, but that's only because the Aussies quite like him. He is an example of what they think the English should be/might have been/once were. He makes them feel a little homesick for the Mother Country.

When I say the Australians, I should say the Coca-Cola Australians (according to the press release, anyway), so if this occasionally escapes my mind, you'll just have to bear with me. Coca-Cola, we are told, is to become the official Ashes drink throughout the summer. Clearly, any soft drink capable of cleaning a corroded fork within hours should not have too much trouble sorting out a rusty England team, although it might be best having it spraying out of the showers rather than asking them to drink it. The prospect of Darren Gough burping his way to the crease with a stomach swollen like a hot-air balloon does not immediately fill one with confidence. England would be well advised to employ a dressing-room attendant this summer whose sole job it is to pour isotonic sports drinks into old Coca-Cola bottles.

Australia have arrived fresh from a Test series victory in South Africa, which has confirmed their status as the best team in the world, but rarely has the best team in the world looked so vulnerable. They look a seam bowler light, and others contend that a heavy schedule has left them mentally exhausted. Their record in the last seventeen Tests – won ten, lost seven – suggests that they are far from invincible, but many of the seven Test defeats have come with the rubbers already won. As Mark Taylor says: 'Losing a dead rubber after already winning the series is not a bad habit to get into.'

Not so long ago, the prime objective of an Australian cricketer on a long-haul flight to London was to offset jet lag with an assault on the world in-flight tinnie-drinking record. Not so the 1997 Australians, who, with the help of a stopover in Hong Kong, arrive so chipper that they can talk of nothing else other than the whereabouts of the nearest gymnasium.

Taylor looks more haggard than anyone, but jet lag is less the cause than a Test sequence now extended to twenty innings for 360 runs and no half-centuries. Turning the clock back is no hardship when he wakes up every morning to the hellish suspicion that it has been turned back twenty-four hours, leaving him to endure the same old debilitating questions. However politely they are phrased – and they invariably are – they add up to the same thing: Have you lost it? How much longer can you go on?

Taylor looks drawn, his eyes dart around with self-doubt, the obligatory phrases tumble out automatically: 'My form has been terrible. But I'm glad to be back in England and hope that the series will turn my form round. You're only one innings away from finding it again.' Steve Waugh, not as much vice-captain as captain-in-waiting, sits alongside him inscrutably, his eyes only flickering slightly when he feels obliged to pick up a glass of Coke and drink it.

In the three weeks since Australia left South Africa, Taylor has addressed his mental exhaustion rather than technical shortcomings. He has done a lot of fishing, probably because casting accurately does not require too much footwork. He also manages to announce that he has 'spent some time with the family' without sounding like a disgraced British cabinet minister contemplating the end of his career.

Australia lost their last Test, in New Zealand; England won their last two, in New Zealand. But however much Taylor diplomatically refers to the series 'beginning at nil-nil', he expects to win easily. Although he says that he will willingly resign if his own predicament becomes disruptive, he does not really expect it to come to that. He is only one innings away from salvation and the English counties have a habit of being all too accommodating. He reckons that four one-day matches before the Texaco Trophy series should do the trick.

Malcolm Conn, cricket correspondent for *The Australian*, believes that too. He has previewed the tour thus: 'There is little challenge and hollow joy in beating an opponent who has forfeited all reasonable rights to fight in the same division.' Connie depicts the whole caboodle as a bit of a holiday and arrives at Lord's for the first practice session with his arms folded defensively, as if he is half expecting to be arrested for crimes against the Empire. Instead, he receives a press pass and a cheery 'Good morning.' Even Athers, upon first sighting, wishes him 'an enjoyable holiday', although in this case the barb is clear.

The weather, though, proves more antagonistic to the Australians. According to Teletext, their opening victory is against the Duke of Norfolk, who predictably is not quite up to the challenge. After a rain-affected victory against

Northamptonshire (who are playing so poorly, the Duke would beat them with ten overs to spare), Australia's third one-day warm-up is at Worcester. If there is any occasion designed to befuddle an Australian touring party still adjusting to English conditions, this is it. Swans idle on an abundant Severn, the team coach becomes wedged in the mud, and a warm and overcast spring day ensures a pitch to quicken the enthusiasm of any self-respecting English seamer.

Before the match, Australian TV crews shoot footage of the cathedral, radio mikes are pointed towards the bells, and spectators waving national flags pose for pictures with Worcestershire's mascot, Peter Pear. Two hours later, Australia's world is pear-shaped as Gavin Haynes's ebullient ten-over spell of four for 40 against the top order is followed by David Leatherdale's abrupt dismissal of the tail.

When David Graveney, the chairman of selectors, called for the counties to harry the Australians at every turn, Haynes and Leatherdale can hardly have been foremost in his thoughts, but the crowd is incredulous as they bowl out the Australians for 121. Worcestershire stroll to a five-wicket victory with more than 14 overs to spare, and the one Australian innings of substance, albeit only 32, is produced by Tom Moody, Worcestershire's captain, who could not even make the touring squad.

Taylor, who has begun with scores of 45 and 76, looks out of touch before edging Haynes to the wicketkeeper Steve Rhodes. He terms the defeat a wake-up call, and the Australians' next wake-up call arrives in Chester-le-Street when their final preparatory one-day game, against Durham, is abandoned without a ball being bowled. Their itinerary has been so unsatisfactory that even England might not have accepted it. Now the Texaco Trophy is upon them. These are the players they have chosen to defend the Ashes:

THE AUSTRALIANS

Mark Taylor (New South Wales, 32 years old, captain): Excellent tactician, marvellous ambassador, but Tubby's woeful batting form has got Australia chewing the fat. Fifty-fifty to survive the series.

Steve Waugh (New South Wales, 31, vice-captain): Cool, gum-chewing temperament and immense will to succeed, he averages more than 100 in Tests in England. Could outdo Clint Eastwood in a shoot-out.

Matthew Elliott (Victoria, 25): Reliable left-handed opener who has displaced Michael Slater, which is a shame because he is much duller. Australia also expect him to be prolific.

Greg Blewett (South Australia, 25). Scored hundreds in his first two Tests in 1995 – and England were the victims. Double hundred in South Africa has won back his place, probably at number three. Handsome driver.

Mark Waugh (New South Wales, 31). Graceful and gifted. Younger than Steve by four minutes, he is infuriated by accusations of under-achieving, which means he is often infuriated. Clint Eastwood casting: the talented sidekick, who would die in the last reel to widespread grief.

Michael Bevan (New South Wales, 26). Moody, complicated, introverted. Combative left-handed batsman and brilliant field. His sudden breakthrough as a chinaman bowler is regarded in England with disbelief.

Ricky Ponting (Tasmania, 22): Talented as he may be, 'Punter' Ponting would not bet on himself to break into the Test side with nine specialist batsmen in a squad of seventeen. Victim of Australian selectorial confusion.

Michael Slater (New South Wales, 26): When Slater kissed the Australian badge on his helmet after completing his maiden Test hundred at Lord's in 1993, it was advanced as a natural display of patriotism seen too rarely in England. Captivating opening batsman with self-destructive tendencies.

Justin Langer (Western Australia, 26): Likeable middle-order batsman with a fine Sheffield Shield record, this could be Langer's last opportunity to make the breakthrough.

Adam Gilchrist (Western Australia, 25): Reserve wicketkeeper, and heir to Ian Healy. A fine batsman in his own right – he made 189 at a run-a-ball in the Sheffield Shield final. So why have the Aussies brought nine more?

Ian Healy (Queensland, 33): Abrasive wicketkeeper who keeps brilliantly to the spinners, gets runs when most needed and is never short of a word of advice for floundering opponents. Man for a crisis, he might also cause a few.

Jason Gillespie (South Australia, 22): Pony-tail, earring, goatee beard, Gillespie is a fast bowler designed for media stardom. The only problem for the English tabloids is that he doesn't talk a lot. Pretty quick, with a mean short ball and a meaner expression.

Glenn McGrath (New South Wales, 27): Australians rate him as the finest fast bowler in the world and Brian Lara (dismissed by him five times in six last winter) might agree. Tall, lean country boy, with an intense desire to succeed.

Michael Kasprowicz (Queensland, 25): Wholehearted, if not outstanding, for Essex in 1994. Australia claim vast improvements since, quoting his robustness and his outswinger. Still, hardly fearsome.

Brendon Julian (Western Australia, 26): Unconvincing selection whose useful all-round performances for Surrey last summer might have tipped the balance. Inconsistent with bat and ball, he should at least be genned-up on London nightlife.

Andrew Bichel (Queensland, 26): Fast-medium bowler who has so far not pulled up any trees at Test level. England expect him to remain environmentally friendly.

Shane Warne (New South Wales, 27): Aw, c'mon, everyone knows about Warnie: the reformed surfie, the jewellery, the blond highlights, the endless magazine shoots, the weight problem, the rumours about the chronic shoulder/finger injuries. Oh, yes, and the leggie, the googly, the flipper, the top-spinner, the zooter, the latest mystery ball...

19

English Oaks

IF there is a more optimistic mood afoot both in the country and in English cricket, then the Texaco Trophy squad captures it perfectly. Teenaged talent has routinely been regarded with suspicion, but the inclusion of Ben Hollioake, alongside his elder brother Adam, is an encouraging signal from the new triumvirate of selectors that old habits are being abandoned. Ben, 19 and still uncapped by Surrey, is a genuine product of the age-group system and put down his marker in the season's curtain-raiser between England 'A' and The Rest at Edgbaston. Stretching his ability before the treadmill of county cricket begins to eat away at his ambition makes sense.

'It's not out of the question that there'll be a few more of his age playing in the Tests this summer,' promises Lloyd. 'We're out to target people early and accelerate their progress. You have to back your judgement and push players regardless of how much county cricket they have played. I mean, look at Imran and Pakistan. He used to claim he discovered 'em in bus queues. Ha!'

Bumble can never quite decide whether he is a serious England coach or an after-dinner speaker. He has pitched up in a sweater, and fields lighthearted enquiries about whether his casual dress is flouting England's new corporate dress code: 'Eh? You're not calling me scruffy, are you? It's Jaeger! You can't beat a Jaeger!'

There have been some winter casualties, notably Irani, the day-dreamy Mullally, and Cork, whose groin injury threatens to wreck his entire season. As Cork's strutting did not exactly endear him to his colleagues in New Zealand, few tears are being shed about that.

In the 1997 *Cricketers' Who's Who*, Ben Hollioake laments that 'Youngsters are not backed enough in the big games,' and, along with a few more of us, might now have to revise his view. This opinion appears alongside the information that one of his nicknames is 'Bedroom Bully' and that his favourite form of relaxation is 'Making sexy chit-chat with women.' He is grilled about this by Mark Baldwin of the Press Association, in a pre-match press conference in the Headingley players' dining-room (opening question: 'What's all this about you being a bedroom bully, then?'), and is relieved to discover that it is all a bit of a wind-up. Adam, playing the protective older brother, then shepherds Ben through the rest of the interview by answering all the tough questions, in the same way that when they are batting together he might take it upon himself to see off the most dangerous bowler.

These guys have attitude, which is an important asset for any England cricketer. Even more essential is a nickname, and Adam has them in abundance. Smokey, Smokin' Joe, Wolf, Rock, Rambo, Holly, Strong Dance, Millionaire, Oaky, The Oak, Hokey Cokey, Abo (his first captain at Surrey, Ian Greig, fooled by his Balinese blood, reckoned he was an Aborigine), Bong, Stumpy, Raj Maru, Gatt and Judgy should see him through the summer, along with whatever new ones spring to mind.

Someone has to invent all these names, and David Bairstow, the former Yorkshire captain, was a nickname factory. When Ian Swallow stood under a skier at Scarborough in the late Eighties, Bairstow managed to boom four out while the ball was in the air: 'Chicken! Swalls! George! Young 'Un!' Swallow failed to respond to any of them, leaving Bluey red-faced and apoplectic behind the stumps.

If confidence and vitality will settle the Texaco series, then England are already overwhelming favourites. No England side has dared to claim that against Australia in the past decade, but then no England side has ever fielded the Hollioake brothers. Adam's brashness is not shared by Ben, whose confidence has a smoother, more placid feel, but they have sharpened their competitive instincts against each other since childhood.

'We never finished a game of table tennis,' says Ben. 'It got to nineteen-all, then the bats would be thrown down and we would accuse each other of cheating.'

Adam then causes the collapse of stout parties. 'If we went to the toilet together, I suppose we would see who would get it further up the wall.'

In many newspapers such comments are morally off-limits, but the *Guardian* has no such compunction. The last time I filed 'f***' (quoting a Brian Lara tirade during the last World Cup), they thoughtfully filled in the missing letters. It was a bad week. One day, my mother was hurt that Rory Bremner had condemned virtually all cricket writers as scumbags; the next day, my mother-in-law was concerned by my language.

The Hollioakes' strong accents betray their Australian roots. They were born in the Victorian town of Ballarat, about an hour north-west of Melbourne, and the family emigrated to England when Adam was twelve and Ben six. By the time that their parents, John and Daria, decided to return, Adam had progressed through the England age-group sides and won a place on the Surrey staff. Ben initially returned to Australia with his parents but remained there for only a year before Surrey, alerted to what they might be missing, also offered him a contract.

No journalist is hankering to question their rights to play for England, but Adam (forewarned by his captaincy of England 'A' in Australia) meets the subject head-on just the same. 'There is an easy answer to those who complain about our background,' he says. 'Everything we have learned about cricket has been derived from the English system.'

The Hollioakes' father, who played once for Victoria, would admire such conviction, but Adam's boldness must owe as much to Australia's social and cultural influences as it does to English education. His appetite for sledging might also be regarded as essentially Australian, whilst his admission that 'I regret the times I have gone out of my way to upset someone and it has put me off my game' is more typically English. Arguably, he has had the best of both worlds. And those worlds are about to collide.

*   *   *

First Texaco Trophy international, England v Australia
Headingley, 22 May
Australia 170-8, 50 overs; England 175-4, 45.1 overs (Thorpe
75 not out, A Hollioake 66 not out).
Result: England win by six wickets.

Wouldn't it be nice to wander outside and sample the
excitement of an English crowd wallowing in a rare Ashes
victory? You must be joking. Outside Headingley's sound-
proofed, air-conditioned press box, where by mid-afternoon
oxygen levels have reached crisis proportions, the real world
consists of lousy facilities, lousy weather and a lousy pitch. If
we want to capture the atmosphere, we have to turn up the
sound on Sky Sports, although as that is not the done thing
nobody ever suggests it. Not that I have a chance to watch
that much. I'm filing copy to the *Guardian*'s ground-breaking
Ashes web-site and answering to a temporary press box
nickname of *Hopps@yetmorecrap.com*. So far the software is
proving as prone to collapse as Thorner's middle order. I can't
say with confidence how well England are bowling, but boy, do
I know that Internet Explorer thinks I have performed an
illegal operation.

The conditions, though, are just what England need. Coats
and thick sweaters are donned with optimism and drizzle is
brushed off ham and tomato sandwiches. Darren Gough,
Yorkshire's most widely adored cricketer since Fred Trueman
in his pomp, dismisses Taylor for seven with a ball that lifts
and leaves him, and when he returns for the 33rd over he again
sends the local populace into paroxysms of delight. Bevan and
Blewett are staging a recovery from 43 for three, but in
successive balls, Thorpe runs out Bevan from midwicket and
Blewett drags – on a wickedly-inswinging yorker. With Croft
also providing a nuggety spell of off-spin, conceding only 16 in
his ten overs as he adjusts his grip to give his freezing fingers
more purchase, Australia subside to 170 all out.

Adam Hollioake's medium pace takes two late wickets in the Australian innings, but his keenest challenge is to walk out with the Headingley scoreboard reading England 40 for 4. This is quite a surprise, as often at this stage the Headingley scoreboard prefers to read œ%%@@@@*&*&. My internet software is fail-safe by comparison. So, even, is Thorner's middle order.

Hollioake inspires little confidence in his first half-hour at the crease. It is no exaggeration to suggest that an England collapse here could bring a doom-laden response that might be impossible to shift all summer; Mark Waugh's comments about English players lacking togetherness spring easily to mind. Instead, English tenacity prevails and by the end of an unbroken stand of 135 between Hollioake and his Surrey team-mate, Graham Thorpe, England are unstoppable. Hollioake even provides the big finish, pulling Gillespie into the Western Terrace for six to win the match with nearly ten overs to spare. Is this real?

All that is left is for Adam to pass on the Man of the Match champagne to his mum and dad, whom he only confirms are at the game when he spots them on the big screen while batting. Daria would have preferred the offer of a tracksuit top, Heathrow's airport staff having managed to lose her luggage.

Back on Sky TV, you can tell that England have done well, because Charles Colvile cheerily finishes every interview by telling people that he'll see them later.

Such excitement is not universal. The BBC receive complaints from some listeners that they cannot hear *Test Match Special* because the crowd are making too much noise. One even suggests that the producer stroll down to the front of the Western Terrace and order them all to keep quiet. Not quite possessing the Reithian faith that the BBC runs the world, the producer demurs. Generally, the crowd is well-behaved and if the price we must pay for their enthusiasm is the drowning out of an occasional phrase from Aggers, then so be it.

Few had given England a prayer. Atherton discovered as much when he went out to a Leeds restaurant the night before the game. 'I sensed there wasn't much hope in the public at large,' he says, recounting the story of how his meal had been gatecrashed by a couple of burly blokes with loud opinions. Atherton recalls the rudest was a man called Tremlett, who possessed a hint of a Scottish accent and a tendency to exaggeration. It's amazing how people return to haunt you.

Press watch:
Daily Telegraph (Martin Johnson): 'In direct contravention of the England and Wales Cricket Board's new sartorial guidelines, the first Texaco Trophy contest wasn't even a close shave. Whether England can keep this up for the Ashes is another matter, as the last time the urn resided here, not even Father Time had much of a beard.'

Second Texaco Trophy international, England v Australia
The Oval, 24 May
Australia 249-6, 50 overs (M Bevan 108 not out, A Gilchrist 53); England 253-4, 48.2 overs (M Atherton 113 not out, A Hollioake 53 not out).
Result: England win by six wickets.

As his career progresses, Michael Atherton finds it ever harder to get the adrenalin pumping. Once upon a time, he was nervous walking out to bat for Manchester Grammar School. After he left Cambridge University, the thought of playing for Lancashire was enough. When he first played for England, he was made restless by the ultimate achievement, but occasionally even that no longer stirs him like he knows it should.

Atherton does not possess the run-gathering hunger of Graham Gooch or Steve Waugh, an obsession that is slightly out of kilter with a normal lifestyle. Neither does he communicate the simple joy of batting like Mark Waugh. He simply likes to succeed at something he is good at, to prove people wrong. He is at his best when England are in dire need

– his immense, match-saving Test hundred in Jo'burg 1995–96 or the innings that salvaged England's tour of New Zealand, played in Auckland only a few months ago. During one Test against Pakistan last summer, he deliberately picked an argument with Moin Khan when he went out to bat because he knew he felt too relaxed for his own good. English observers misguidedly concluded that Moin, who has the reputation of a back-chatter, was up to no good again.

Today, Atherton has been infuriated by Geoffrey Boycott, who has suggested in the *Sun* that his batting is too slow, and too limited, for one-day internationals. England, according to Boycott, would have been better advised to give Adam Hollioake the one-day captaincy. This rankles with Atherton; if Boycott was an express train, no wonder all our motorways are overcrowded.

On such unplanned occurrences are matches won and lost. Atherton, proud of his captaincy record of never having lost a one-day series in England, does not feel daydreamy when he walks out at the Oval. He is supremely motivated. Australia's total of 249 for six on a good Oval batting track is also to his advantage – just enough for him to plan a score of note, not too many to disturb his natural game. Because in a way, Boycott is right: Atherton's one-day game *is* limited. If he does not sheet-anchor the innings, it is difficult to envisage his role. That was one reason why England were so reluctant to follow the pinch-hitting trends during the 1996 World Cup. The next World Cup, however, scheduled for England in early summer, will make pinch-hitting less desirable.

Atherton makes an unbeaten 113 and with bright contributions from Alec Stewart and Adam Hollioake, whose quality of strokeplay and temperament in making 53 not out from 41 balls moves him ever closer to his first Test cap, England again win by six wickets, this time with eight balls to spare. It is much more comfortable than it sounds and Charles Colvile is so happy in the post-match interviews that once again he is cheerily telling everybody that he'll see them later. So much for Atherton's abysmal early-season form.

England's fielding draws gasps of admiration. Three of the Australian top five – Mark Waugh, Mark Taylor (after scraping 11 in thirty-five balls) and Michael Slater – are run out. Only a century from Michael Bevan, impressively positive without entirely cutting loose, and a half-century by Adam Gilchrist make Australia's total respectable. Gilchrist is purportedly on tour as a reserve wicketkeeper, but here he is playing as one of six specialist batsmen in a squad which contains nine of them. Curious business. Since losing the World Cup final, Australia have only won nine out of twenty-seven one-day internationals, yet as far as Tests are concerned they retain their classification as the best team in the world. As England celebrate the winning of the Texaco Trophy, it is worth remembering.

Press watch:
The Observer (Vic Marks): 'To think some of us had the temerity to advocate Atherton's omission from the side.'

Third Texaco Trophy international, England v Australia
Lord's, 25 May
Australia 269 all out, 49.2 overs (M Waugh 95; D Gough 5–44); England 270-4, 49 overs (A Stewart 79, B Hollioake 63, J Crawley 52).
Result: England win by six wickets.
England win series 3-0.

Most one-day hundreds are forgotten almost as soon as they are made, but at Lord's we are watching a dreamily exhilarating innings that will be recalled with joy for years to come. Ben Hollioake's 63 is almost surreal, a casual destruction of the Australian attack by a 19-year-old who seems oblivious to the pressures of an England debut. Hollioake is the first teenager to represent England since Brian Close in 1949, and his insouciance makes a mockery of such a conservative selection policy. It is inconceivable that for nearly half a century, even in the bleak years, no teenager has possessed the talent, the toughness and the nous to play for England. English cricket has been brightened and emboldened.

Ben Hollioake is a veteran of five first-class matches, such a novice that he has never visited Lord's before and has to ask for instructions about how to get from the dressing-room to the outfield. He has no wish to emulate David Steele more than twenty years before him and end up in the gents toilets.

His introduction is quite dramatic as he straight drives his second ball, from Glenn McGrath, for four, ruffling the fast bowler so much that he responds with a bouncer. It is automatically called a no-ball and the crowd jeers. Another McGrath over goes for fourteen and he responds by flashing a one-finger salute at the chortling banks of spectators.

In all, Ben Hollioake strikes 11 fours and a six (depositing Shane Warne over square leg) before striking his 48th ball, from Jason Gillespie, to backward point.

It is rare in the garden-party atmosphere of Lord's that a crowd applauds football-style, with its hands above its head, but for Hollioake they summon a show of rare emotion. Even here, there is a sense of a country relaxing. Hollioake raises his bat tentatively and stares at the ground through the grille of his helmet. Adam's comment upon his brother springs to mind: 'Ben's the one with the good genes.'

I watch much of Ben Hollioake's innings in the corner of Lord's' south turret. Crammed in this wind-tunnel, barely able to see the square, is Nick Slade, who is huddled over a sixteen-inch TV screen, single-handedly logging every ball into a cricketing database. I am face to face with England's Ashes secret weapon.

Nick familiarized himself with the world of video cameras and computers during a thesis on fast bowling, as part of a sports science degree at Liverpool John Moores University. He has just graduated and, in between the one-day internationals, has driven back to Liverpool to collect all his gear. At Headingley, he was housed in his own hospitality box, complete with waitress service, but in case he has developed too much of a taste for the good life, Lord's provides more spartan conditions. Alongside him are all the necessary survival rations: a carton of slim-a-soups (he is not noticeably overweight), tea bags, coffee, dried milk and plastic cups. A few yards away, a pre-packaged lunchtime salad bearing the name 'Ian Botham' is becoming more irresistible by the minute. How lightly we treat our sporting heroes! A pre-packed salad? Sixteen years ago, against the Australians, they were feeding Both on raw steaks.

If, over the coming weeks, David Lloyd orders incidents of Ben Hollioake driving Shane Warne's flipper and finds instead that he is watching Alec Stewart twiddling his bat (amazing how it always ends up the right way round), then this interview will probably be to blame. It is quite a challenge for Nick to remember his own name as he presses up to fourteen different keys after each ball. He will always register the basics – the type of delivery, the stroke and the outcome. He might also record the line and length of the ball, the batsman's footwork (back or front foot) and whether the ball is struck on the ground or in the air. So far, Lloyd has had a voracious appetite for Shane Warne in Sky TV's super slo-mo.

To recall a particular over takes a couple of minutes; to collate something more complicated, such as all Warne's flippers over the series, might take half an hour. Quite a responsibility for a 21-year-old who describes his active cricket career as 'pretty casual stuff'. For the sake of the nation, I ask him if he can identify Warne's flipper. 'I can pick it as well as the England batsmen,' he jokes. So far England are picking it exceedingly well, so perhaps we can all relax. Overcome by his concentration levels, I return to the press box for a lie down.

Australia's 269, reliant upon a sublime 95 by Mark Waugh, has set England a challenging target, but their confidence is transparent. Atherton apart, every batsman contributes with freedom and spirit, and Adam Hollioake is left to strike the winning runs with an over remaining. 'Big brothers always have the last word,' says Ben. There has only been one previous instance this century of brothers appearing together in the same England side – Peter and Dick Richardson playing against the West Indies at Trent Bridge.

The birthplace issue hardly causes a stir. It might be that Australian-born cricketers have become such a common feature in the England side that the issue has become redundant. It might be that the protectors of 'Englishness' have surrendered to the imperatives of a more mobile world. Or it might be that we are so desperate to refresh our cricket, to encourage verve and dynamism and confidence, that we will happily embrace any English-qualified player if they suggest that they care. The problem with Graeme Hick was that he never conveyed his desire for England to succeed. The Hollioakes can talk bullishly about their commitment to England in Australian twangs and their enthusiasm conquers all.

Bestowing nicknames has always been a customary sign of acceptance in England and the Hollioakes now have another, being lovingly referred to by the *Guardian*'s sports editor as 'the Hollyhocks'. In this nation of obsessive gardeners, there will be an overpowering urge to hack them down to size by midsummer, but the selectors might uproot them first: neither can be entirely confident of selection for the first Test at Edgbaston.

England, 7-1 to win the Ashes only a week ago, have shortened to 7-2. At least it now sounds like a contest. Meanwhile, on Sky TV's post-match interviews, Charles Colvile is still promising to 'see everybody later'. It must be a hell of a party. And don't England deserve one.

Press watch:
Daily Telegraph (Christopher Martin-Jenkins): 'Prepare for much talk about a second Ian Botham and this time prepare to be agreeably surprised.'

20

Scream II

IF the England Cricket Board had not kindly alerted all village clubs to the task of saving English cricket, this might have been a sickeningly jovial little tale.

It would have opened with fanciful talk of moles, about how the little blighters were forever popping up in the middle of the outfield when least expected, and how extra cover on the top side of the ground was in perpetual danger of disappearing down a mole run.

It would have fondly related that we have even caringly adopted the mole as our club motif, which is now proudly worn on club sweaters – well, on First XI sweaters anyway, our Second XI preferring to model an assorted variety of woollies knitted by favourite aunties, bought for a few coppers at Scout jumble sales or found lying behind rubbish bins in opposing changing-rooms.

It would have delighted in relating the larks we had when 'Wobbly' Wharton almost gave me a coronary by placing a fake molehill on a new practice pitch over which I had slaved for an entire season. The fact that the molehill was perfectly symmetrical did not immediately provide a clue, realisation only dawning when I noticed that it was lying in the middle of the artificial bowling end.

But those days have gone.

Now we are taking our place in the England Cricket Board pyramid seriously.

This year, we've poisoned the beggars.

The moles might well have been banished, but other forms of wildlife are proving more troublesome. Another cold, dry winter has left the outfield in a dreadful mess and my over-enthusiasm with the weedkiller has left the practice pitch looking like a Portuguese camping site. Any of our batsmen following the coaching advice in the nets about 'sniffing the ball' when playing forward will find themselves in Leeds General Infirmary for a nose job.

The outfield was already well below standard last September, but no one did anything about it. This was partly because the Hon Sec's circular about the 22 September work parties inconveniently landed below most letter boxes on 23 September, and partly because no one can be bothered to turn up anyway, having more pressing matters to occupy them such as wandering around local garden centres, idling a few hours away on the sofa, or watching the sumo wrestling on Sky Sports 3.

After the trauma of Sri Lanka, I seek solace in an emergency reseeding operation. It proves entirely futile. Squadrons of rabbits advance from Bottoms Wood at nightfall to scratch holes in the repaired areas. What seed is not scratched up by the rabbits is eaten by an increasingly rotund pheasant. We have barely trailed off the field after our first-day victory against Amaranth when the pheasant struts onto the outfield with an offended air that suggests its supper has been inconveniently delayed. I almost feel obliged to wander up to apologize and promise that in future home matches we will endeavour to bowl our overs more quickly. Either that or draft Jack Clark back into the first team because he is a dab hand with an air rifle.

Until the Eighties, the adjoining field was full of cows, which periodically pushed through the wire fencing and fertilized the square. Those halycon days departed soon after a prize milker wandered through an open gate and ended up in an outdoor swimming pool.

Instead of cows, we now have horses, two of them, so attentive that they rank as our most knowing spectators. The friskier of them invaded the field during a match last summer and it took us the best part of half an hour to lure it towards the gate. Ten yards from our objective, it was scared off again by a blundering fool who lurched out of the pavilion and tried to arrest it single-handedly with a head-on charge. He turned out to be a retired policeman.

I digress. A month into the season, not one blade of fresh grass has burst onto the outfield, even though Yorkshire's drought has broken with a vengeance. Even allowing for the rabbits and a pheasant with a waistline to rival Pavarotti's, this is hard to understand. I bemoan the fact to our groundsman Dave Wake and he sniffs the air and scratches his 'W G Grace' beard with all the wisdom that he can muster.

'Did you use all that old seed in the black dustbin, like I told you?'

'Yeah...'

'Ah, well, no wonder. It's no good that stuff, the mice have been at most if it.'

'Well, why did you tell me to use it, then? (with slight exasperation).

'Well, I'm not going to let you use the good stuff. Not for the outfield. It's sixty quid a bag!'

Almost as reluctant to show as the grass seed are the players themselves. Village cricketers are often reluctant to appear until optimum temperatures have been reached, which in Yorkshire normally covers a couple of Saturdays in mid-July. Every season brings an avalanche of innovative excuses. In the first few weeks, I log the following cry-offs:

Tom Jordan: Retreated to Essex to complete a dissertation. Essex has the advantage of a quiet room, a computer and his mother's cooking. 'I can't write in Leeds,' he says, 'I get a mental block.' No doubt to be followed by batsman's block, if he ever returns, a possibility which becomes more unlikely when his floppy disk goes haywire and re-orders his entire dissertation. I consider whether to put Thorner's middle order on a floppy disk in the hope that it can also reshuffle that. We have been experimenting in Tom's absence with 'attacking the ball'. Tom is our finest fielder, but attacking it from Colchester every week seems a bit too ambitious, even for him.

Phil Warren: Revising for a solicitor's exam; meant to cram earlier in the week, but went to the pub instead. Oh yes, and the mountain-biking weekend in the Peak District. Warren never stops talking which provides another good reason to nickname him 'rabbit'. It is disconcerting to have a rabbit going in at no. 3, but our weak early batting performances make it entirely appropriate.

John Eagle: House up for sale; rugby coaching; holiday. Take your pick really.

Andrew Laycock: 'I never play in April, David. You know that.'

(Andy does not play at Kippax, either, on the grounds that it is not a village. He has an austere view of this that must make him a force to be reckoned with in a court of law. Quote, c1994: 'The Wetherby League is village cricket, David. Village cricket should be for villages. I like to be able to hear the church bells.')

David Wharton: 'Wobbly' is a compulsive wind-up merchant. Among the 103 reasons he has given me for his unavailability for the first month of the season might lurk a real one. I shall never be certain which one it is, but it might be the rugby league cup final.

Ed Day: Struggling with a back injury. This fills me with optimism on the grounds that it is a proper sporting excuse.

Ian Both: Our chief transfer target, we have tried everything to tempt him but Interflora. Next time, we'll have to get on the phone to Nicola Florists – he's staying with St Chad's.

Nick Spencer: Still churning out the football reports for the *Daily Tel*. He delays his seasonal debut, saying: 'I'm a football writer. How can I not watch the FA Cup final?' Easy, I'd have thought. He's already watched 130 matches this season, which should be more than enough for anyone, especially as a large number have involved Leeds United. He is also still driving a Mazda sports car, which makes him totally useless for giving people lifts to away grounds.

Phil Ralli: Isn't love wonderful? Not when it means he has to spend one weekend in four in London, it isn't. As if that isn't bad enough, he dislocates his little finger in the first round of the Fred Fleetwood Cup failing to hold a return catch. Nobody knew that a Green Hammerton batsman could hit it that hard. Instead of yanking it back in himself and getting on with the game, Phil faints twice in the dressing-room with shock and is then driven off to hospital. No wonder the health service is overloaded. The NHS get their own back by failing to put the dislocation back in properly. Eleven days later, with the help of a block and tackle, they finally get it right and blithely announce it will be six weeks before he is fit again. He returns with his index finger pointing at an angle of ninety degrees from the ball, like a dowager about to sip a morning cup of tea; if not quite the best off-spinner in the league, certainly the politest.

Chris Walker: Wakker has not actually said he is unavailable. But every week, when he doesn't slouch up until five minutes before the start, you think that maybe he *has* told you and you've forgotten. When he does finally arrive, he is amazingly reluctant to get changed, giving the impression that he cannot quite remember why he is there. Wakker is a grand bloke but he is not a leader of men, and after taking over the captaincy against Green Hammerton, he is mentally shot within an hour. 'Now I know why you and Ralli are so stressed-out,' he says. 'We'd only played three more overs and they were all shouting at me.'

Village cricketers used to regard every Saturday afternoon as an unchanging ritual. Holidays were taken in early April, late September, or from Sunday to Friday. Wedding invitations received a note of apology and a Marks & Spencer gift voucher. The cricket was sacrosanct. Andy Young, a stalwart Wetherby League seam bowler, summed up the change in attitudes when he flicked through our scorebook during a match against Walton in mid June. 'Bloody 'ell,' he said. 'They've had all of Thorner playing for 'em!'

This season we do not inspire confidence. As well as losing Hartley to Scarcroft and Adrian to the discovery of his inner self in Australia (like Australia's inner self, it will probably turn out to be entirely barren), we have not repeated the experiment of the past two seasons of inviting over a young Sri Lankan cricketer for the summer. Rajan, our first overseas player, had a mean leg-spinner and a sunny smile that made him immensely popular, especially because we got promoted and he creosoted the pavilion fence. Romesh preferred a mean bouncer, a more introverted personality, and claimed to be allergic to creosote. About the only sentence he ever uttered to Gren and Andrea, who were putting him up, was to point at the TV one night and order: 'BBC 2.' Andrea not being in total accord with his assumptions about male superiority, and much preferring *Coronation Street*, his digs did not quite last the season.

All these shortcomings leave Ralls to estimate, in what passes muster as the least uplifting pre-season comment in the club's history: 'We've lost our top three bowlers and all our middle-order batsmen. That's seventy-five per cent of our runs, and seventy-five per cent of our wickets.'

When he dislocates his finger, it is a surprise that he does not underline his pessimism by announcing as he leaves the field that the figure is now nearer ninety per cent. As I rely heavily upon him to point out the deficiencies in my field placings, the prospect of him returning with a crooked index finger deeply concerns me. One gesture of 'You want your extra cover over there' could cause havoc.

Amaranth is our only league win in an opening nine weeks ravaged by rain and cold. Spinners feel the chill more than most and, on the opening weekend, Amaranth's leggie, John Wood, attracts the sympathy of Billy Daniels, who is umpiring at square leg and can just be seen behind a haze of tobacco smoke. 'Come and field 'ere, lad, and warm your hands on my pipe,' he says. Woody does just that.

Most disconcertingly, we seem to be developing a weekly habit of falling out with umpires. Our game at Rufforth is the only one to survive the weather. As we repeatedly troop on and off the field for showers, confusion reigns. One umpire informs me in no uncertain terms that the rules state that if (as the side batting second) we are not left with at least 25 overs to bat, the game becomes null and void. With 28 overs left in the game, we don't look like bowling Rufforth out, so I deliberately bowl two overs of full tosses to persuade them to declare. They milk about 30 runs and, instead of declaring, bat out their entire allocation of overs.

'Why haven't you declared?' I admonish an opposing player. 'You've killed the game.'

'No, we haven't,' he replies. 'The umpire's talking bollocks.'

I put this to the other umpire, who says the next time I want some advice about the rules I should wait until he has got his reading glasses.

Chasing 151 in 21 overs, far more than necessary, we finish on 143 for 7...

Another unnerving aspect to the season is that we have signed a player whose competitive instincts make Adam Hollioake look like an apologetic patsy. When Chris Maycock fails to attack an impossible long-on 'catch' off Ed Day's bowling at Sherburn, Ed (one of the few genuine bowlers we have left) repeatedly rants about the superior fielding talents of his grandmother. I take him off as a disciplinary measure and then realise I've got nobody left to bowl the 'death' overs. This leads me to bowl them myself, and the first full-toss soon invites several players to wonder if I'm deliberately repeating the Rufforth tactics again.

At Bramhope, another abandoned match, the home side respond to a light shower by locking the equipment shed and getting changed. We are not amused. Ed's impressive response is to grab a fork and strop out to the square to do their groundwork for them. Bramhope being a well-to-do suburb, we can only suspect that they have mistakenly given their servants the afternoon off. At 4.29pm (one minute before the cut-off time) the umpires finally pronounce that the game can go ahead. Ten seconds later, one of them happens to step in a squelchy bit of the square and immediately changes his mind.

Another Ed-case is reserved for an lbw decision that he

suffers against Scholes. He is so far down the pitch that he could have whispered his misgivings into the umpires' ears. Instead, he expresses them more loudly, and because as he leaves the field he swears in earshot of the Scholes scorer (the wife of their captain, no less), the umpire marches off to wave a notebook at him and pronounce that he is 'on report'. Ed eventually avoids a likely suspension by apologising loudly to all and sundry, but Scholes's scorer fails to hear a word of it, being immersed in adding up the leg-byes. 'If we had known she was deaf, we needn't have bothered,' says one of our lads.

After an easy first six matches, we should theoretically be in the top three, but clearly the table is upside down. In an attempt to lift confidence, I Blu-tack a poster on the dressing-room wall, depicting the art of the forward-defensive stroke, but it is soon displaced by the pitch rota, which is far more important. We have also started our under-13 team and might even try to teach them something if anyone ever manages to leave work early enough. The advent of sunshine nearly improves us. Against Wetherby, who are heading for the top, we only lose by two runs thanks to a herculean all-round effort by Ed (four wickets and 60-odd runs), spoilt only by his inability to remember the stumping regulation, which leads to his dismissal two balls from the end even though the wicketkeeper initially treats us to a juggling act worthy of a summer season at the Hydro Hotel, Katowice.

Kippax is the sort of grating fixture around which half our side book their holiday weeks, and introducing Ed to the denizens of Kippax is like combining Hydrochloric and Sulphuric. This year, we have to worm our way to the ground through a pretty down-at-heel council estate. Officially, this is because the normal approach road is under repair, but I suspect it is tactical, a blatant attempt on their part to strike fear into the hearts of cosseted middle-class opponents.

Most Kippax batsmen are incapable of hitting skiers without bawling 'He'll do well to catch that bugger,' as loudly as possible. Ed's hackles soon rise at such gamesmanship and, as he is slogged three times in a row, he advances down the pitch in finger-jabbing mode. As Kippax are 230 for 3 in 33 overs at the time, and planning a declaration, they tend to the opinion that they can slog as much as they like. I've no energy to get involved and pass the time by wondering whether we've got Mark Taylor out yet at Edgbaston.

Kippax's constant stream of sledging, chuntering, bitching and piss-taking makes the average Australian Test player seem a vision of decorum, and I gravely warn our players over the tea interval not to be sucked in. This advice all goes to pot after three overs when my bat cracks and I signal for a replacement.

'It's not the f------ bat that's crap, it's the f------ batsman,' shouts a scruffy youth from point.

Clearly, the optimum moment has arrived to set a captain's example.

'Look, I'm the bloody batsman, it's my bat and I know if it's bloody cracked,' I say. 'You're just a lippy twat who knows f--- all.'

After this interesting exchange of views about the durable qualities of the willow, the levels of sledging do not noticeably diminish and it is not long before one of the umpires, seeking fair play, instructs Kippax's fielders to 'Remember Law 42.' They look at him, bemused. For all they know, Law 42 might as well be a new Wakefield nightclub. Our batting collapses, as usual, but we take great delight in playing out time for a draw. It doesn't get us many points, but it sure screws up their promotion challenge.

There is a theory that all this umpiring trouble is to do with my weak captaincy. I know that because it's my theory. I don't take too kindly, though, to a peculiar reversal of roles during our home match against Walton when an umpire sledges the players. One fielder takes a pop at a batsman for not walking and I'm suddenly cast as a weakling. 'The trouble with you Thorner lot is your captain's got no control,' pronounces the umpire in a stage whisper. Indignant, I stop the game and rail that his job is to umpire, not analyse my captaincy. Had I been suspended, I could not have had the slightest complaint.

It was a total embarrassment. When I pop into an under-13 match the following week, Matthew Fisher rises to his full 12-year-old height and tells me: 'That was disgraceful, what you did.' He is right, too, and I tell him never to forget it. When he is older, we'll ask him to sort out Ed.

Put it down to life's little insecurities. The sad fact is that if square leg does as much as raise an eyebrow at my request for him to move a little squarer (and Phil Warren has done just that a few minutes earlier), I imagine all sorts of conspiracies, feel entirely exposed, and visualise what it would be like to resign immediately and stalk off down the road to the pub.

At such times, I understand why Mike Gatting had a spat with Shakoor Rana, even though all logic insists that his behaviour was unacceptable. I also wonder at such moments how on earth Atherton handles the pressures of leading England, where every decision is routinely considered by driven, opinionated team-mates, analysed by TV experts or misinterpreted by critics not even present at the game. A steady drip, drip, drip of gripes, objections and denunciations. He doesn't half deserve the good days.

This year, at least, we are living in comparative luxury. The club kit bag has been replenished with a new bat, purchased the previous autumn after Ralls' final act as captain was to spend countless hours poring over the end-of-season catalogues. Ralls, like the England Cricket Board, is a firm believer in the adage that 'You have to look smart to play smart,' his own kit bag being easily distinguishable from the club bag on the grounds that Ralls's bag is at least twice the size.

Ralls's list of Wants ran into several hundred pounds, but as all expenditure is only passed after several committee meetings, he felt obliged to ask the chairman to pass his own judgement. So it came to pass that Fred wandered up to the field one morning. After much riffling through equipment, wise counsel prevailed.

'We could do with a strap-on box,' he concluded.

We're still on the lookout for one, if they still exist. If we

find one, we're going to give it to Athers. It will be something
for him to keep the Ashes in.

21

Team England

First Cornhill Test, England v Australia
Edgbaston, 5–9 June.

Michael Atherton prepares for Edgbaston, and the start of the Cornhill Test series, in an atmosphere he never dared expect. Cab drivers beam at him, wine waiters are dangerously enthusiastic about filling his glass with Chardonnay, and old women cross the road to greet him just so he might offer to help them back across again. 'Ta very much,' he repeats a thousand times. 'It was OK, ta very much.'

Atherton is about to equal Peter May's record of forty-one Tests as England captain, and his job is only just free of incessant obstacles. If it was not the intrusion of the infamous dirt-in-the-pocket affair, when he was accused of cheating during a Test against South Africa at Lord's, it was the confidence-shaking dismantling of his first touring party by Raymond Illingworth, done in the name of 'stopping the bleeding', but which stopped the circulation instead. To take a step forward, he has first had to hack away at the creepers around his feet.

Adversity has always caused Atherton to lift his game to new levels. There was the epic match-saving innings at Jo'burg, when he batted nearly eleven hours for 185 not out; the 99 at Headingley as the media howled for his sacking after the ball-tampering incident; his run of Test scores in New Zealand last winter of 80, 30, 94 not out and 118 when England's failure to win the series might have forced his sacking; and his hundred at the Oval in the Texacos when his fitness as a one-day batsman was being widely questioned. Pressure stimulates those who succeed as much as it stimulates those who fail.

Now, though, there is no adversity in sight, and Atherton is inspired instead by the rare sense that the nation is on his side. So far so good, but England's dilemma is how to transmit this one-day enthusiasm into the Test side. How much dare they discard to satisfy the different demands of the five-day game? Atherton is relieved that he no longer has to give his energies to the problem. The selectors leave out Nick Knight and Ben Hollioake (the latter to some protests, as even the *Daily Mail* has used its front page to tell its readers what a handsome lad he is), and call up Surrey's Mark Butcher, a member of the triumphant England 'A' party in Australia, and the old stager himself, Devon Malcolm.

Malcolm is about as reliable as Damon Hill's new motor, but considerably quicker on the good days. His feud with Illingworth is no longer a problem and he has been in spanking form for Derbyshire. The only other convincing fast-bowling option is another Surrey teenager, Alex Tudor, whose ability to withstand the pressure is as yet unproven and who is invited along to the nets for experience. After the teenage joys of Ben Hollioake, some journalists view Malcolm's selection as a retrograde step. Lloyd zaps them with the Positive Thinking gun. 'Never mind 19-year-old Hollioake. The country can get the same buzz about a 34-year-old Malcolm. Is he on trial at 34? Of course he isn't! He's glad to be back, rarin' to go, fit and strong, on the top of his game; he's in good shape, good shape!' When Lloyd is sacked, I want him as an agent.

If England's improvement is to prove long lasting, then Australia can take much of the credit. Lloyd incessantly repeats a dressing room mantra to his players which is based on a paragraph about Australian strengths by Christopher Martin-Jenkins in the *Daily Telegraph*:

'Sharply-honed and dedicated players. Attacking bowling. Superb fielding. Orthodox batting with flair. A message that they must be tough and ruthless.'

CMJ has already picked up a reporter-of-the-year award. Should England win the Ashes, the unlikely title of Mr Motivator may soon follow. But why stop there? Just imagine the mantra that could be adopted by choosing suitable sentences from *The Sport*: 'Stick it up the Aussies! You Kangaroo't of this one! We've Got Yer By The Didgeridoos!'

But Australia, oddly enough, remain in turmoil, and the ruses of the tabloid press are playing their part. At Bristol, where the tourists are playing Gloucestershire, Mark Taylor is greeted by a facsimile of a three-foot wide bat, amid gloating in the *Daily Mirror* that his woeful form represents Australian cricket's biggest crisis since Bodyline more than 60 years earlier. Taylor chooses not to pose next to it. 'I don't think I should have to stand next to a three-foot wide bat to prove I've got a sense of humour,' he complains. The English appetite to reduce everything to the absurd is insatiable. Australia then lose at Derbyshire, whose run chase is triumphant at the last. That makes five defeats in their last six matches... and the whole of England is gleefully counting.

Accusations abound that Taylor's poor form is detrimental to the team, a self-fulfilling prophecy if ever there was one. About the only former Australian captain not to call for Taylor's resignation is Sir Donald Bradman, and The Don does not make a habit of such things. Australia feel hounded. During Tuesday's net session, they politely lock the gates to keep the media out.

First day: Australia 118, 31.5 overs (Warne 47; Caddick 5-50, Gough 3-43); England 200-3, 56 overs (Hussain 80 not out, Thorpe 83 not out).

David Lloyd sits in the Edgbaston press conference wearing an exhausted grin and that ultimate symbol of childhood achievement, a Blue Peter badge. It is an appropriate award on a day when English cricket resembles a childhood fantasy: Australia skittled for 118, and England already possessing a considerable first-innings lead. Is this really the side once quoted at 7-1 to win the Ashes? And that was by their own bookmakers. In Australia, you could get pretty much what you pleased.

Lloyd talks fervently again of the advent of Team England: how the groundwork had been laid during the dog-days in Zimbabwe when, ridiculed as the worst Test nation in the world, the players fielded a visit from Ian MacLaurin and the ECB's chief executive Tim Lamb; it was about the first thing they had fielded properly for weeks.

Team England involves rights and responsibilities, enthusiasm and self-belief, ordered thinking, modern coaching which takes on board technological advances, brighter fielding routines and nutritional knowledge, and selectors who still have their cricket gear in the boot of the car. A feeling that the whole nation is sharing in the win. Brilliant stuff, but MacLaurin's plan for the long-term restructuring of English cricket has yet to be revealed. Can it possibly last?

The same question is being asked about the Edgbaston pitch. Steve Rouse's first two creations have been so disastrous that officialdom has placed Edgbaston on 'final warning'. This has led Rouse to meet requests from England's new selectors for a pitch that 'does a bit' with a certain amount of impatience. All he wants it to do is travel from one end to another in a reasonably straight line. He might be feeling suicidal, but he does not actually want to commit it himself.

But the selectors are right. Australia's recent record suggests that they are vulnerable in low-scoring matches and, whatever the groundsman intended, this looks like being another one. There are still twenty-four minutes remaining before lunch when the eighth Australian wicket falls, and at that point Mr Rouse is not taking visitors. He has graduated to the role of persecuted groundsman once played so brilliantly by Keith Boyce at Headingley, although, unlike Boyce, he has yet to be reduced to baking soil samples in the oven alongside the apple crumble.

Rouse is easy to spot – he is the only Englishman looking apprehensive. The ball is swinging, far more than Mark Taylor expected when he won the toss and chose to bat, but the bounce is a bit 'iffy' and there are previous offences to take into consideration.

England's innings defeat against the West Indies in 1995 was one of the shortest Tests on record and Atherton, who did not appreciate being barracked by spectators before lunch on the third day, condemned an uneven surface as the worst he had ever seen. Against India in 1996, the match sneaked into the fourth day and England won, but the verdict was not much better.

This, though, is The Ashes and, as long as it is Australia up against it, Rouse can expect to be treated to the order of the Blind Eye. After collapsing to 50 for three themselves, England recover through an enterprising stand between Nasser Hussain and Graham Thorpe which is worth 150 by the close. Even the Australians tone down their pitch condemnation after that. English newspapers are too busy scrambling for graphics of every Australian wicket to worry about the consistency of the bounce, with even *The Times* opting for a mass of red cricket balls, and on page one to boot.

There is so much to relive. Gough's verve demolishes the top order. This is high-class swing bowling, going both ways at pace. Elliott is bowled through a stiff front leg, and Blewett does well to edge an outswinger to third slip. In England's mind, there is also a fullish length which lulls Mark Waugh into dreamland and Gough finds it, swinging the ball back to strike his off stump. Goughie is full of himself. He is the Hovis Kid again, cheerily pedalling his pushbike, loaded with fresh loaves, down a cobbled Yorkshire street, waving at passers-by and whistling a summery tune that insists it's good to be alive.

Taylor, whose decision to bat might have been influenced by his own batting traumas – no captain so close to the edge wants to be accused of running away from his problems – manages seven before a horrible drive at a wide ball from Malcolm lands in the hands of second slip.

This is England's most exhilaratingly controlled spell of pace bowling for years. What Gough begins, The Cad finishes.

Steve Waugh and Healy both touching outswingers to fall to Caddick's poker-faced cool in the space of five balls, while Bevan's perceived shortcomings against the short ball are exposed by Malcolm. At 54 for eight in the 20th over, it is possible to offer an arithmetical progression that predicts that the match will be over tonight, but Warne and Kasprowicz put an end to such a notion as they double the score with a forthright stand. Australia's innings finishes with a plunging catch at third man by none other than Devon Malcolm. There could be no more unlikely, or uplifting, finale than that.

Gough exclaims afterwards that if people don't get behind England after this, they 'need beheading'. Perhaps Peter Hayter, the *Mail on Sunday* correspondent, is mindful of this phrase later in the evening when he insists upon ceremonially beheading me in the Prince of Wales pub for allegedly having been too supportive of the previous reign of Raymond Illingworth. While swinging the imaginary axe, he rambles something about 'Bolly', but I cannot make out whether this is another scathing reference to the past influence of Brian Bolus, Illingworth's sidekick, or merely Hayter's pleasurable recollection of his visit to the Bollinger marquee.

Hayter was consistently Illingworth's most trenchant critic, believing him negative, destructive, out of touch with the modern game and obsessed with his own self-importance. Such a stance cannot be taken lightly. As well as attracting Illingworth's ire, Hayter also irritated some of his colleagues who were more than happy to accept the chairman's daily diet of controversy. He is relieved that it's all over.

It is nice to drink to England success. The only worry is this: after one memorable day, claims can already be heard that England's problems are only cyclical. They are only cyclical if people act decisively to sort out the bad times.

Press watch:
Daily Mail (Ian Wooldridge): 'I would prefer to record my

sheer joy at the prospect of not being requisitioned, at least for the next couple of months, to write some sociological explanation why England lagged behind Malta and Lapland as the Remove of the sporting universe. The simple truth is that all sport is cyclical.'

Second Day: Australia 118; England 449-6, 129.1 overs (Hussain 207, Thorpe 138).

Nasser Hussain has just made a princely double century, and all England cannot quite believe the turnaround. 'Roy of the Rovers stuff?' asks Stuart Pike, the IRN reporter. 'Well, not quite Roy, perhaps,' suggests Nasser blithely, 'but it was a good day.'

It has been a captivating day: after the demolition of the Australian batsmen on Thursday, Hussain and Graham Thorpe have trod the sunlit uplands. They extend their stand to 288, an England record for the fourth wicket in Ashes Tests. By the time Thorpe miscues an ambitious hook at McGrath soon after lunch, Australia's demeanour is hang-dog. To make matters worse for them, Gillespie has torn a hamstring.

Hussain can hardly sneak a quick single for England without references to his history as a member of the Brat Pack. The phrase was first coined for three England 'A' batsmen – Hussain, Thorpe and Mark Ramprakash – to depict times when their commendable ambition occasionally spilled over into testiness or haughtiness. There were fears that their temperaments might ultimately prove flawed, but now that very ambition, matured by the passing years, makes Hussain and Thorpe Test cricketers to be reckoned with. Perhaps the advent of the Middlesex captaincy after Mike Gatting's resignation might yet do the same for Ramprakash. Hussain knows that the bad old days will be relived again on the morrow – one petulant kick at Mark Ilott's kit bag in the Chelmsford dressing-room some years back has achieved more notoriety than if he had single-handedly invaded Poland.

Nasser's sister Benazir is a principal dancer with the Royal Ballet and it is not too fanciful today to equate this with his own balance and movement. A year ago, on this ground, a comeback century against India owed much to resolve and discipline. Now he drives and cuts at Test level with a style he has never exhibited. He has only one close call: playing no shot at McGrath during the bowler's peppery introductory spell, he is relieved to see that umpire Bucknor is unmoved.

Thorpe's uncertainty has also vanished. His cross has been the statistic of two centuries in his first thirty-four Tests, but now the left-hander has made three in four games. His partnership with Hussain gains much from their long association, drawing strength from trust, understanding and humour. It is an apt illustration of the importance of continuity, and at last England have three selectors who recognise it. 'I told Nass just before lunch that I was feeling a bit tired,' Thorpe recalls. 'He said, "Well we've nothing else to do, we might as well stay in."'

Hussain's omission from the Texaco squad had hurt his pride, but David Graveney ensured that it did not unsettle him when he telephoned to explain that he was still part of England's Ashes plans. An innings ago, Nasser was arguably the most vulnerable of England's top six. Now he is a fixture for the series. Like Lloyd twenty-four hours earlier, he gives recognition to Team England. 'The selectors now involved are the right people,' he says. 'They are fully with us. What is happening behind the scenes is great.'

Hussain falls fifteen minutes before tea, touching a Warne leg-break which Healy catches in his right elbow. He has batted for seven-and-a-quarter hours, striking 38 boundaries, and raises his bat with meaningful thanks to the spectators on the popular side.

The Rea Bank has become a heartily happy, if slightly smutty, receptacle of popular culture. Two Elvis impersonators vie for attention and a group of teenage lads, their faces painted with the cross of St George, walk single-file down a gangway in The Coconut Parade. Each one wears two half-coconuts on bare chests and despite a predictable chorus of the football refrain, 'Get Your Tits Out For The Lads,' they maintain a sense of decorum.

Not everyone in the press box relishes the tone of modern Test matches. 'It sounds like the Eurovision song contest,' says one broadsheet representative. 'Not what we expect from an elitist sport.' But if English cricket truly is to redevelop as a great new alliance, then the relationship between the crowd and the players is a vital element. Elitism can go to hell.

The crowd's unbridled joy is enough of a reminder of Euro 96 to send a shiver of expectation down the spine, but an even greater shudder occurs when Hussain, closing upon his 200, uppercuts a short ball from Kasprowicz to the point boundary. The umpire, Steve Bucknor, is uncertain whether the ball has carried and his attempts to call in the TV umpire to adjudicate are stymied by inadequate BBC camera positions. While they await the decision, the Rea Bank sings: 'It's six, and you know it is,' to the tune of Village People's 'Go West'.

The last time that tune was heard in an England context? Bulawayo, December 1996, when England had failed by one run to beat Zimbabwe and David Lloyd had just issued his 'We bloody murdered 'em' speech. Late that night, in the hotel bar, Ronnie Irani stood on a chair, arms extended, and sang to the Zimbabwe players: 'You bowl wides, and you know you do.' Ronnie Irani...poor tour, poor tour report and perhaps never to play for England again. Zimbabwe, the low point of English cricket. It seems a world away.

Up in the posh seats, Bob Bennett, chairman of the England management committee, is playing host to John Major, who beams and applauds as much as anybody. As Alan Lee remarks in *The Times*, Bennett could be forgiven if he passes on a few tips about how to transform a losing team.

Press watch:
The Times (Michael Henderson): 'So superbly did Master Thorpe and Master Hussain play that one wanted to stand on the nearest rooftop and shout (extremely loudly): "Hurrah!"'

Third Day: Australia 118 and 256-1, 80 overs (Taylor 108 not out); England 478-9 dec (Kasprowicz 4-113).

Had Mark Taylor had the fortune to be born an Englishman, his head would have been turned into a root vegetable months ago – a sprout probably. Australia are facing an overwhelming defeat they can hardly comprehend, Taylor has not played an innings worthy of the name for eighteen months, and his captaincy could fall with the flick of a bail. Just like Atherton in Auckland a few months earlier, he goes out to bat knowing his very survival depends upon it. And just like Atherton, he makes a century in adversity. These Ashes captains are as tough as any of their illustrious predecessors.

It is a chastening day for New England. On a rain-interrupted day, their only wicket comes when Croft bowls Elliott for 66, sneaking a delivery past his outside edge, although Elliott is so fidgety against the England off-spinner that he is fortunate to have survived so long. Taylor plods on regardless. It is a plucky innings, not a commanding one, assisted in its early stages by the inaccuracy of Malcolm and Ealham, and even though he still plays and misses outside off stump, he seems to have become immune to it. When he pushes Caddick for a single to reach his century, his response is deadly serious. It is not the time to think of throwing a party. He returns to the Australian dressing-room to receive semi-formal handshakes from the entire squad.

English observers, by contrast, continue to clink glasses. It took one day for the notion that sporting success is always cyclical to raise its depressing head above the ramparts. It takes three for Mike Brearley, in *The Observer*, to argue that England's improvement is largely down to confidence. He disputes the 'journalists' truism' that England were churlish and unfriendly in Zimbabwe, that their minds were closed to the local culture and, moreover, that this attitude somehow affected their performance adversely.

Brearley concludes that 'both parts of this received wisdom are highly contentious'. He depicts Zimbabwe as hostile on the grounds that white Rhodesians declared unilateral independence thirty-two years ago; presumably when Australia dares to become a republic, we can be excused for treading there fearfully, too? He goes on by asking, 'Since when has interest in local culture been a reliable guide to a touring team's sporting success?'

To suggest that England were pilloried for not visiting historical ruins does such an intelligent and analytical man no justice. The fact was that England, for the most part, were homesick, bored and unoriginal, a deadened state of mind that contributed to their sub-standard performances, indeed, gnawed away at the very confidence that Brearley rightly holds in such high regard. Had he been present in Zimbabwe, it is inconceivable that Brearley, as one of England's greatest captains, would not have recognised the dangers. It bears repeating, even in such a blessed state of euphoria: only New Zealand have been defeated by England in an away Test series in the past decade.

Nevertheless, the last few days have been wonderful. I even find that Janice has been tuning in to *Test Match Special* again, and she hasn't done that since she had a teenage crush on David Gower (in what became known as his 'curly-haired kitten period'). So far, her turning of the dial hasn't met with the best of luck: two rain-break chats about the Packer Circus, a long monologue by Fred Trueman about meeting up with his old mate Peter Parfitt again, and an amble down the highways and byways of Anglo-Saxon curses courtesy of Jeff Thomson.

Press watch:
The *Observer* (Mike Brearley): 'If your side does badly, it must be down to moral failings and such things as designer stubble: when they do well, the same players are resilient and courageous and can have what they like on their chins.'

Fourth Day: Australia 118 and 477, 144.4 overs (Taylor 129, Blewett 125; Ealham 3-60, Gough 3-123, Croft 3-125);

England 478-9 dec and 119-1 (Atherton 57 not out, Stewart 40 not out).
Result: England win by nine wickets.
England lead series 1-0.

Suspense shrouds Edgbaston as Taylor and Blewett resume Australia's second-innings only 104 runs behind, with nine second innings wickets remaining. Few English voices dare express it, but the fear lurks that this Test might yet turn itself on its head. England could not lose from here, surely? To do so would be devastating after their domination of the first two days, but it would hardly be out of character.

Blewett plays handsomely. His driving, which matches Hussain's of two days earlier, is another bonus on an inconsistent, if not devilish pitch. He square-drives Caddick to become the first batsman to score centuries in his first three Ashes Tests. He has only made five all told.

Australia trim England's lead to only 33, and a breakthrough is sorely needed. But Taylor has not been quite able to raise himself again after his emotionally draining century. He bats guardedly as if no longer able to trust his own judgement and, after six-and-a-half hours, Croft deceives him with a semblance of flight and turn, causing him to jab back a simple return catch.

This Edgbaston crowd could hardly have been more partisan, with Warne, in particular, copping the boos, the ridicule and the derisive songs. But this is a more symbolic moment and the ovation for Taylor from all areas of the ground is heartwarming. Just because modern crowds prefer a noisier atmosphere does not automatically mean that they are any less knowledgeable.

Australia lunch only eight behind, but three wickets in the first hour thereafter regain England's ascendancy. Croft, exaggerating his follow-through to offset the buffeting of a stiff breeze – on the advice of his Glamorgan mentor Don Shepherd – is bowling more rhythmically than on Saturday and has Blewett caught at silly point off pad and glove.

Persistent suggestions that he is 'England's best off-spinner since Emburey' might soon be wide of the mark. He is spinning the ball more than Emburey ever did. Michael Henderson from *The Times*, remarks that a mate of his, Giles, penned a few lines, *Private Eye* style, in the Albertine wine bar in Ealing on Emburey's retirement from first-class cricket:

So
John Emburey
You've turned it in then?
That's more than you ever did
As a Bowler.

A slippery spell from Malcolm goes unrewarded, but Gough's boisterous intervention proves decisive. Bevan, for the second time in the match, proves fallible to a short ball into his body, just as England calculated he might. Mark Waugh has just returned from hospital, where his suspected appendicitis has been diagnosed as a stomach virus, and he soon edges an excellent lifter to the wicketkeeper. When Gough has Steve Waugh leg-before, Australia are notionally 71 for 6.

Even then, Healy and Warne stage a recovery and Atherton's gamble upon on Ealham's medium pace is met by scepticism, not least by his vice-captain Hussain. Ealham's first over is dross, just as it had been the previous day, and Australia's lead passes one hundred. Hussain urges his captain to take him off, but Atherton is content that the ball is swinging. The force is with him, as it might once have been with Brearley. Ealham takes three wickets for no runs in ten balls: Healy hacks a virtual wide to gully; Kasprowicz is unhinged, second ball, by extra bounce; and Gillespie (batting with Bevan as a runner) is run out for nought. Warne is so nonplussed that he knocks back a return catch.

England's target is 118 and they rush there on an evening tide of adrenalin. Atherton, an accepted master when it comes to tenacious resistance, is intoxicated into drives on the up against McGrath that he will never better in his life. Stewart despatches Warne as if it is totally irrelevant whether he can read him or not. That both are dropped once just underlines Australia's continued staleness in the field.

England's jubilation is unbounded... until Atherton begins his press conference, that is. No loose talker, he. He pronounces on a victory that has moved a nation with an unbendingly grim expression and determined monotone more suited to a Minister of Defence announcing that the war has been lost with the Cook Islands. His sentences are imprisoned in caution, so short that they end impatiently, often before they begin. Secretly, he has rarely been happier.

> *'They were singing "The Ashes Are Coming Home", Michael.'*
> *'Yep.'*
> *'Good tune?'*
> *'Good tune... long way to go.'*

Once, he would have been pilloried for such an uninspirational approach. Now he is treasured as England's Mr Realism.

'I'm pretty good at keeping my feet on the ground,' he adds, which might well have been an in-joke. But by then, even we gentlemen of the press are floating heavenwards, quite unable to hear his warning about not getting carried away.

Press watch:
Daily Telegraph (Christopher Martin-Jenkins): 'A team performance which should delight all British cricketers from Lord MacLaurin to the humblest of village players.'

SUMMER 1997

22

Wet Blankets

Second Cornhill Test, England v Australia
Lord's, 19–23 June.

BY now you might be blithely assuming that English cricket is looking forward to the Lord's Test in a spirit of anticipation and accord. You poor, deluded thing. Complaints have been received that we have all become a bit too boisterous.

The team is winning, the selectors are a repository of common sense, and Michael Atherton, freshly honoured with an OBE, is about to captain England in a record forty-second Test. Lord MacLaurin estimates that we are as much as 'fifteen per cent of the way into our plan to become the best team in the world'. There are endless reasons to be cheerful, but instead Lord's is fretting again about the game's morals and manners. And for the MCC, there is no subject more certain to occupy the waking hours.

According to Roger Knight, the MCC's secretary, spectators stand to be ejected during the Lord's Test for the following outrages: hissing the Australians, booing the Australians and chanting mindlessly, in particular about the Australians. Those caught frowning at an Australian are liable to escape with a warning, at least in the first instance. Knight has condemned such behaviour during the first Cornhill Test at Edgbaston as 'objectionable and unsporting'.

The MCC would like to remind us that our guests deserve us to be, well... more English.

Justin Langer has also had a dig at English crowds on the Australian Cricket Board's official web-site. Langer is one of the most fair-minded of Australians, but when he complains about the 'obscenities' of English crowds, and expresses his relief that Grandma Langer did not hear them, it occasions the summer's first official appearance of the 'wry smile'.

Nothing so far has rivalled the insanely drunken and aggressive verbal onslaughts upon Phil Tufnell during the last two England tours of Australia.

England's players beg to differ. Michael Atherton praises the Edgbaston atmosphere as the best he has ever experienced, and cautions: 'Lord's is the most subdued of our Test grounds... I hope they get behind us as well.' Nasser Hussain, Atherton's vice-captain, agrees that the crowd was 'phenomenal... they made a great noise.' Unfortunately, Bumble's observations escape me, but they are something excitable, along the lines of 'Great! Tremendous! Great crowd! Great!'

Now, I can do without mind-numbing chants of 'Atherton's Barmy Army.' For one thing, Athers would never want to lead a barmy army, he would rather read a book. There also comes a time when repetitive tunes about shagging, sheep and Shane Warne begin to get on my nerves. And if I hear any hint of racism or sexism, then, pray, send in the SAS without delay. But there is a danger that if we also curb the delightful flippancy of a modern Test crowd, we will curb the game itself. Social moods are changing, and if cricket is serious about becoming a broad-based, successful sport, it has to adapt sensibly.

In their campaign for peace and quiet, traditionalists are guilty of the most outrageous generalities. A letter in *The Times* from the Reverend Ian Gregory, published less than forty-eight hours after England's Edgbaston victory, is symptomatic of the strange priorities that still exist: 'Has anybody perfected a TV control unit that deletes the idiots' chorus from Test match transmissions? If so, please will they send me details.... Good sportsmanship is still around, but TV prefers to broadcast the baying masses rather than the very important good example of true sportsmen appreciating the efforts of their opponents.'

Presumably when the 'baying masses' offered such heartfelt applause to Mark Taylor for his courageous, career-saving century, Rev. Gregory was still recovering from the after-effects of his Sunday sermon.

Had Taylor's innings been played at Lord's, he would have walked off to half-empty stands, unnoticed by thousands of spectators remaining true to their curious afternoon tradition of treating a sporting event like a garden-party luncheon. And at Lord's, it is worth underlining, England have not beaten Australia since 1934 when fifteen wickets in the match for the Yorkshire left-arm spinner Hedley Verity gave them victory by an innings. In fact, that is their only Lord's win in the past 101 years. Silence has hardly done the business.

*   *   *

Whereas before Edgbaston, Mark Taylor had to fend off questions about his own batting, before Lord's, Australia's captain fields questions about the well-being of his chief bowling asset, Shane Warne. Warne's introduction in the last Ashes series in England had been mind-boggling, a lavishly turning leg-break which bowled Mike Gatting and shattered England's confidence in the process. To term it The Ball of the Century, as many did, for once sounded no exaggeration. At Edgbaston, though, Warne looked a pale imitation, taking only one wicket for 137 runs.

Taylor offers a theory. It's all down to the balls, he argues. Warne is used to Kookaburras in Australia, but in England the chosen manufacturer is Dukes, who produce an altogether more hardy ball. Warnie is having trouble gripping it. The *Sun* responds with the derisive headline, 'Shane Can't Squeeze His Balls,' and one half expects Roger Knight, flanked by a couple of Taste Police, to be hiding in wait for their cricket-writing trio – Messrs Etheridge, Boycott and Sheehan – when they traipse through the Grace Gates on the first morning.

Kerry O'Keefe, the former Australia and Somerset leg-spinner, offers a more technical analysis to Scyld Berry in the *Sunday Telegraph*. He concludes that Warne's tendency to drop his right shoulder at the point of delivery has become even more exaggerated. Result: he is slinging the ball out with his right arm, bowling with a lack of 'body' and not generating his normal quantities of loop and bounce.

Warne's modified action may be just a technical hitch, but it may also be a response to the wear and tear on a shoulder which, at various times, has needed cortisone injections and massage to keep it serviceable. Another doubt concerns the operation a year ago on his fourth finger to tighten a tendon, which also seems to have reduced the potency of his leg-break. Perhaps this most demanding of arts is beginning to take its toll.

In 1993, Warne had also been assisted by the conditions. If the pitches were not firm and dry, offering turn and bounce not only to Warne but also to the Australian off-spinner Tim May, there was always the advantage of bowling into the rough caused by Merv Hughes's lumbering size twelves. Four years on at Edgbaston, when Warne needed encouragement he found only a slow, low seamer, and what rough there was never really came into play. Warne was thrown onto the defensive and England's batsmen (in particular, Hussain and Thorpe) were allowed a leeway they barely could have imagined.

But that was Edgbaston. In preparing for Lord's, Australia have used their time between Tests well. Paul Reiffel, who should have been named in the original party, has been summoned because of injuries to Gillespie and Bichel. Reiffel took nineteen wickets in the last three Ashes Tests in 1993 and he shows up well in consecutive matches against Nottinghamshire and Leicestershire. England face a more demanding task.

First day: No play - rain.

This is how England honours a man who is about to captain England in a record forty-second Test:

(i) Tepid Lord's applause when he walks into the drizzle to collect a silver salver from the chairman of the ECB, Lord MacLaurin.

(ii) The judgement by a sixty-something former selector, Fred Titmus, that he is 'one of the worst England captains since the war'.

Second day: England 38-3, 21 overs.

As befits a man educated in the social graces, Roger Knight, the secretary of MCC, commences his address over the public address as every polite Englishman should, with a few niceties about the weather. How nice it is to see that it is nicer than it was yesterday; how nice, indeed, if it remains nice for the nicest part of the day. Then there is a small pause, indicating that he has something more consequential to say:

'I would ask you for your support in preserving the traditional atmosphere of sportsmanship at this ground... to give enthusiastic support for your teams and to acknowledge good play on both sides.'

The MCC ties applaud politely, chivalrously even. They know that the schoolmasterly ticking-off is not directed at them, but that it is a subtle message to the oiks at Edgbaston, and the other provincial grounds up and down the country: cricket's dignity must be preserved. Lord's, at least, can be relied upon to stand firm against the booing, the jeering and the obscene singalongs. As if we didn't know.

Mark Taylor has inserted the opposition on only one other occasion in his twenty-nine Tests as captain – Australia's stirring victory against South Africa in Port Elizabeth earlier in the year, and even then they had to recover a large first-innings deficit – but this time the decision is automatic. Thick, grey clouds scud overhead, and rain rushing in from the west is forecast to arrive by lunchtime. From the outset, the ball swings and bounces lavishly. As England's innings lurches forward, the rain cannot spare them soon enough.

Rumours are circulating in the English camp that Glenn McGrath has not fully recovered from the foot injury he suffered in South Africa. Since his lacklustre Test at Edgbaston, he has bowled only nine overs: is that not proof that something is amiss? A new-ball spell of three for 21 in ten overs goes much of the way to scotching the suggestion. The gangling Australian is a far more challenging proposition, maintaining a spritely pace and an 'English' length. Here is one Australian not about to be unsettled by his first taste of the Lord's slope.

Butcher's double failure on his debut was the most disappointing aspect of England's Edgbaston victory, and his second Test proves even more exacting. Reiffel, immediately at home, bellows twice for lbw, and McGrath is squirted over the slips for four, before Surrey's left-hander pushes forward in McGrath's fourth over and is caught, bat and pad, by Blewett at short leg.

Atherton has his silver salver, his OBE and Peter May's record. He also has a single, but after nine overs of wary reconnaissance, that is where it ends as Taylor clings to a low catch at first slip. Stewart is then bowled, leaving a delivery that jags back down the slope. Stewart is the most enthusiastic advocate of playing the national anthem before the start of every international match, a proposal that the ECB has rejected for fear of provoking excessive nationalism. Had he played just after the war, he would have insisted in batting in full army uniform, with the Band of the Coldstream Guards playing in the background.

England, 13 for three, momentarily seem to be 14 for four. Ian Healy initially claims to have caught Graham Thorpe off McGrath, plunging to scrape up the ball on the half-volley. Umpire Shepherd, by no means convinced, calls in his colleague Venkat at square leg for a confab and as they mull it over, Healy jogs up to express his doubts. Umpire Shepherd, with the sort of podgy handclap which he might attempt on a crisp autumn day outside his Devon sub post-office, coaxes the Lord's crowd into a round of applause for Healy's good sportsmanship. Knight's pre-match address has had a remarkable effect: the crowd is sporting, the Australian wicketkeeper is sporting, and the pitch is far too sporting.

Healy's gesture is certainly well-timed, the Lord's video

replay proving that the ball fell well short. It is worth considering which alternative conversation took place in the Australian slips.

(a) *'I am determined to uphold Lord's reputation as the repository of good sportsmanship. That ball did not carry.'*

(b) *'Shit, Heals, don't forget the video replay, mate!'*

Press watch:
The Times (Alan Lee): 'The thousands who had come to celebrate a new dawn for the England team retreated to their damp and deflated picnics wondering if it had been just another delusion.'

Third day: England 77, 42.3 overs (McGrath 8-38); Australia 131-2, 43.2 overs.

Glenn McGrath has remained strangely unobtrusive. We have debated Mark Taylor's batting woes or Shane Warne's restrained start, but nobody has given much attention to the man the Australians regard as the best fast bowler in the world. How that has changed. Today, McGrath is striding from the outfield with eight for 38 to his name, the third-best analysis in Australian Test history. England have also updated a few statistics, although they prefer not to talk about it. Their 77 all out is their fifth lowest total since the war.

As McGrath makes his awkward, bony exit, a man striding off as if to mend a fence post, the reasons why England should fear him come flooding back. This is the fast bowler who reached 100 Test wickets as quickly as Warne, and only one Test slower than Dennis Lillee; the fast bowler who has set himself a target this summer of 30 Ashes wickets; and the fast bowler who spent much of the last Australian winter making Brian Lara look mortal, and a pretty tattered mortal at that.

McGrath is willing as well. 'Ask me to bowl every second over in this Test series, and I will,' he said at the start of the series. But in South Africa, McGrath's excellent fitness record came under pressure. He tore a tendon in his foot and pulled out of the one-day series. Looks pretty much fit to me, mate.

He remains what Australians, with a tremor in their voices, romantically call a 'country boy'. He was born on a farm in Narromine, New South Wales, and his first acquaintance with Sydney's traffic nearly persuaded him to turn right around again. He has invested his financial rewards from cricket in a 34,000-acre farm north of Perth, an area the size of Greater London. For the moment, it is merely somewhere to escape once in a while, a place to camp or to shoot wild pigs from the back of a pick-up truck, but if you want to speak to Glenn McGrath in years to come, prepare to walk a long way before you find him.

Before then there are many more Test wickets to take and McGrath's chief Ashes memory consists of Terry Alderman, a softly-swinging ball delivered from close to the stumps and a host of lbws. Alderman's 41 wickets in 1989 make McGrath's aim of five wickets per Test sound modest by comparison. His exploits in the morning session have kept him up to the mark.

McGrath bowls with skill, speed and stamina. Content with his rhythm, he does not curse or fret as he did at Edgbaston but inexhaustibly pounds an unreliable, damp and cracked pitch, unaffected by the frequent showers or the threat of them, his mood as arctic as that of Lillee or Hughes was once ablaze. Bob Massie shook England with equal force twenty-five years ago when his Lord's outswingers claimed sixteen wickets, and he is present to see it. Or at least would have been had he arrived at the Grace Gates with the right tickets. By the time he returns, England have already been dismissed.

In 10.3 overs, McGrath has added another five wickets to the three he took on the second day.

Thorpe is the first to go, removed by Reiffel as he deflects a ball to short-leg off bat and pad. Then the McGrath count rises: Crawley, edging to Healy; the dogged Hussain, his concentration broken by a rain-break, leg-before; Croft, fending inexpertly, also caught at the wicket; Gough's fleeting counter-attack ending with a failed hook shot; Caddick, lbw, completing the picture. Only Arthur Mailey, in 1920-21, and Frank Laver, eleven years before that, both against England, had ever surpassed his figures for Australia.

By stumps, Australia are 131 for two and for the first time this summer, England's fielding revives memories of Zimbabwe. Four catches and a run-out are scorned – Matt Elliott being the main beneficiary, and Devon Malcolm the most ridiculed as he fumbles a sitter from Elliott at long leg. In the dressing-room afterwards, Devon contemplates the replay. 'I don't understand it, coach,' he tells David Lloyd. 'I catch those ten out of ten.'

John Crawley keeps wicket for England because of Alec Stewart's back spasms and does well enough to suggest himself as a candidate for cover-wicketkeeper on the winter tour to the West Indies. Crawley's past fortnight has not been without confusion. In the glee that followed Edgbaston, he was dubbed on the *Daily Mirror*'s women's page, in a contest to judge England's sexiest cricketer, as a 'blond, floppy-haired beefcake' and was awarded eight marks out of ten. One of the Cornhill girls wonders about this grading as she doles out the end-of-innings scorecards. There does seem some inconsistency, it has to be said, in Crawley's 'floppy-haired' rating and the announcement by Advance Hair Studios (the hair-restoring company promoted by Graham Gooch) that they are considering him as their next sporting client. Perhaps the *Mirror* should update its photographic library.

Press watch:
Wisden Cricket Monthly (Tim de Lisle): 'Sporting Index held a dinner for Atherton, David Lloyd and the media, and asked for a show of hands on England's spread, which stood at 210-220. We hacks all voted to sell; captain and coach, muttering about the cynicism of our trade, both bought. Had it been a real bet, they would have lost 133 times their stake.'

Fourth day: England 77; Australia 213-7, 61 overs (Elliott 112).

It is raining again, but John Jameson has not become secretary of the MCC without knowing his duty. Soon after dawn, he is undertaking an inspection of the ground when he feels a bolt of lightning strike the tip of his umbrella. The umbrella might be in the MCC's bacon-and-egg colours, but he has no wish to be the singed black pudding in the middle of a breakfast fry-up. 'It certainly got the pacemaker racing a bit,' he says.

Play does not begin until 5.40pm, to English delight and Australian frustration, and people entertain themselves as best they can. Considering English cricket's ban on musical instruments, a welcome number of musical shows are taking place. Michael Slater sits on the visitors' balcony with his guitar and strums 'Singing In The Rain' before a heavier shower forces him inside (presumably, he does not know the words to 'Wonderwall'). Nearby, on the top deck of the balcony, an MCC member produces a squeezebox from his bag and plays a frisky little sea shanty. If Wayne Morton was top of the bill, I must have been asleep when he came on.

The groundstaff pass the entire, shower-ridden day rolling out covers then rolling them back again. The crowd are so bored that an impromptu rolled-up-cover jumping competition receives a round of applause. In the Australian dressing-room, Matt Elliott, 55 not out overnight, yawns for the umpteenth time. Then the call comes that play will start in twenty minutes. Elliott rises in shock, showers and changes and walks out to the middle without so much as a knock-up in the outfield.

Clearly, he has discovered the secret. After careful practice on Saturday, Elliott's half-century required monstrous good luck. Today, with barely the time to velcro his pads, he spurts to his maiden Test hundred with a series of hooks and drives, oblivious to the fall of wickets all around him. In eighteen overs, he makes 57 of Australia's 82. England begin well, taking four wickets in eight overs, but another shower loosens the bowlers' grip literally and metaphorically, and by the time Elliott succumbs to the hook shot, he has long since proved that he can play it better than Gough and Caddick think he can.

Elliott's Test career was interrupted in bizarre circumstances during the Sydney Test against the West Indies last December when he collided with his batting partner Mark Waugh and missed the next eight weeks with a knee injury that remains no more than 'manageable'. Today the Battle of Wounded Knee is clearly Australia's. They lead by 136, but there is hardly a weather map in sight that is not covered in rainclouds.

Press watch:
The Times (Alan Lee): 'England's shame came from a session in the field, on Saturday, that would have embarrassed a village team.'

Fifth day: England 77 and 266-4 dec; Australia 213-7 dec. Result: Match drawn. England lead series 1-0.

A Lord's Test bedevilled by rain has at least brought an entrepeneurial spirit onto the streets of St John's Wood. Spectators scurrying from the tube station, encouraged by admission prices slashed to £5, are waylaid by an umbrella salesman urging, 'Buy a brolly or you'll be sorry.'

'More rain, no pain,' might be more how England see it, but both they and the umbrella salesman have to contend with a prompt start in watery sunshine. Australia declare overnight, but to England's relief the pitch on which McGrath had wreaked havoc no longer possesses the same devils.

Atherton is hardened to such salvaging operations and, for once, he has company. Butcher's technique has been dissected and analysed; he knows that Fleet Street sports editors are itching to demand 'Butcher For The Chop' just because it is a good headline. Taylor drops a swerving catch at slip off McGrath when Butcher has made only two, and the same bowler strikes him on the helmet – England's newly designed coronet, no less – but gradually he gets his game into decent shape.

It is almost lunch before Australia turn to Warne, and despite enough primeval grunting to excite a female elephant on heat, penetration is again lacking. Michael Bevan's chinamen and googlies, such a trump card in Australia last winter, are yet more ineffective.

Atherton has never made a Test century at Lord's and, on 77, appropriately enough the score that the entire side amassed first time around, the feat eludes him again. He plays back to Kasprowicz, a simple procedure he has carried out since childhood, deflects the ball behind square leg and steps onto his stumps.

He barely hears the polite applause from a Lord's crowd that has always suspected his Northern professionalism. He is immersed in the replay of his error on the Lord's big screen. Even now, with tea approaching, he does not believe the draw is copper-bottomed. A year ago at Lord's, he had led the survival fight against Pakistan but, upon his dismissal for 64, England's last eight wickets crumbled against the leg-spin of Mushtaq Ahmed and pace of Waqar Younis.

This time, England prove more resilient. Butcher bats for four-and-a-half hours and a maiden Test hundred is only thirteen runs away when Warne turns a ball from the rough and bowls him. Excessive friskiness costs Stewart and Hussain their wickets, but England are 266 for four when a draw is agreed at 5.20pm.

Somewhere amid all this, I can't quite remember when, a man slowed by alcohol and an unaerodynamic body streaks across the outfield in a naff pair of underpants and pinches the bails. Welcome to the winner of the Most Repressed Englishman of the Day award. Streaking is pretty foolish at the best of times, but those who do it should at least have the indecency to do it properly.

At the press conference, Malcolm Conn, Atherton's official Australian press adversary, asks how important a century in

THE REFUGE

John Major's first act after losing the 1997 general election was to don the dark glasses. His second act was to announce his intention to resign as leader of the Conservative party and retreat to The Oval to watch some cricket. Here he meets members of the British Universities team. *(Graham Morris)*

THE SHOCK

Australia's captain, Mark Taylor, cannot believe it. England have torn to
victory in the first Cornhill Test at Edgbaston. *(Allsport)*

THE SHOCK-TROOPERS

England's fast bowler, Darren Gough (left), made a dazzling start to the Ashes summer, but by the time the Yorkshireman reached his home Test at Headingley, it was Australia's Jason Gillespie who was irrepressible. *(Graham Morris)*

THE FANFARES

The emergence of the Holloake brothers, Ben (top) and Adam (bottom) was greeted with delight in the media. Adam was immediately billed as the next England captain, while Ben drew comparisons with Ian Botham. For all their promise, their reputation owed as much to presence as performance. *(Graham Morris)*

THE SUPERSTAR

English crowds' treatment of Shane Warne lurched between the amusing and the crass, some of it fuelled by alcohol and the media (bottom). Warne, who came out on top, runs through his full repertoire of emotions during his matchwinning spell in the Old Trafford Test. *(All photos Graham Morris, except bottom, Mark Ray)*

THE FASHIONS

Fancy Dress became a feature of Test crowds throughout the summer, Lord's excepted, of course. Fashions at Headingley varied from a fairly ropy set of Spice Girls to a Roman toga party. *(above Graham Morris, below Mark Ray)*

THE CONTENTMENT

Phil Tufnell returned to England's ranks for the first time in the final Test
at The Oval, and immediately bowled them to an unforgettable victory. Here
he celebrates in traditional fashion; nutritionists and fitness advisers are
advised to avert their eyes. (*Graham Morris*)

THE PLEA

A supporter of Michael Atherton makes her stand during the final Test at The Oval. He did, too. *(Graham Morris)*

his record-breaking match would have been to him. 'Just another Test,' Athers mutters, leading Connie to exclaim: 'Don't you get emotional about anything?... You don't have to be specific!'

Atherton grins hugely. An Australian taken aback by his stoicism, and what's more, an Australian who depicted this Ashes series as an extended summer holiday. Now, that is something to get emotional about. But only in private, only if the Ashes are eventually won, and only long after his retirement.

Press watch:

Daily Mail (Peter Johnson): 'The demons Mark Butcher had to fight did not spring from the cracks in the Lord's pitch but from the corners of his own mind.'

23

Left-Hander!

The battle for supremacy in a village match makes Test cricket seem a haven of predictability. Winning positions are forced with moments of great prowess, then tossed aside with even greater incompetence. On a wet pitch against Bramham, we experiment with Wobbly as a pinch-hitter and a display of devastating straight hitting brings up 100 in the twelfth over. After countless near-misses over twenty years, he scored his maiden century a month ago, and it seems nothing can deflect him from another one. Then I run him out (blatantly), Ed runs me out (equally blatantly), and only a doughty last-wicket stand edges us past 150. Bramham, in reply, lose early wickets before their repeated left-hand/right-hand combinations leave us in total confusion.

'Left-hander!'
'Nick, square leg, please. No, not square leg... point... that was the right-hander.'
'No, Tom's point.'
'No, I'm not, I'm sweeping. I was point, but he dropped me back for the big square-cutter.'
'He's not the big square cutter.'
'Well, if he isn't, he's doing a bloody good impression!'

* * *

'Right-hand!'
'I thought I was here, Foz.'
'You were.'
'That's alright, then.'
'But you're not now, I am. It's a hundred yards to where I should be. Just spread out a bit. It'll be alright. They'll never notice.'

*   *   *

'Left-hand! No, sorry, right-hand. Sorry, boys. They've swopped ends.'
'They do, it's called taking singles. We do it occasionally.'

*   *   *

'Right-hand!'
'Third man, Wobbly.... no, sorry, I want a fine.... hold on Wobbly, go back to third.'
'I've had enough of all this wandering around, I'm retiring.'
'C'mon, Wobbs, I know it's uphill but he's just changed his mind, that's all.'
'You're all bloody mental.'

*   *   *

'C'mon guys, let's try to remember our positions occasionally, it's not that bloody difficult.'
'Hoppsy, you're in the wrong place yourself, you're over there.'
'What? Damn!.... Yeah, very bloody funny.'

*   *   *

'Every time I look round, someone's been moving my field!'
'Well, it's not me, Ed. I gave up hours ago.'
'Well, who the hell is it, then?'

*   *   *

'Rod, are you sure you had five on the leg side?'
'Yeah, about twenty minutes ago, but not deliberately.'

*   *   *

'Spenny, what you doing here?

'This is where I am, roughly.'

'No, you're not. I've got a mark here.'

'Wakker, you've got marks everywhere. You've got so many marks that you've done more damage to the outfield than the rabbits.'

*   *   *

Thorner win by five runs with three balls to spare, our first league victory since April. In the pub, Wakker suggests we should all swap our cricket boots for a pair of Clark's Commandos. 'You know, those shoes that used to have a compass in the bottom...'

24

Hot Streak

Third Cornhill Test, England v Australia
Old Trafford, 3–7 July.

TUESDAYS before Test matches can be the bane of a cricket writer's life. Tim Henman and Greg Rusedski are steaming towards the Wimbledon quarter-finals, the British Lions have wrapped up the Test series in South Africa and Mike Tyson has bitten a chunk out of Evander Holyfield's ear. Unless something remarkable happens, no one will be much interested in a drizzly England practice session. But here we all are, hanging around the front of the Old Trafford pavilion and fielding the usual distrusting looks from players who calculate that a pack of journalists hanging around are bound to be up to mischief. In truth, we're so bored, we're up to nothing at all.

Simon Wilde has driven up from London for *The Times* and there is a promising flurry of activity as he untangles his tape recorder from his pocket. Those anticipating the sharing of a few earth-shattering quotes are disappointed when all that can be heard is Gayle, his wife, singing 'Jingle Bells' with the kids. If Michael Atherton suddenly trots up to announce his resignation, this could present 'Wild Man' with an awful dilemma. His immediate priority will be to tape every pedestrian utterance. Woe betide him in ten years' time, though, if he does: 'Simon – where's that nice tape of the kids singing Jingle Bells? I've tried this one, but there's just a man on it, muttering.'

Peter Marron wanders past, sniffing the wind direction as Test groundsmen are wont to do, and encapsulates the complications of a wet Ashes summer. 'Someone tried to flog me a computer which could predict the weather every fifteen minutes,' he says. 'I told him that if I could press a button to stop it coming, I'd be interested.'

As if on cue, a charcoal cloud looms from behind the pavilion and splatters Lancashire's long-suffering groundsman with another shower. He dons his waterproof jacket with an air of resignation and trudges back out to the square. Mike Kasprowicz joins Australia's fielding practice in a raincoat: a suitable symbol for the summer. The weather continues to hound Australia and, after the practised gentility of Lord's, so will the crowd. 'At least the crowd will be able to shout at this ground,' says David Lloyd, 'and say "Well done."'

Four years ago on this ground, Shane Warne delivered his Ball of the Century, a hugely turning leg-break which bowled Mike Gatting and gave Australia a psychological hold that they never relinquished. If he tries to repeat that ball on Thursday, the feeling is that on this surface it will trundle straight on for two leg-byes. No one carps much when Phil Tufnell is released again to rejoin Middlesex's championship challenge.

Tufnell is fated to drive up and down motorways to no apparent purpose all summer. He does not seem unduly forlorn; in view of all his cigarette smoking, motorway pollution is probably no more than a bit of a drag. He takes an enthusiastic part in England's fielding practice, which is increasingly rivalling the professionalism of the Australians'. One of the more imaginative routines involves catching and saving tennis balls, which are efficiently served by the strumming physio, Wayne Morton, and which can be struck much harder without the fear of broken fingers. This routine seems to have two main benefits:

(i) It quickens reactions.
(ii) It allows Wayne to make a lot of noise.

Expectations are that England will retain Mark Ealham at number seven, which leaves Devon Malcolm to vie with two new seamers, Gloucestershire's left-armer Mike Smith and Kent's Dean Headley. Headley stands to be the third generation of the same family to play Test cricket. His dad, Ron, and grandad, George, both represented the West Indies, George with such distinction that he holds the third-highest

Test batting average of all time and was dubbed 'The Black Bradman'.

Headley dutifully churns out the old story about how he met George for the first time in the back garden in Stourbridge when he was eleven, and how it felt more like meeting a famous cricketer than his grandad. We all dutifully write it down; most of us dutifully file it; some people might dutifully read it. It's hardly new, though. One of those days, really.

First day: Australia 224-7, 69 overs (S Waugh 102 not out).

Michael Atherton was deemed last winter to be unconvinced by Dean Headley's prowess as a Test bowler on the grounds that he could not bowl an outswinger. Atherton was extremely irritated by the suggestion and exchanged faxes from Zimbabwe to say so, which at least spared him an hour listening to people strumming 'Wonderwall'. What matters right now, though, is that, by tea on the opening day of the third Cornhill Test, Headley has three wickets on his Test debut and Australia, at 162 for seven, are fighting for their lives. Only Steve Waugh (with an unbeaten 70 of great discrimination) has batted with any assurance.

As to whether Headley can bowl an outswinger, for the moment no one really cares. Australia are again fielding three left-handers in the top six and he has dismissed them all, snaking the ball away from Mark Taylor and Michael Bevan and also benefiting from a stroke of luck when Matt Elliott is adjudged caught at the wicket from a delivery which, replays suggest, brushes his left elbow.

An impressive performer on the England 'A' tour of Australia, Headley is finally relishing a Test debut which, at 27, is testimony to his perseverance. He left Middlesex and Worcestershire before settling to a career with Kent. Injuries have slowed his progress and every time he enters the pavilion, you wonder if you will ever see him again.

Life is not going as smoothly for Dad. Ron Headley is in a

traffic jam on the M6. He measures the progress of the Test by service stations. When Dean is officially presented with his Test cap, Ron has reached Keele; by the time Dean takes his first Test wicket with his eighteenth ball, he is within sight of Sandbach. As the wicket is described on *Test Match Special*, Ron leaps around with delight in the driver's seat. On every side, pissed-off motorists, replaying old cassettes or listening to recaps about the Budget, wonder what right he has to feel so happy with life.

Sir Colin Cowdrey was once so excited about son Chris's first Test wicket, on a tour of India, that he drove the wrong way up a one-way street. You can imagine it even now.

'Do you know this is a one-way street, sir?'

'Apologies, officer, but Chris Cowdrey has just taken his first Test wicket... He's going to captain England one day.'

'Chris Cowdrey? Do me a favour! Would you mind blowing into this bag?'

A seaming Manchester pitch might have been designed for Headley, a most fluid of movers, possessed of a slightly slingy action and a gleaming stud in his left ear. Taylor, courageously electing to bat, is soon squared-up by a seaming delivery, which he edges to slip. Elliott and Bevan follow in Headley's second spell. Bevan's retention for Headingley, his adopted English home, looks unlikely.

By tea, Alec Stewart's tally of catches has risen to five. But there is a thorn in England's side, a thorn becoming more embedded by the minute and beginning to undermine their sense of well-being. Steve Waugh's previous two Ashes tours have been a tale of unremitting success: a Test batting average in England of more than 100, constructed with utter certainty in a period of overwhelming Australian superiority. The 1997 Australians lack that authority – the best side in the world are being given a run for their money – but Waugh's authority is undiminished. He reaches his century in the penultimate over, from 152 balls, when he square-cuts Croft to the boundary.

Fourteen intemperate overs late in the day, after more rain and bad light, grant Australia another 51 runs. Waugh's innings deserves to be ranked with any of his previous three Test centuries in England, or, indeed, his twelve others worldwide. He thinks so too. He punches narrow-eyed drives through the offside, his defence is astute and defiant, his mental approach pared down to the essentials.

Two balls after Waugh reaches his hundred, Reiffel, sound in support, edges Croft faintly into the wicketkeeper's gloves. Stewart completes what would have been a record-equalling six catches in an Ashes innings, but umpire George Sharp remains unmoved. The first hour tomorrow will be vital. It could even settle the whole series.

Press watch:
the *Guardian* (Frank Keating): 'Lay the ghost of Warne once and for all these next few days and England will be looking mighty good for the Ashes.'

Second day: Australia 235, 77.3 overs (S Waugh 108; Headley 4-72, Gough 3-52); England 161-8, 81 overs (Butcher 51).

On my way to the press box, I bump into David Graveney. 'The first hour this morning will be vital,' he asserts. 'It could even settle the whole series.' Funny, I've just typed that. All over England, people must be saying the same thing. 'I'll just have a tin of sliced peaches as well, please, Grace. I'll tell you what, the first hour's vital today and no mistake!'

And the first hour goes wonderfully well. Australia's first innings is wrapped up within forty minutes. Steve Waugh finally falls as Gough bowls him off the inside edge for 108, an innings so meritorious that it is even applauded by Atherton, who is not a man given to gushing shows of appreciation. And Stewart equals his record when Headley dismisses Gillespie without scoring.

To a decent first hour can be added two more. Atherton and Stewart have departed, but England are 94 for two and

Butcher is solidity itself. One more good session and England will be strong favourites to win the Test, perhaps even the series. The cricket is grindingly slow, but the anticipation is building, so much so that the *Guardian*'s Ashes web-site is heading for a hundred visitors a second. How's that little ditty go again about the Ashes Coming Home?

England have even survived Ball Of The Century II, which like most sequels is not half as successful as the original. Shane Warne's dismissal of Mike Gatting four years before assured him of immediate fame. 'The greatest ball I ever bowled... it changed my life,' was how he rated it. Warne is enough of a showman to attempt something equally dramatic here, but when a leg-spinner rattles fast and low into Mark Butcher's pads, Butcher manages to whip it through square leg for runs.

Australia's leg-spin lead has not taken five wickets in an innings for sixteen Tests, the technicians are doubting his action and the groupies are shifting their attentions to Wimbledon and Pat Rafter. Even England's batsmen are beginning to venture how it is all just a matter of countering his ploy of bowling round the wicket by daring to play against the spin. Then the sun comes out. And all it takes is a couple of sunbeams to dance through the dyed-blond locks for the Ashes series to be turned on its head. Spin bowling might no longer be an innocent adventure for Warne – too much has occurred in the intervening years for that – but once a great sportsman discovers his greatness, the most appealing option is to keep confirming it.

By the close, he has five for 48 in 28 overs, the last twenty-five delivered unchanged from the Warwick Road End. The turn is evident, but hardly awe-inspiring, and there is swerve too, but nothing to excuse England's loss of six wickets for 29 runs in 19 overs. Australia even summon up Bevan's chinamen with success, as Butcher misses a full toss down the leg-side and is expertly stumped by Ian Healy. Warne needs only 26 deliveries to banish Thorpe, Hussain and Crawley, the last two nibbling deferentially at wide leg-spinners wandering wider; Gough is befuddled by a devilish straight one; Stewart, the first victim, edged one to first slip before lunch. As the sun goes in again, Ealham and Caddick stage something of a recovery. England are losing this Test match by degrees.

Press watch:

the *Sun* (John Etheridge): 'He has had surgery on his spinning finger, daily massage on his sore shoulder and his wife has even just had a baby. There has been talk that he is washed-up, a flush busted by the strain his craft applies to his body. But the blond-haired former beach bum proved he is still a joy to behold and a devil to bat against.'

Third day: Australia 235 and 262-6, 85 overs (M Waugh 55); England 162 (Warne 6-48, McGrath 3-40).

It is time to list England's lost opportunities in the Old Trafford Test. Adopt a suitably affronted air:

(i) First day: Chance to bowl out Australia cheaply. Failed.

(ii) Second day: Chance, from 94 for two, to build a decisive first-innings lead. Failed.

(iii) Third day: Chance to stage a remarkable recovery when the first three Australian wickets fall for 39. Failed again.

Disturbingly, Australia's key players are all running into form. McGrath at Lord's, Warne in England's first innings, and Steve Waugh twice in this Test. After his first-innings century, Waugh finishes Saturday unbeaten on 82, even though he is suffering from a hand injury caused by persistent jarring against the bat handle.

In the time it takes Waugh to advance to 82 on the telly, Amaranth beat Thorner by eight wickets. Our only consolation is that, collectively, we score at five times the speed and are unlikely ever to suffer from team bat-jar. However, we do appreciate the problems of press harassment as a photographer from the *Wetherby News* sidles around the boundary for a few seconds to take a snap or two. Amazingly, he captures the sight of Jon Eagle driving flamboyantly, a feat he has only ever previously achieved in his company BMW.

After I'm dismissed, I spend some time scoring alongside Betty Chadderton, whose commitment to village cricket is unlimited and who could talk the Australians to death. Maybe England could call her up if all else fails. Betty has valiantly tried to force the Department of Transport to re-route the A1/M1 link road because of the potential noise nuisance on Barnbow Common, but they don't seem too likely to oblige. Still, there are compensations – judging by the length of the grass on the outfield, there is not much chance of any additional noise from motor mowers.

'I spoke to the top man,' says Betty, a trifle put-out. 'Or at least, he said he was the top man. He said, "Mrs Chadderton, I have my finger on the map at this moment and I can assure you quite categorically that the motorway link does not come within a mile of your cricket ground."'

Now my judgement of distances is unreliable, especially over twenty-two yards, but that swathe of hacked-out earth is somewhat closer. Next season, if we stop the bowler whenever traffic moves behind the bowler's arm, we could escape with a losing draw. Officialdom has condescendingly tried to defuse Betty with the promise of a few trees, but even now she could be planning to launch a rush-hour lie-in protest in the middle lane. Swampy, eat your heart out.

As for the Old Trafford Test, why not spare yourself the agony? Steve Waugh, it seems, was immovable, Nasser Hussain's claim for a catch at slip to dismiss Greg Blewett was upheld, even though Sky TV cameras suggested the ball fell well short (BBC pictures, not for the first time, proved inconclusive)... and England are going to lose by a distance.

As for Thorner, to be in Nasser Hussain's position would be luxury. We drop the real catches, and those that fall short we miss completely. By the time we find them in the long grass, the opposition have run seven. Even a *Guardian*-reading umpire is of no assistance. He busies himself during my innings assembling a quiz question about Gloucestershire off-spinners who have played for England. Or is it 'should have played for England?' Slogging one to mid-on at least spares me the admission that I don't know the answer.

Press watch:
Sunday Telegraph (Peter Roebuck): 'His innings had all the familar traits: defiance, a terrible stillness at execution, chiselled defence... Waugh's innings was clipped, capable, discriminating and withering. Every ball passed through the laboratory of his mind and no stroke was played without the most careful consideration.'

Fourth day: Australia 235 and 395-8 dec, 122 overs (S Waugh 116, M Waugh 55, Warne 53; Headley 4-104); England 162 and 130-5.

It is mid-afternoon and England's second innings has just begun, to the full accompaniment of the terrace songbook. The Ashes are still coming home, the waves are still ruled by someone called Britannia, although I don't see how she will ever stab many fish with a fork like that, and Shane Warne is still allegedly engaged in curious sexual practices. England, faced by a notional 469 for victory, have to bat for a minimum of 122 overs to save the match. Atherton, who might be relied upon to adopt the role of the Young Curmudgeon (the Old Curmudgeon, Boycott, long banished to the commentary box), has just gone mad and hooked Gillespie for six. The Barmy Army seem to think we're going for 'em.

Australia have declared at 395 for eight. When Steve Waugh drives Croft through midwicket, with the pavilion clock around midday, he joins Denis Compton, Arthur Morris, Wally Hammond, Herbert Sutcliffe and Warren Bardsley as the only batsmen to have made centuries in both innings of an Ashes Test. Morris and Compton last achieved the feat, in the same Adelaide Test, fifty-one years ago, so it can safely be ventured that Waugh's achievement is the first to be celebrated on the Internet. The *Steve Waugh Is God* site lauds him thus:

> *'Our Stevie,*
> *Who Isn't Yet In Heaven,*
> *Thy Kingdom Come,*
> *Thou Shalt Get A Ton.'*

Waugh's second hundred is also more workmanlike than poetic. At nearly six-and-a-half hours, it is more than two hours slower than his first, but his steadfastness has drained England's spirits. No one else has managed more than 55.

As Atherton plants his six into the crowd at square leg, Mark Taylor stands behind him at slip pondering a conversation he has had with Peter Marron. 'It's all down to Warnie now,' Marron has advised. 'This surface has become so slow that the quicks won't take another wicket.'

Taylor is shrewd enough to have shared this opinion with the dressing-room and Gillespie is bowling as sharply as at any time on the tour. Atherton's six irks him further and, in his next over, he has England's captain lbw. Warne is already ensconced at the Warwick Road End and, before tea, he adds the wicket of Stewart, whose lurch forward to be bowled through bat and pad, as he meekly attempts to compensate for leg spin which never materialises, brings the bowler his 250th Test wicket.

After tea, the procession continues. Australia, still infuriated by Hussain's 'catch', have devised a special welcome for him: ten minutes of reproachful silence followed by every rebuke they can muster. The plan never reaches its second stage as Hussain is adjudged leg-before to a ball from Gillespie that looks slightly high. Surely not a case of the Umpire Strikes Back?

Butcher then hooks Gillespie and is astoundingly well caught at long leg by McGrath, who collapses like a giraffe with ruptured Achilles tendons. Thorpe falls cheaply to Warne for the second time in the match, cutting at a wide ball which drifted wider. England are 84 for five and, briefly, it seems that the match might yet finish tonight.

Old Trafford is suddenly struck by a maudlin recognition that the summer might never be the same. Behind the stands, hundreds of spectators mill slothfully around fat-stained fast-food outlets, or slump in disbelief against walls, empty beer barrels and sun-blistered green seats. Discarded lager cans drip their contents onto the tarmac.

On the other side of the stands, as if in protest, a persistent stream of streakers disgorge themselves onto the square, but Old Trafford's security men are requisitioned from Salford rugby league club and the first wave are tackled before they barely cross the gain line. The stewards gradually tire, however, and John Crawley, whose resistance at least takes the game into a fifth day, is hardly helped when one club-wielding drunk, dressed in a Viking helmet, is ambushed in the middle of the pitch in a cloud of dust by three flagging tacklers. Salford? Perhaps Lancashire should have employed the Brisbane Broncos.

Soon after the close in the Lancashire library, Waugh is about to reflect upon his two historic hundreds when he finds himself usurped at the microphone by John Bower, Lancashire's chief executive, who is still obsessed by streaking. It is the first time that Waugh has conceded ground to an Englishman for four days.

Bower vows that Manchester police will prosecute streakers (in their purest – or impurest? – form) for a common-law offence against public decency, with the possibility of a four-figure fine. This, of course, is entirely irrelevant, Manchester streakers preferring to keep their clothes on.

'You can't charge clothed streakers, because they have committed no offence,' Bower says. 'You just hope that the Salford lads hit them quite hard and leave them a little breathless. I wanted to keep their clothes for twenty-four hours and turf them outside, but the police wouldn't let us.'

Lancashire's approach is psychological nonsense. By

employing rugby-league playing stewards, they have encouraged a laddish competition in which the aim is to break as many tackles as possible. If they just let them run on, look foolish and run off again, the sport would go out of it in no time.

Press watch:
the *Guardian* (Matthew Engel): 'What everyone now knows is that the gloves are off in this Test series. If not, in every case, the trousers.'

Fifth day: Australia 235 and 395-8 dec; England 162 and 200 (Crawley 83; McGrath 4-46, Gillespie 3-31).
Result: Australia win by 268 runs.
Series 1-1 with three to play.

It takes Australia only ninety minutes to capture the last five wickets and wrap up the third Test, assisted by John Crawley's mishap when he treads on his own stumps, but that is long enough for England to rule that there will be no panic. In an attempt to maintain team unity, and suppress endless press speculation, they announce an unchanged squad for the next Test at Headingley almost two weeks ahead of schedule. Unfortunately, they decide to announce it through Richard Little, the ECB's corporate affairs manager, and he doesn't get round to mentioning it until the following day. Happily, a new media officer is on the way and, as it is Brian Murgatroyd, the Sky TV Memory Man, he should at least remember to pass on the occasional message.

Atherton drops heavy hints about the policy in the press conference. 'I'll give good money at the bookies that we'll have the same squad at Headingley,' he says. Well, he would, wouldn't he? He is in the middle of a record benefit year. Most of us write 'England unchanged' in the manner of a £1 each-way bet, apart from the *Daily Express* man who stumbles across David Graveney in the car park and therefore feels able to put his mortgage on it.

England also plan another management training course before Headingley, under the supervision of a company run by the former England rugby union captain, Will Carling. The players turfed up suspiciously to one in pre-season, resenting press stories that they were being sent to a charm school after their surly behaviour in Zimbabwe. Then they found that they were taking part in team-building exercises such as driving Land Rovers blindfolded through forests (teaching them to trust team-mates' advice) and thoroughly enjoyed it.

While England clamber up mountains, reminding themselves that Old Trafford was their first defeat in eight Tests, Australia's schedule is more concerned with social climbing: a elitist one-day match at John Paul Getty's private ground in the Cotswolds and a trip to Buckingham Palace to meet the Queen. The sharpened Australian appetite for republicanism clearly has not dulled their appreciation of the English class structure. Not too much harm can come of it, although the Queen might be advised to check the underside of the coffee table for chewing gum.

Warne could also do with some instruction in the Royal Wave. He has soaked up the crowd's baiting all summer in good humour, so during Australia's victory celebration he sticks out his stomach, gives it a hearty pat, and follows up with a light-hearted one-finger salute. You would never see the Queen Mother behave like that, so this is presented in at least one tabloid dreamworld as poor sportsmanship. Warne could not care less – he has negotiated a few days out of the tour to go and see his new-born baby.

England, meanwhile, must take heart in Arthur C Clarke's prediction that, a thousand years hence, humans will be communicating largely by telepathy. That means there are only another 250 Ashes series to go before England can read Warne quite easily.

Atherton, intent upon remaining upbeat, risks several press conference pronouncements:

(i) 'Our batsman are confident in their ability to play Shane Warne.'

(ii) 'I'm confident that we can bowl Australia out twice and win at least one of the next three Tests.'

(iii) 'The measure of a side is how well you come back from a setback. I'm backing my team to do just that.'

Press watch:
Daily Telegraph (Christopher Martin-Jenkins): 'McGrath took four of the last five wickets in a 31-ball spell, costing him only 15 runs, and, perfectionist as he is, he begrudged every one, scowling like an angry scarecrow at the offending batsman.'

25

Screaming Pitch

Fourth Cornhill Test, England v Australia, Headingley, 24–28 July.

SINCE Yorkshire proudly announced their intention to move to what their president, Sir Lawrence Byford, immodestly termed 'the best cricket ground on the planet,' the Americans have managed to land an unmanned spaceship on Mars. Nearly a year later, Yorkshire are no nearer to touching down at Durkar, balked by the substantial figure of Paul Caddick, the owner of Headingley and a master of intransigence.

Assumptions are that Headingley is doomed to eventual closure, but Caddick intends to scotch them. He has refused to release Yorkshire from the terms of their lease, which still has more than eighty years to run, and matters are in the hands of our legal friends. As the solicitor on Headingley's board just happens to be Andy Laycock, the secretary of Thorner CC, this theoretically offers me the rare prospect of a mole. As if afraid I might accidentally try to poison him, Andy remains stubbornly underground.

England and Australia prepare for the Headingley Test with the argument over the ground's future raging behind the scenes. Headingley have produced a rival £32 million development plan, promising £20 million improvements in time for the 1999 World Cup; Yorkshire still insist that their own £50 million super stadium is feasible. But neither has a hope of lottery funding as long as the dispute continues, the Sports Council having refused to arbitrate on the merits of the rival schemes. Byford and Caddick are not even on speaking terms and blame each other for the impasse. Around Yorkshire is the sound of grating egos. Meanwhile, Headingley degenerates.

Yorkshire's members voted three-to-one to move to Durkar

at the spring annual meeting at Leeds Town Hall, but that is not quite as convincing as it sounds. The motion was couched in terms approaching: 'Do you want to escape Headingley's decaying hovel and move to the best stadium on the planet that won't cost you a single penny?' Not surprisingly, most people said yes, and those who were of a mind to argue from the floor were suppressed by Sir Lawrence in a style that he would argue represented strong leadership, but which made me wonder uneasily how a former chief constable could gain such a muddled sense of democracy.

Headingley's attempts to interest the national media in their development plans prove pretty futile because:

(i) They haven't laid on a lunchtime buffet.

(ii) The golf tee-off times have been booked.

(iii) There is the pressing matter of the annual Headingley pitch row.

The official Test pitch was relaid five years ago under such strict supervision from the TCCB's pitch inspector, Harry Brind, that he was allocated his own parking space. At the time a succession of low-scoring Tests on undependable surfaces had contributed to Headingley's uncertain future as an international venue. The intention was to implant a clone of the Oval up t'North, so maximising revenue with as many fifth-day finishes as possible. The evidence of the first three years suggested that the replacement pitch was as flat as southern beer.

Yorkshire folk being suspicious of incomers, even ones which arrive in bags on the back of a lorry, there was much opposition to the TCCB's interference. But criticism was not just restricted to the Broad Acres. Graham Gooch, then England captain and now an England selector, was aghast at the change, believing that a good home side should prosper on a Leeds pitch offering classically English conditions: liberal amounts of seam and swing.

England's last Test win at the dilapidated old ground was five years ago, on the old Test surface, when Gooch top-scored in both innings and Pakistan were bowled out twice by a trio of everyday English seamers: Neil Mallender, Tim Munton and Derek Pringle. Even more striking was England's 115-run win against the West Indies a year earlier. Gooch regarded his unbeaten 154 as his finest Test innings and England exhibited the levels of discipline of which the best Headingley victories are made.

Now England will seek to reawaken Headingley's reputation as the most hazardous batting venue on the circuit after an intervention, ironically, by Brind himself, accompanied by the chairman of selectors David Graveney. The justification is that the substitute pitch has 'a more even grass covering'. Andy Fogarty, Headingley's inexperienced head groundsman, is decidely unchuffed, but the switch goes ahead anyway. To offer Shane Warne another bare turner would be insane fair-mindedness. The Australians soon complain self-righteously of skulduggery and foul play. Taylor calls the new pitch 'under-prepared' and the coach, Geoff Marsh, expresses the hope that England 'can live with themselves'. The one thing Australia seem to have learned from England is the capacity for whingeing.

As Keith Boyce, Fogarty's predecessor, follows the dispute, his ruddy, weather-battered face breaks into a smile. For seventeen years, Boyce laboured to combat the unpredictability of the Headingley pitch, and when he was finally forced aside nearly two years ago, he was little nearer to understanding the nature of the most fickle square of sports turf in the land. His sole responsibility these days is for the rugby league side of Headingley's operation and he reckons that Fogarty is welcome to the aggravation.

'There's a bastard in my family and it's sitting out there!' Boyce once memorably exclaimed on the eve of a Headingley Test. However much he tried to nurture the Test wicket towards responsible adulthood, it would rebel as sulkily as a recalcitrant adolescent.

Boyce affectionately clothed the Headingley pitch with all types of grasses, treated it to all manner of soils. Soil institutes throughout Britain proffered advice, letters were written to *Gardeners' Question Time*. Boyce even took to baking soil samples in the oven to learn more about... well, what happens to soil samples when they are baked in the oven, I suppose. If he had inadvertently relaid the pitch with bread-and-butter pudding, things could only have got better.

When the Test pitch still seamed and bounced erratically, Boyce tried to batter it into submission with a twenty-ton road roller. On one occasion, he was so exasperated by his problems, he inadvertently squashed the roller key into the middle of the pitch and a championship match had to be suspended while he dug it out.

Criticism became part of Boyce's life and there was no time bleaker than the mid 1980s, when he was refused permission to dig up the square.

'Until I was allowed to re-lay the square in 1988, we had to keep moisture in it to stop it cracking,' he said. 'Too little moisture, as in 1981, and the pitch would crack; too much, like for Pakistan in 1987, and it would seam too much on the first morning. Then when we did re-lay it, we didn't dig deep enough and used over-light soils.'

Headingley's square caused Yorkshire captains to rage, and England captains to awaken abruptly from tormented sleep. David Gower once put Australia in, watched helplessly as they made 600 and then listened to Raymond Illingworth play the role of Headingley sage. 'I told him,' said Illy. 'Two degrees too cold to swing today.' On another occasion, Headingley's drains were deliberately blocked to retain the square's water levels, but there was a heavy overnight storm and the start of the Test was delayed the next morning as water bubbled up from beneath the bowlers' feet.

Whether Headingley really does possess its own weird micro-climate, or whether it has merely been cursed by a dog of a pitch, nobody ever quite agrees. Fred Trueman grumbles to this day that things have never been the same since they chopped down some poplar trees in the Sixties.

Boyce became the most famous, and most hounded, groundsman in the country. 'It'll be a belter,' he would annually predict, before retreating to his bungalow on the ground to study the opening overs on TV. He would emerge, pallid, by lunchtime, after one irregular bounce too many had told him that further criticism was as certain to descend as the next West Yorkshire shower. When the TCCB did force him to re-lay a new Test pitch to their instructions, he dug so deep that he needed a ladder to get in and out of the hole, and could be heard muttering to himself from down below: 'I'll sort this bastard out if it's the last thing I do.'

It was a vanload of this star-crossed soil which finished up on Thorner's practice pitch. Last week, after three years of up-and-down bounces, we conceded the inevitable and covered it with an artificial surface. If Friday night's barbecue is rained off, heaven knows how we are going to pay for it.

First day: England 106-3, 36 overs.

England have arrived at Headingley fresh from their motivational get-together at Rudding Park, near Harrogate. Instead of driving Land-Rovers through woods while blindfolded, this time they settle for riskier pursuits: archery, clay-pigeon shooting and an address by Sebastian Coe.

'Seb came to talk to us about winning,' explains David Lloyd. Presumably as a former Olympic champion, not as the defeated Conservative MP for Falmouth.

Even the Conservatives have caught on to team-building ideas, their new young leader, William Hague deciding to summon all 164 of their MPs to a country-house survival weekend, when they will no doubt attempt to abseil down cliff-faces armed only with copies of the *Daily Telegraph*. One Tory grandee is aghast. 'I'd rather be buried in shit than go away for a weekend with Teresa Gorman,' he says. One hopes that England's unity runs deeper.

The Australians have met the Queen at Buckingham Palace, and their manager Alan Crompton remains misty-eyed at the experience, telling all and sundry how wonderful she is at putting everybody at their ease. One can almost picture the scene:

The Queen (putting everybody wonderfully at ease): 'Are you enjoying England, Mr Crompton?'

Alan Crompton (with distracted air): 'What about this bloody pitch change, your mateship?'

The Queen (regally dismissive): 'Oh, come, come, Mr Crompton, you don't think we're going to give Warnie another bunsen, do you?'

Crompton's charge that David Graveney has surreptitiously influenced the pitch switch – made by letter to Tim Lamb, the chief executive of the ECB – is enough for Lamb to emerge for an emergency press briefing. The Australian media actually enquire whether Lamb thinks the 'reputation and integrity of English cricket has been brought into question.' The Hon Tim has every right to laugh it off, and announce that what pitches we play on is our own business, but being English, he regards this charge extremely seriously and offers a series of rambling justifications, all of which amount to the same thing: the decision to change the pitch was not taken by David Graveney, as chairman of selectors, which would be absolutely wrong. It was taken by Harry Brind, who kept David Graveney fully informed, which was absolutely right. Lamb then announces that Alan Crompton's misgivings have all been allayed.

This is hair-splitting at its finest, and by far the most interesting question is why the ECB has chosen to stage the press conference with Lamb crammed tightly up against a soft-drinks cabinet. Perhaps it is all part of Coca-Cola's sponsorship contract? Roll on the day when English cricket is sponsored by a company specializing in microphones and office furniture.

It is five o'clock, and all this chatter is suddenly interrupted by the sound of bat on ball. The Test has finally begun, six hours behind schedule, and Taylor, winning the toss for the fourth successive occasion, has inserted England in the belief that the ball will jag around in damp and overcast conditions. Atherton is equally convinced that Taylor has miscalculated, relying on past evidence that Headingley's bounce will become increasingly treacherous as the match wears on.

Conditions are perfect for Atherton. Flamboyance is disallowed, excessive caution out of the question. If this is the last Ashes Test at Headingley, he intends to make the most of it. Cheaply dismissed in his previous three first-innings of the series, he survives for two-and-a-half hours in making 34.

Around him, though, England batsmen are falling. Mark Butcher makes spritely progress to 24, then flicks Paul Reiffel fiercely to short leg where Greg Blewett, courageously keeping his shape, is rewarded by a catch which lodges in his midriff. The short catch offered by Alec Steward demands no such bravery or technique. Five minutes from the close, Glenn McGrath prises out Nasser Hussain at slip. At 106 for three, the Test is precariously balanced.

Off the field, arguments have raged about whether the Test pitch might one day be moved fifteen miles down the road. Right now, the repercussions of shifting it a few feet are what really matter.

Yorkshire's other priority is a clampdown on violent and abusive behaviour on the Western Terrace. Alcohol is confiscated at the turnstiles and the only available bar on the ground has queues designed to put off all but the most determined drinkers. A one-way system is enforced so strictly that anyone accidentally dropping an apple a yard to their left has to complete a half-mile circle to pick it up again.

A year ago, in the Test against Pakistan, the stewards proved entirely insensible to racist chants, but ejected a pantomime cow. Once again, they fail entirely to draw the distinction between unacceptable, loutish behaviour and light-hearted merriment. Brian Cheesman, a 51-year-old lecturer in the sociology of childhood at Leeds Metropolitan University, has raised money for charity over the past fifteen years by going to the Headingley Test in fancy dress. In past guises, he has been a lion and a polar bear. On this occasion, he has dressed up as a carrot, which seems to have infuriated the turnip heads in charge of stewarding. They stand Cheesman against a wall, order him to take off his costume and photograph him. He is then frogmarched from the ground (if he dresses up as a frog next year, it will save an awful lot of time). When he telephones the head of security for an explanation, he is told he has been drunk and abusive. He takes legal advice, demands an apology, a refund and compensation, and even writes to *The Times*.

Press watch:
Daily Telegraph (Martin Johnson): 'Cricket has a rare gift for creating dramas out of incidents that the former Pakistani manager, Hasib Ahsan, described as "storms in a cup of tea." Now we have letters being exchanged over who might have vetoed a pitch. What a waste of stamps.'

Second day: England 172, 59.4 overs (Atherton 41; Gillespie 7-37); Australia 258-4, 67 overs (Elliott 134 not out, Ponting 86 not out).

Sprinkled over various parts of the Western Terrace, Thorner CC and guests continue to revel in what is fondly billed as Festival Week (a trip to the Test, a couple of evening matches, a barbecue and a freakish appearance in the quarter-final of the Fred Fleetwood Cup). The week has included a last-over defeat against an Australian Media XI, which hopefully will not prove to be an omen.

At the last minute, Phil Warren has copped out of appearing on the Terrace as a Spice Girl, which, considering the Neanderthal stewarding, is probably no bad thing. He would probably have awoken to find himself chained to a bedpost in a cave just outside Armley. 'Rabbit', in a mood of relentless laddishness, solves the problem of the drinks restrictions by nipping out of the ground at the intervals and throwing back a few pints up the road at the Headingley

Taps. He becomes agitated when two spectators a few rows in front of him are ejected for faking a couple of friendly cuffs towards each other (the sort of thing that England might attempt on another male-bonding session). As the stewards eject them from the ground, he springs to his feet and taunts them with the chant: '40p an hour!' He comes close to ejection himself.

The Festival Week has also been a Sri Lanka tour reunion, and for some of the London crowd experiencing their first taste of the Western Terrace, the atmosphere is particularly disconcerting. Virtually everybody walking in front of the crowd from mid-afternoon onwards becomes an automatic figure of fun and is subjected to a considerable amount of good-natured heckling. Whether they are girls bursting out of skimpy T-shirts, or a man with an impressive beer belly, they are all targeted. In large swathes of the North, this is a display of communal acceptance, a breaking down of social barriers. All part of a fun day out.

Others view it more earnestly. Perhaps Phil, Bernie, Luci and Janet have a keener sense of how such attitudes can easily degenerate into racism and sexism, perhaps they merely exist by a stricter form of London political correctness. Certainly, they are unsettled by an atmosphere redolent of Leeds city centre on a Saturday night. The Western Terrace, for them, is a draining experience. But the fact is that it is society, not Yorkshire CCC, that must draw limits on racism, sexism or homophobia. And that means a government and education system which recognise their obligations in giving a strong and consistent moral lead, and a police force charged with enforcing it.

By mid-afternoon, the Test is again precariously balanced. England have been blown away for 172 before lunch by the pace of Jason Gillespie, but Australia are three wickets down for 50. Taylor has fallen to Gough without scoring, and since his career-saving century at Edgbaston has now made scores of 1, 2, 1 and 0. Gough also accounts for Blewett, and Dean Headley forces Mark Waugh to chip a return catch.

Australia's bleating about the pitch switch could become counter-productive.

England have given a Test debut to Mike Smith, Gloucestershire's Yorkshire-born left-arm swing bowler, who remains top of the national bowling averages and who has been summoned as a Headingley Specialist. Smith is such an unassuming, diffident sort that when he was on the England 'A' tour to Pakistan, one journalist was under the misapprehension that he was just a fan. He looks disturbingly nonplussed to be in such exalted company, but he is already visualising his first Test wicket when some extra lift defeats Matt Elliott and a looping, head-high catch sails invitingly to first slip, where Graham Thorpe drops it.

Up on the Western Terrace, Simon Gilhooly is flabbergasted. 'Bloody hell, Wakker, *you* could have caught that!' he says. Wakker's fielding, admittedly, has improved this season – he no longer escorts the ball to the boundary like a confused cocker-spaniel – but his nod of agreement is unconvincing. He shirks slip catches like a matador dodges a bull. Then Steve Waugh is out to the next delivery, plopping Headley to short leg, and Australia are 50 for four anyway. 'I could have caught that one, too,' says Wakker. Even this relies on the assumption that he would have been brave enough to stand there. When Wakker is at short leg, it is as much as you can do to get him close enough to save the single.

That Thorpe's miss might be a defining moment of the series is not immediately apparent, as Steve Waugh's wicket acts as a convenient smokescreen. By the close, though, the extent of his miscalculation is clear. Australia are virtually unassailable at 258 for four, and Elliott and Ricky Ponting, recalled for his first Test of the summer, have added 208 in forty-nine overs. On a breezy, sunny afternoon, the pitch flattens out and both bat with draining authority. Eleven wickets fall in the first half of the day; none in the second. Smith does not swing a ball all day. The next Headingley specialist might as well be requisitioned from St James's Hospital.

Many catches are missed, and where Elliott is concerned, England have been dropping them all summer. Thorpe does not deserve to become a scapegoat. Nevertheless, the opportunity spurned when Elliott had made 29 of his unbeaten 134 develops into one of the most painful experiences of his career.

Only a few months ago in New Zealand, Thorpe was prominent among players who achieved fielding levels not matched for years. This summer, he has held roughly fifty per cent of his opportunities and has misfielded an inexplicable number of times for a player of his quality. All these bonding weekends driving trucks blindfold through forests are all very well, but you would have thought they would have allowed Thorpey to take the blindfold off for the Tests.

Thorpe has looked troubled for most of the summer. His personal life has been under great strain after allegations in the *News of the World* about an extra-marital fling during England's tour of New Zealand, and this has contributed to his restlessness. It is another case where the media has not exactly assisted England's cause, but he cannot retain an aggrieved and distracted look for ever.

On the brink of tea, Elliott, on 63, slashes Mark Ealham to gully, where Atherton stoops uncomfortably and is struck on the boot. England revert to Plan B, which concludes that this tall, angular Victorian is weak against the hook. When Gough summons up the energy, in the penultimate over, for one last bouncer, Smith drops the catch at fine leg. You can imagine Gough chuntering: 'I said 'e were useless agenst 'ook.' Elliott is 132 at the time.

Gough's frustration leads one vocal Australian to barrack him from the Western Terrace.

'Hey, you great puff, Goughie,' he taunts.

A burly 6ft 4in Yorkshireman, who has soaked up enough Australian disdain for one day, lurches calmly towards him and issues a businesslike tap to his shoulder.

'Eh!' he says. 'This is Yorkshire and Goughie is a Yorkshireman. If Goughie's a puff, *we'll* tell *you*.'

The antagonists are united in the recognition that the day's finest fast-bowling has come before lunch from Gillespie, a threatening sight with his stony expression, ferocious goatee and glinting earrings, who has steamed down the slope to take six-23 in forty-seven balls. His return of seven for 37 is the best by an Australian at Headingley, outstripping Charlie Macartney's seven for 58 eighty-eight years ago.

Once Atherton falls hooking Paul Reiffel, having laboured for nearly four hours over 41, Gillespie hounds England into submission. John Crawley is bizarrely caught at short leg when the ball rebounds off Blewett's boot into the fielder's hands. England's innings ends when Smith backs so far away to leg that presumably he still thinks the match is being staged on the official Test pitch.

At the close of the second day, the Headingley stewards, having dealt with the carrot, turn their attentions to another pantomime cow, which is frolicking in the outfield. It takes four of them to tackle it and a fifth to crash it into the advertising hoardings, whereupon eyewitnesses speak of hearing 'a loud crack'. This confrontational style could have had calamitous consequences. Branco Resik, who is in the back end of the cow, briefly loses consciousness and is treated for nearly half an hour on the outfield by medical staff. To everyone's relief, he is released from hospital late that evening. Newspapers which a year ago called for the yobs to be dealt with do the same again. Only this time, they are talking about the stewards.

Press watch:
Daily Mail (Peter Johnson): 'There is a moment, sometimes only a split-second, in most Test series when you know instinctively that the game is up, the dream irreparably shattered. Graham Thorpe did not need the groan from 15,000 throats to tell him yesterday that he had just lived through one of the worst.'

Third day: England 172; Australia 373-5, 95.2 overs (Elliott 164 not out, Ponting 127).

That Graham Thorpe catch is still on everybody's mind. Mike Brearley, writing for the *Observer*, recalls the dropping of Don Bradman at square leg by RWV Robins in the third Test of the 1936-37 series in Australia. England, two Tests up, were never the same again.

'I'm awfully sorry,' Robins apologized.

'Don't worry, old chap,' his captain Gubby Allen is alleged to have replied, with considerable foresight. 'You've probably lost us the match and the series, but don't let it bother you.'

Brearley muses that in the Greek tradition, error and sin are inextricably linked, whereas in the Christian tradition, they are determinedly kept apart. He concludes that, while Thorpe's dropped catch is not a sin, our characters do contribute to our fate. English cricket continues to suffer from a malaise of national character: a lack of grit and self-confidence, and the pleasure we tend to draw from our own mediocrity. Australian cricket succeeds because it is hard, ambitious and uncompromising.

The *News of the World* is roughly on the same lines. Its message is:

*'Chuck Out The Wallies
Bring In The Hollies.'*

The campaign for the inclusion of Adam and Ben Hollioake, England's Texaco Trophy heroes, has officially begun.

Rain by lunchtime allows endless opportunity for reflection. Ponting has departed, for a self-assertive and cultured 127, but Elliott is 164 not out and Australia's lead 201. Atherton, who ignored Smith for the first new ball, ignores him for the second, even though conditions are conducive to swing bowling. When Atherton does not rate a player, everybody gets the message.

As the rain tipples down on an unprotected Western Terrace, the carousing continues. The funniest fancy-dress caper involves the Three Little Pigs (variously labelled Taylor, Waugh and Warne) being pursued by the Big Bad Wolf (Goughie). I wish.

Press watch:
Sunday Times (Graham Otway): 'Once again ineptitude has been the common currency of players who, it was hoped, would benefit from continuity in selection and strategic assistance from the sporting gurus – the dieticians, fitness assessors and motivation experts – that crowd the modern dressing-room.'

Fourth day: England 172 and 212-4, 63 overs (Hussain 101 not out, Crawley 48 not out); Australia 501-9 dec, 121 overs (Elliott 199, Reiffel 54 not out; Gough 5-149).

It is another wonderful day to be an England captain. Michael Atherton trails from the field at lunchtime with Australia about to declare at 501 for nine and the Ashes series resembling the awful mismatches of recent years. In helpful bowling conditions, England have conceded 128 runs at nearly five an over against a lower order cavorting around as happily as the pantomime cow before it was so rudely interrupted. Much of the fielding has been lazy and incompetent. Having missed key opportunities, for the second Test running, the game is running away from England and they have lacked the wherewithal to respond. People are obsessed with Atherton's body language again. It is not particularly positive, but let's retain some perspective. If strutting around in the field is the first mark of a captain, why not just give Dominic Cork the job and be done with it?

One MCC member sitting alongside the England dressing-room accurately proclaims the performance to be 'garbage', a comment which goads Atherton so much that he approaches him and tells him to repeat the charge to his face. Something about Atherton's mood conveys that this might not be a good idea. 'I wasn't addressing you,' says the spectator. Atherton mutters something along the lines of 'MCC twats' and stalks off. He is the grammar school boy suspecting that the public school brigade is out for his blood. Later, when he meets the press, the hoi-polloi will cause him equal trouble.

Elliott's hook shot still looks fallible, especially on a pitch of irregular bounce, but it proves productive. On 199, Gough finally defeats him with a yorker. And, in the mind's eye, Goughie is still harping on a familar theme: 'I teld ye he didn't like 'ooking. That's what he were expecting, another short one!'

England's pace attack has under-performed. Gough has been inconsistent, Headley's rhythm affected by the Headingley slope, and if Smith is top of the national averages then the county championship is a joke. That leaves Ealham, who would only catch Atherton's eye if he streaked across the middle of the pitch and stole the bails. Professor Hindsight is already lambasting England on two counts:

(i) Why did we field three medium-quick bowlers with only ten Tests between them?

(ii) Why did we prefer Smith to Caddick when Caddick's additional height would have been an advantage on a pitch of irregular bounce?

The answer to (i) is that inexperience is inevitable when everybody keeps screwing up, and to (ii) that even if Caddick had played, things would probably have gone just as badly. Then the same people would have been asking why Caddick had been preferred to Smith when Headingley had a reputation as a haven for swing bowling.

By tea, Atherton's mood is not improved. Four England wickets fall for 89, including the captain himself who receives a lifter from McGrath. Upon his dismissal, Atherton passes his vice-captain, Nasser Hussain. 'Fight,' he snaps. Hussain knows that he must. Since outraging Australian sensibilities at Old Trafford by claiming that disputed catch, he has been about as popular as a redback in a dunny. At least one England selector privately fears that Hussain might have to be dropped by the end of the series because he is not handling the sledging particularly well.

Hussain is treated to the Great Australian Oathbook (the cruder, unabridged version) but proves resistant. His double century in the first Test at Edgbaston had been an exhilarating innings at a time of bouyant English spirits. This time, met by the twin perils of Australian acrimony and English depression, he produces a brilliant unbeaten century which drives Australia to distraction and guards England against catastrophe.

McGrath welcomes Hussain with a mean bouncer and a speech substantially longer than the lifetime's press conference sayings of Jason Gillespie. There was a time when Taylor might have intervened, but his batting form is in tatters and perhaps he is no longer so confident of his authority. Hussain's response speaks volumes for his character. McGrath, a country boy who would recognise the dangers of a redback in a dunny, is bitten back with feeling as he concedes a stream of regal cover drives. On 95, Hussain is struck on the pad by Warne's full toss and Healy's petulant response behind the stumps when the lbw appeal is refused also stretches the line between disappointment and dissent. Hussain's century demands Australian applause; his three hundreds in England since his recall a year ago have all come on exacting, unreliable surfaces.

'The Australians have great mental strength,' Lloyd praises. 'You have to be able to match it and give a bit back. Nasser did match it. Many players would buckle underneath that type of test.'

Fleetingly, Hussain almost did. He might have joined that afternoon procession when he chanced a risky single to extra cover to get off the mark. Ponting's shy flashed past the stumps for overthrows. It had not seemed the sort of day when Hussain could invite an Australian, 'Give me five!'

After Friday's assault on the pantomime cow, Headingley's stewards are under orders to be less confrontational. The inebriated streaker who invades the outfield as Hussain nears his century could not have been treated more considerately had he been ushered away by a glamorous gameshow hostess to collect his pop-up toaster.

Press watch:
The Times (Simon Wilde): 'Situation desperate, situation normal.'

Fifth day: England 171 and 268, 91.1 overs (Hussain 105, Crawley 72; Reiffel 5-49); Australia 501-9 dec.
Result: Australia win by an innings and 61 runs.
Australia lead series 2-1 with two to play.

If Michael Atherton is of a mind to consider alternative employment today, he could always consider auditioning for the vacant role of Tinky Winky in the Teletubbies. Judging by the colour of the character's costume, at least then he would always be assured of being in a purple patch.

Atherton would be well-schooled for the part. *Teletubbies*, the replacement for *Playdays* as BBC TV's regular pre-school programme, attracts criticism for its inarticulate language and repetitive plots, which makes it sound exactly like an England press conference on a bad day. Today, there has been another one, with England beaten one ball into the afternoon session. Hussain's early chip to short extra, followed by the tail's capitulation against the second new ball, has ended thoughts of stalwart English resistance.

Atherton utters cricket soundbites as if a *Teletubbies* script would be a blessed relief. At Old Trafford, he had affirmed that good sides bounce back from adversity and imagined a Teletubby land of happiness and bright colours. 'I'm sure that we can win one of the next three Tests,' he said. Today, with England trounced, the same question pops up. One out of three is no longer good enough, so Atherton, with a world-weary show of optimism, is forced to raise the stakes. 'There are two games left and we have to win both to win the Ashes,' he says, sick of having to express the bleedin' obvious. 'It's a hard task.'

Tinky Winky would be right up Atherton's street. As the sacked actor who played him has been telling all and sundry, he is the daring one who takes all the risks, such as falling off his chair and rolling over. Atherton is now precariously close to rolling off his for good. Past England captains might have been suited to alternative roles in Teletubby Land. David Gower was born for Laa Laa, a flaxen, curly-haired Teletubby. Graham Gooch would have been cast as Po, on the grounds that he could be particularly po-faced on a bad day. That seems to leave Mike Gatting as Dipsy, an odd-looking Teletubby with a horn sticking out of its head.

Atherton has argued throughout his captaincy for a Teletubby England, where the characters become well loved and consistency is valued above change. The selectors, so far, have concurred. He is still on press-conference autopilot, mumbling about 'lost opportunities' and 'doors that are ajar and which need walking through'. He then sees a door and illustrates exactly what he means by walking through it. In a more surreal existence, Shane Warne would have intervened in the uniform of a Headingley steward and bawled: 'I'm sorry, you can't come through here without a pass!'

Press watch:
Shane Warne (in newly published biography): 'When the pressure point comes, English cricketers crumble.'

26

Fixes and Fudges

NO change is not an option, Lord MacLaurin warned cricket's Reactionary Tendency when he took over as chairman of the England and Wales Cricket Board. The Great Shopkeeper's hawkish introductory pronouncements last Christmas while England made a hash of things in Zimbabwe encouraged dreams of a great revolution. Yet here he is at Lord's, outlining a series of proposals which, although far-reaching in parts, are largely designed to mollify the most stupefied of county clubs.

A lifetime in the supermarket business has taught MacLaurin that you cannot sell people what they do not want, and he knows that the first-class counties must ultimately fling the product into the trolley at a full ECB board meeting in September. A two-divisional championship, with automatic promotion and relegation, is the only sensible option to regenerate the first-class game, but in his discussions with the counties, MacLaurin has recognized the extent of the hostility to it.

'Life is a progression and this is not the limit of our plans,' he says. Until then, what is available, and adorned in 'BARGAIN!' stickers, is a mixture of fixes and fudges.

England's top-heavy first-class system, with eighteen counties contesting a one-divisional championship, is wholly inadequate. It is understandably cherished for its sense of tradition, its cheerful festival weeks, and as a mellow retreat from the outside world. But the talent is spread too thinly and there is an emphasis on quantity rather than quality. Players, made stale by too much cricket, spend their free time on the golf course rather than perfecting their off-drive in the nets. Those whose ambitions have long since departed cling to county contracts in the hope of a lucrative benefit, and so block the progression of younger players eager to make their way. As there is no fear of failure, so there are limited rewards for success. It is a system that fails to serve the needs of the England Test side, and, as such, it automatically puts the long-term health of the game at risk.

The MacLaurin solution is a mess: an American-style conference system – three conferences of six counties, each playing the twelve remaining counties in the other two conferences. Explain that to an enthusiastic ten-year-old. The season then reaches a climax in September with a series of play-offs to determine the county champions. This being England, play-offs will also exist for the minor placings. The attraction of watching three counties battle it out for thirteenth, fourteenth and fifteenth place is not immediately apparent.

Each side's number of championship matches would be reduced from seventeen to fourteen in 1998, a reduced workload intended to offer players the opportunity for more serious practice time. Reorganisation of one-day cricket is also envisaged, with the proposed implementation of a 50-over league, to include two divisions, with promotion and relegation. In another complicated formula, here counties would play sides in their own division twice and the other division once: a total of twenty-five matches. Another decision designed to appease the reactionaries, who all fear an impecunious existence in the Second Division.

The proposed increase in one-day cricket sits at odds with the much-touted belief that its proliferation has caused a fall in playing standards. The net practice that MacLaurin envisages will allow budding England players to hone their defensive techniques could house bits-and-pieces limited-overs specialists perfecting a series of risky strokes in preparation for the next one-day thrash. Bowlers, equally, might abandon the art of the leg-cutter in favour of rehearsing an endless succession of blockhole balls. Counties sensing more kudos and financial reward in one-day success will employ bits-and-pieces players ahead of specialists.

The blueprint's title, Raising The Standard, possesses subliminal messages of the great battles in English history, but MacLaurin is not exactly crying God for Harry, England and St George. It is a solution that might have been devised by ACAS.

Disconcertingly, the county boards are charged with much of the restructuring work down the scale. With the help of cricket development officers, they must combat the decline of cricket in comprehensive schools. They must provide mentors for promising juniors, to ensure that they do not play too much cricket. They must bridge the gap between the professional and recreational games by establishing a national network of premier leagues by 1999, with two-day games contested over consecutive Saturdays. They must create the framework in which a revitalised amateur game will assume the responsibility from county second XIs for producing potential first-class players. Are they remotely up to the challenge?

David Lloyd, England's coach, has played Aunt Sally long enough to develop a scathing disregard for those local officials already obstructing a pyramid system of local leagues. At Trent Bridge, where England are preparing for the fifth Test, he describes the proposed introduction of premier leagues as 'radical... an unclogging of the system'.

'The leagues have to come to the party,' he pleads.' They must forget their parochial interests and take the wider view. If they digest the report properly, they will find they will get better facilities, a better game of cricket and better players. Some will respond with that insular, "We're alright, thanks" attitude. Well, they are not alright and they have got to understand that.'

What arouses the media more is the anticipated Test debuts of the Hollioake brothers. Ben will become the youngest England Test debutant since Brian Close in 1949, and this injection of brazen and youthful talent has been widely applauded. Lloyd praises Ben as 'a shining light of the Under-19 system,' and points out that England's recent policy of fast-tracking our best young players through representative cricket, rather than waiting endlessly for the counties to produce them, is paying dividends.

On the day that Lord MacLaurin proposes an overhaul of the English system, Ben Hollioake's lack of first-class cricket with Surrey is striking: 11 first-class matches, 422 runs and 21 wickets. County cricket has been virtually redundant in his development. Ben Hollioake is a confident cricketer, and might well be a highly-talented one. But nobody could remotely call him battle-hardened. While England talks fondly of a Boy's Own Story (suitably, even that comic-book image is forty years out of date), the Australian system is based in reality.

First day: Australia 302-3, 90 overs (Elliott 69, Taylor 76, Blewett 50).

The man from the *Daily Sport* has just accused Michael Atherton of being a useless tosser, and no one is arguing. Even a lucky Isle of Man coin does not prevent Mark Taylor correctly calling tails for the fifth Test running. The pitch gleams with promise of runs galore and England, who must win to prevent Australia retaining the Ashes, must wonder how on earth they can achieve it. Perhaps Atherton should toss with more optimistic body language?

Darren Gough is injured, and Devon Malcolm has been recalled despite a mediocre Trent Bridge record. Atherton tries not to reflect upon his England debut in similar circumstances on this ground eight years ago when Taylor and Geoff Marsh posted 301 for nought by the close.

This time Dean Headley and Andrew Caddick, in particular, bowl with admirable discipline and the fielding is trusty, but Australia's 302 for three carries echoes from the past. In baking heat, which makes the Nottingham crowd even more inanimate than usual, Elliott, Taylor and Blewett make fifties in turn and are exasperated at getting out in such ideal conditions. The band that struck up the theme tune from *Mission: Impossible* before play began clearly got it right. When the Hollioakes dreamt of playing for England in their back-garden childhood fantasies, the pitch was a bit bumpier.

Ben Hollioake does not quite make the scintillating debut worthy of such media commotion, but he does have his first wicket. Atherton benignly protects him from punishment after his first three overs cost 23, and when he is allowed another gambol after tea, he has Greg Blewett caught at the wicket. It is a reasonable enough delivery, but Blewett, seeking to glide to third man, rues his lapse of concentration.

Press watch:
Daily Express (Colin Bateman): 'Some things in life just naturally belong to Australia: big beaches, frozen beer, bronzed sheilas and bad television are among them. So are the Ashes.'

Second day: Australia 427, 121.5 overs (S Waugh 75, M Waugh 68); England 188-4, 57 overs (Stewart 87).

Watch the Gaffer go! Alec Stewart, re-established at the top of England's order, bristles with hectic authority. His strokeplay is crisp, cool and commanding. His game is scrubbed and polished to perfection, so much so that one imagines he can see his reflection in his boots. Any minute now, expect him magisterially to stop the bowler in his run-up while he adjusts a starched collar or reties an irksomely crooked bootlace. His 87 has represented one of England's most uplifting moments of the series.

After an hour's reconnaissance, Stewart has clipped his last 72 runs from 73 balls, ridding the ball from his midst as if flicking a speck of dust from his sleeve. Gillespie's second over costs 18; Warne, Stewart's persistent tormentor, is lofted into the legside spaces with effrontery. Despite keeping wicket for more than four sessions in enervating heat, Stewart is at the height of his game.

He had entered the Test in such poor form that there was a powerful case for dropping him down the order, even omitting him altogether. Instead, to accommodate the Hollioakes, Mark Butcher was dropped and Stewart was forced to reaccompany Atherton at the top of the order. Right this minute, the decision smacks of ingenuity. While Stewart bristles, Atherton potters alongside him with the slightly abstract air of an amateur gardener planting his dahlias, his occasions on strike serving in the crowd's imagination as Stewart resting stations. But Atherton has gone, pushing cagily at a Warne leg-break, and after an opening stand of 107, the breach has been made.

And there is to be no miraculous England fightback; Shane Warne so decrees. In seven overs, this most tantalizing of leg-spinners virtually ensures what we have grown to expect: that the Ashes are about to be regained by Australia. Stewart misses an off-drive at Warne and, vexed with himself, edges the next delivery to Healy, who deflects the ball over his own head and twists to catch the rebound. Stewart stalks off promptly, probably to smarten up his kit bag. It is Healy's 300th catch for Australia and 100th against England. When Nasser Hussain, working Warne towards the leg-side, loses his off stump to a ball of outlandish flight and break, Warne has summoned no better delivery all summer. Crawley follows, and Thorpe might well have followed too, to a TV umpire's run-out, had the ECB bothered to station their own cameras square of the wicket.

A day that had threatened to become a long and dreary Australian march to supremacy has overflowed with entertainment. Australia's last seven wickets have produced only 135, and the notion has been scotched that the Waugh brothers, well-established overnight, could score a hundred in the same innings, a feat they have only achieved once before, against the West Indies in Jamaica. England's pace attack maintains a full length and strict line, on a hazy morning offering persistent swing and extra bounce. Headley again looks the finished article; Malcolm, perhaps stung by not getting the new ball, escapes his lethargy of the first day; both take three wickets.

Steve Waugh briefly threatens to give Ben Hollioake nightmares, driving him square for three boundaries in as many overs, but Malcolm rattles a quick delivery into his off-stump. Young Ben has been well looked after. Even the dismissal of McGrath, a contender as the worst number eleven in Test cricket, possesses special significance. It is the first time that England have got him out all summer.

Press watch:
The *Guardian* (Frank Keating): 'The blond maestro bewitched Nasser Hussain into that splay-footed French-cricket prod of his and England were behind the sandbags again, all the gaiety and gumption of the day's stirring fightback defused.'

Third day: Australia 427 and 167-4 (Blewett 60); England 313, 93.5 overs (Stewart 87; Warne 4-86, McGrath 4-71).

Just as Adam Hollioake has become the media flavour of the month, so the knives are out for Michael Atherton. The *Sun* causes a stir with an exclusive story that Atherton offered to resign the captaincy before the start of the Nottingham Test, but was persuaded to stay on over dinner by Lord MacLaurin and Bob Bennett, chairman of both Lancashire and the England management committee.

At such times, the cricket becomes almost incidental. Atherton dismisses the very thought as 'rubbish' before the start of play, and an ECB statement advances the same argument in more long-winded fashion by lunchtime. However insistent the denials, though, the list of alternative candidates as England captain is already being drawn up: Nasser Hussain, vice-captain in Zimbabwe and New Zealand and the notional 'vice' this summer; Alec Stewart, on the grounds that he does almost everything else; and Adam Hollioake, whose Test experience will amount to three days by the evening.

Adam has at least gained respect on the county circuit as a solid performer – even if his Surrey side are regularly castigated as prima donnas for their on-field excesses – but

Ben, what has he done outside a couple of glamorous appearances at Lord's? For all the comparisons with Ian Botham's entrance into Test cricket, Ben's bowling remains naïve by comparison. His batting, though, briefly turns attention back to the cricket. He is lithe, elegant and still at the crease, and his first scoring shot in Tests, from Reiffel's ball of good length, fairly zings to the midwicket fence. Only Denis Compton scored his first Test run at a younger age. Heady comparisons are also made all day with another famous entrance into Test cricket, David Gower's nonchalant hooked four off the Indian medium-pacer Liaqat Ali. But for all that, Ben is out around lunchtime and Australia are in command by the close.

Press watch:
Independent on Sunday (Stephen Brenkley): 'It was like seeing the future and realizing that it worked.' *(On Ben Hollioake's first runs in Test cricket).*

Fourth day: Australia 427 and 336, 98.5 overs (Healy 63); England 313 and 186, 48.5 overs (Thorpe 82 not out; McGrath 3-36, Warne 3-43, Gillespie 3-65).
Result: Australia win by 264 runs.
Australia lead series 3-1 with one to play, and retain the Ashes.

Darren Gough, resting his knee injury back home near Wakefield, paces up and down his lounge in a state of disbelief. Since breaking into the Test side, Gough has endeared himself to English and Australian crowds alike with his uncomplicated exuberance, and it is precisely this buoyant, warm-hearted innocence that makes watching Australia's celebrations on TV so difficult for him to bear.

It is not just that Australia have retained the Ashes – that fear has been lurking at the back of Gough's mind for weeks. It is the extent of England's final collapse that is so hard to stomach. Gough has drawn pride from the way that England have fought hard, in his absence, for three days, and the Yorkshireman faithfully believed that the cause would continue deep into the final day. Instead, beginning their second innings at three o'clock, and set a notional 451 for victory, England embark upon a calamitous collapse which sees the Ashes conceded by early evening.

Gough prides himself on 'not joining the knockers,' on giving absolute support to his captain and his team-mates. He is still convinced that Atherton remains England's toughest professional and best captain, a man retaining the respect of the dressing room. But Gough's pride has been badly shaken. He suddenly understands why English cricket can attract so much criticism. He turns off the TV as if trying to blot out a painful memory, stares out of his lounge window, past his back-garden putting green and down the hill to the local village cricket club. He cannot settle.

He does not know it, but shoved in a litter bin along Bridgford Road in Nottingham, lies a broken, lifesize, Darren Gough cardboard cut-out, finger raised in triumph. As a symbol for England's distant euphoria of early season, it could not be more appropriate.

England, trailing by 285 at start of play, remove Steve Waugh with the second ball of the morning. Five wickets left - knock over the tail and there would remain a glimmer of hope that they could level the series, and settle the destination of the Ashes at the Oval. Instead, England's bowling is shoddy and Ian Healy collects 63 from 78 balls with an ease that breaks hearts.

England collapse in only 48.5 overs, in a shamelessly fatalistic batting display which crosses the dividing line between positive cricket and sheer recklessness. Once Atherton falls to another cruelly lifting short ball from McGrath, England's shot mental state becomes clear. Stewart falls loosely, off a leading edge, and Gillespie, bowling largely tripe, removes Hussain, Crawley and Adam Hollioake in an insane six-over burst of three for 52. After a strokeless half-hour, Ben Hollioake is leg-before to Warne; Ben Hollioake is trying to play like a batsman and the batsmen are playing like Ben Hollioake. Croft slogs to mid-on, Caddick completes a pair and Malcolm, appearing to ribald cheers like the clown in a Shakespeare comedy, edges the penultimate ball of the day to slip. Even Thorpe's unbeaten 82 possesses an unacceptable death-wish. A testy swing of the bat at a streaker, as defeat looms, invites the question as to whether he would have crashed him to the square boards or edged him to third man.

Steve Waugh has described Atherton as a cockroach – people keep stamping on him, but he just won't die. England's Ashes challenge, though, has proved so ephemeral that it owes more to the Mayfly. 'Top side, Australia,' England's players repeat that evening, with a reverence only truly granted to beaten men. 'Top side.'

England could have saved the fifth Test today had:
(i) The temperature in Nottingham risen so inexorably that the umpires called off play for the welfare of the Australian fielders.
(ii) The contractors redeveloping the Radcliffe Road End moved their diggers onto the outfield to begin work at 8.30 in the morning.
(iii) Tony Banks, the Minister for Sport, ruled that all competitive sport, apart from Premiership football, was a complete waste of time and should cease forthwith.
(iv) Cyril Mitchley stopped not giving people out lbw and not giving them out caught or bowled either.
(v) Shane Warne performed the anatomical feat for which English crowds have been chanting all summer.

Press watch:
Daily Telegraph (Simon Hughes): 'Whoever captains England this winter, he will lead a nucleus of spirited, thoughtful cricketers who discuss the game fervently and stimulate each other. They are learning their lessons and fighting their battles.'

27

Resignation

I FIRST suspect that all this Thorner captaincy business might be getting too much when I wander up to Ed in mid-July to discuss field placings (an unnerving task at the best of times) and ask something like: 'Do you want another two barbecue tickets on the legside?' It is a relief to be met with the sort of look normally reserved for incoherent tramps in railway station doorways. On another day, Ed might have responded: 'You stick to the sausages, I'll put the bloody fielders where I want to.'

This episode takes place against Rufforth, the bottom club, where we achieve the heights of a winning draw, but where Ralls observes my field settings with barely concealed impatience. After eight pints, he tells me so – so I quickly buy him another one and by the time he has demolished it, he has agreed that he wants nothing more than to resume his rightful role as The Man With The Asterisk.

Never give a *Guardian*-type the captaincy of anything. Life just possesses too many uncertainties. Consider this simple question:

'Skip, do you want me in front of square, or just behind?'

The disturbing fact is that I rarely mind. Do I want him in front or behind? Well, in front, I suppose, or perhaps behind. In a bit, or out? Wider, or squarer? Crouching or walking in? Younger, almost certainly, and fitter. And a bit of 'Heads Up, Lads!' and general lifting of the troops from time to time would not go amiss. But apart from that, why worry? The overriding law near the foot of the pyramid is Sod's Law. Introduce all the normal guidelines about pace of pitch, style of bowler, strength of batsmen etc, and they are swamped by a host of imponderables.

Gareth Andrews, up from London for the Headingley Test reunion, treats me to his skit on a *Guardian*-reading captain:

'Do *I* prefer you in front of square or behind? Well, I don't *really* have an opinion. Which would *you* prefer? Which position could you most *relate* to? Where do *you* feel more comfortable? Where do you think you could most *grow* as a human being?'

The subconscious reason that I daren't bowl Tommy Jordan's off-spin is that I fear the setting of *his* field would take several days. I would shrug and say that I didn't overly mind, he would expand upon a Nietzsche philosophical tract to justify why the stationing of a sweeper on the cover boundary would enable him to overcome the manifold frustrations of his present bowling average and explore the possibilities of a more perfect mental state. Tommy, unusually, has also taken to dropping catches in the deep; after three in one afternoon at Amaranth, I offer to loan him the *Test Match Special* sunhat, complete with earplugs, so that he can soothe his mind with a burst of Radio 3.

Ralls' more focused captaincy takes a while to filter through. To ensure that team spirit remains intact during this most bloodless of coups, we spend hours drafting a players' letter to announce the switch. The following Saturday, Thorner collapse to 44 all out against Scholes. So much for the powers of English literature. Relief soon follows, however, as two fellow strugglers, Long Marston and Sherburn, are beaten in successive weeks and we sneak away from the bottom three.

There is (those of you yearning for neat thematic tie-ups, take note) an Australian influence here. Richard Gibson, who has spent a year playing club cricket in Adelaide, joins us in mid-July, awash with Australian aggression and enthusiasm. One year's exposure to Australian habits and he treats every game like a Test match. We all become permanently deaf, gain lots of new nicknames and learn to chant phrases such as It's All About Desire, There Are Eleven Of Us On This Field, and It's Coming, Boys, It's Coming. If it is, it's sure taking a long time.

Ed's mood does not entirely lighten, post-revolution. At

Long Marston, he runs himself out in a mix-up with Wakker, whose only response to the call 'Let's have a third' comes in the Fox around 9pm every Saturday night. Ed is so distraught at his dismissal that he tears off his pads and berates Wakker's every shot from the boundary's edge. 'He even asked me why I haven't got a girlfriend at the moment!' Wakker complains.

Long Marston grumble with some reason about 'Thorner's bloody Australian,' which is not entirely apt, as Ed hails from Birmingham. He has been there, though, and the day he returned to Heathrow, he wanted to grab hold of everyone on the tube and shake some life into them. His reaction to the opposition is intriguingly polarised. The sides we beat are hailed as 'as good as anyone else we've played,' which is designed to make us feel we can beat anybody. When we lose, our opponents are invariably 'crap,' so refusing to accept that anybody might actually be better than us. It is all, doubtless, sound psychological stuff, but I can't help feeling it's the wrong way round.

But the good days make it all worthwhile, and against the might of Sherburn, assisted by a flat pitch, a sweltering afternoon and a deal of luck, the Hopps/Eagle opening partnership finally achieves its five-year ambition of a ten-wicket win. Jon is adamant that our concentration levels have been slipping and proposes that we play the innings a section at a time. His method of counting stages becomes so complicated that during one drinks interval, I am almost persuaded to exchange my thigh pad for a calculator. I think he might be a closet mathematician.

At 41 for nought, he wanders into mid pitch to suggest, or so I presume, that the next target should be to get to 50.

Instead, he urges: 'All we need is another ten, then we're only eight runs away from getting half their total.'

That staging-post safely (well, not entirely safely) negotiated, he volunteers a new fact.

'C'mon,' he says. 'If we get another nine in the next four overs, we only need two-an-over for the last fifty.'

I advise him that I'm not quite so good at complicated take-aways, so would he mind awfully if we could stick to simple addition, and if he is thinking of inspiring me in a few overs' time with a couple of logarithms, could he please think again.

Jon's best arithmetic is reserved, though, for the panic-stricken realisation that, in the final shake-up, he might miss his fifty. 'You're on strike, I need seven, and we need four to win, so if you get a single, I can still do it with a two and six,' he says, 'or if I lose the strike again, even a...'

He is still dividing small numbers into bigger numbers when a deliberate misfield at extra cover by a man who probably did not enjoy his maths lessons at school makes the whole thing spurious.

After our peevish match against Kippax, the return in late August takes place in an atmosphere of sweetness and light. Kippax pile up several thousand on a damp wicket, and then reduce us to 36 for seven after nineteen overs. Raising the Standard, the ECB's proposals for the regeneration of the English game, has just been published, full of worthy plans to improve club cricket. Michael Brennan deserves a mention, then, for the sterling way in which he blocked out the last hour, alongside his captain, to secure us a losing draw. Millfield could be proud of him. His reward, though, was not immediately apparent: all his mates got tired of waiting and went out clubbing without him.

28

We're Right Behind You, Captain!

Sixth Cornhill Test, England v Australia
The Oval, 21–25 August.

Have you ever felt the need for a personal motivator? Perhaps they will soon be commonly available, a constant companion encouraging us to make that phone call, retune that video and explore our lives to their maximum potential. It is rumoured that in South Kensington, people are already insisting that they can't live without one. But what if your motivator turns out to be Michael Atherton?

As England prepare for one last hurrah in the sixth Test at the Oval, Atherton's resignation is being demanded by all who doubt his motivational qualities. In a particularly spiteful piece of journalism, the *Daily Mail* responds to defeat at Trent Bridge with the headline, 'Dead duck: Michael Atherton – you are charged with impersonating an England cricket captain.' And don't blame the writer; he found the whole affair so stressful that he suffered a minor heart attack.

The knives are out. Around the country, the theory abounds that England's periodic displays of slovenly fielding, undisciplined bowling and indiscriminate batting can be laid at the door of a captain who failed his GCSE in body language. We are obsessed with motivators. Premiership football is with us again, and nearly every goal scored in the first ten minutes of the second half will be attributed by someone to a manager's half-time pep talk. In football, motivators need to rule for ninety minutes, in rugby even less, but a Test match spans five six-hour days. For Atherton, the challenge is more complex.

Atherton spends the time between Tests fishing, musing and seeking the advice of friends and mentors. He has long been resigned to the fact that part of the baggage of the

England cricket captaincy is to be told you are infallible one minute, an imbecile the next. David Graveney, the chairman of selectors, has expressed his preference that Atherton skipper England in the West Indies, although even that honest opinion has a smattering of convenience until a natural successor comes forth. No matter how thick Atherton's hide, there comes a time when it is simply not worth the hassle any more.

Thrashed in the past four Ashes series, England's realistic goal this summer has been to compete, to challenge and occasionally to win. Not very uplifting, but what right have we to expect anything better? Since Mark Taylor first contested an Ashes series, Australia's margin of victory has followed a shrinking mathematical progression: 4-0 in 1989, 3-0 in 1990-91, 4-1 in 1993, 3-1 in 1994-5. For England to fail 3-2 this summer might logically be presented as progress.

Of course, a captain must inspire his players, command them and fathom their moods. But for England to bat so recklessly at Trent Bridge was a common abdication of responsibility. Atherton had a right to expect his team-mates to work a few things out for themselves, such as the fact that a drawn Test, and therefore the chance of a drawn series, was still something worth fighting for.

Nasser Hussain blames county cricket, in a back-page piece which does the *Mail* more credit. 'This softness comes from playing county cricket, which is all very matey and lovey-dovey,' he says. 'We're all mates out there, and it's about a few cups of tea and maybe a Pimm's or two afterwards. The gap between that cosy little world and Test cricket is immense. The Aussies, even in their grade cricket, are abusing you and rucking you. Our club cricket, in comparison, is like a social gathering.'

Sod's Law then inconveniently intervenes. The day after this analysis, a NatWest semi-final between Glamorgan and Hussain's Essex at Chelmsford ends in uproar when Robert Croft and Mark Ilott push and shove each other as they dispute whether the game should be suspended for bad light with Essex two wickets and six runs away from victory. They are such good mates that, at the time, their wives are sat in the crowd arranging a foursome for dinner. Both players are fined £1,000, newsdesks blather on about cricket's 'collapsing morality', and Hussain's comments are widely misconstrued.

'I am not condoning sledging or fighting, I am talking about inner strength, inner toughness,' Hussain implores. 'These players overstepped the line, but these things happen in the heat of the moment. English cricket needs more games like this.'

Mark Taylor has his own problems. His own mediocre batting form means that he might not survive as Australia's captain, even though the Ashes are safely gathered in. But he finds time to offer Atherton encouragement.

'Just by changing the captain, or the coach, or the team, you're not going to change the way things are going,' he says. 'This is the time to offer encouragement, not criticism. Compared to Michael, I was lucky. I had a good side to help me out.'

Perhaps a great side. When it comes to the crunch, Australia believe in self-determination. Motivate yourself, make no excuses, relish pressure. It was not Taylor's doing when Steve Waugh stood up at a team meeting and movingly explained, as the only Australian in the party who had ever lost an Ashes series, how he never wanted to experience the feeling again. It was not Taylor's body language which inspired Steve Waugh to make two centuries at Old Trafford when his hand was bruised by bat-jar, or encouraged Jason Gillespie to roar down the slope at Headingley to take seven wickets, or revealed to Ian Healy how to assemble the adventurous innings which finally ended England's Ashes challenge at Trent Bridge.

What produced those moments was a host of things: world-class players hardened by a demanding domestic system, a nation which takes unabashed pride in the achievements of its sportsmen and women, and a united dressing room which feeds off pressure rather than fears it. For England to match

Australia requires not just a change of captain, or even a change of system, however vital that is, but a country that teaches itself the value of self-motivation. For the moment, though, they are playing for personal pride, and to express their allegiance to a captain under siege.

First day: England 180, 56.4 overs (Stewart 36, Hussain 35; McGrath 7-76); Australia 77-2, 241 overs.

For the first time, *Test Match Special* is broadcasting via the Internet, a development which could safeguard its future now that the BBC is showing an ever-shrinking commitment to its continuation. The *TMS* commentary team announce the Internet address with clumsy embarrassment, as if faced by an undesirable foreign language. But for the thousands of British youngsters gaining access to the Net every month, the danger is that it is cricket itself which will become the foreign language, as the sport fails in its responsibility to embrace the future.

For the first time, in countries as diverse as Brazil, Lithuania and the Solomon Islands, ex-pats are exclaiming: 'He's got to go, Atherton, hasn't he?' The evidence is building by the minute. When it is essential that England cussedly protect the captain's future, they bat neurotically. When Atherton needs to draw encouragement from a talented and courageous batting display, he receives sheepish looks and mumbled apologies. If he hasn't already decided to resign, this is enough to tip him over the edge.

Reasonably placed at lunch at 97 for two, England are dismissed for 180 by tea. The Oval pitch, normally so true and firm, is notably inconsistent, with the ball going through the surface from the outset. Shane Warne responds with verve to the unexpected presence of first-day spin, but the most potent performer is Glenn McGrath, the summer's perpetual antagonist, who bowls straight and aggressively to collect seven for 76. 'Pigeon' has never quite stirred the imagination of the English crowds but, since his false start at Edgbaston, he has completed his English education. For England, the Oval looks a Test too far; for McGrath, it provides further confirmation that he is the finest quick bowler in the world. Paul Reiffel and Jason Gillespie might have returned home early with injuries, but a couple of large problems still remain.

Atherton relishes the long, grudging innings – but not this summer, as McGrath reminds us when he has the captain caught off an inside edge. Mark Butcher, recalled after a Test's absence, under-edges a hook against McGrath onto his stumps. Alec Stewart and Nasser Hussain ride their luck until lunch, after which McGrath works them over. Graham Thorpe crashes 27 like a man on borrowed time, before McGrath switches around the wicket and rattles an exposed leg stump. He bowls with glorious consistency.

Two other dismissals arguably possess greater import. The populist media refrain for Adam Hollioake to replace Atherton as captain grows from an obsession with style over content, nothing if not a sign of the times. Hollioake is brash, confident, strong-willed (good luck to him), but he reveals none of those qualities when he allows a straight ball from Warne to trundle into his stumps. Mark Ramprakash, for a long time the classiest batsman on the county circuit, has also been recalled. Atherton, shrewdly, chats constantly to him before he goes out to bat, in an effort to lessen the tension that has blighted his Test career, but Ramprakash makes only four before deflecting McGrath to short leg. Ramprakash needs much more than a comforting chat with his pads on: he needs a first-class structure that extends him, and a national identity that fills him with pride. England, meanwhile, need a hell of a turnaround.

Press watch:
the *Guardian* (Mike Selvey): 'McGrath's progress since his adaptation to an English length in the aftermath of the first Test has been relentless; a video of his technique and method

is now compulsory viewing for any prospective England bowler.'

Second day: England 180 and 52-3; Australia 220, 79.3 overs (Blewett 47, Ponting 40; Tufnell 7-66).

Phil Tufnell's Ashes figures before this Test approximated to the following: five stock and slightly tongue-in-cheek conversations with Michael Atherton for the captain to apologise for the fact that he was not in the final eleven; 1,200 motorway miles; 100 overs in the nets; various calls home; a dozen team talks and roughly a million fags. To that he can now add seven Australian wickets – it has been a triumphant return.

Tufnell is playing his first home Test for three years, and is determinedly flip about the reasons for his absence. 'I suppose I've played more on tour because someone thinks I'm such a brilliant tourist,' he jests, as if headbutting hotel rooms was on the approved list of Things To Do for bored England cricketers abroad. Sure beats strumming 'Wonderwall'. The Lovable Rogue image is also flaunted to the full when it is suggested that Australia have no qualms about his bowling, and that Steve and Mark Waugh, in particular, quite fancy him. 'Yeah, well I'm a pretty good-looking chap,' he says. His tinge of disrespect does no harm in an England atmosphere, at least where Australia are concerned, of developing subservience.

Tufnell has never bowled better for England. His challengy-cheeky, street-urchin expression, scrawny build and mischievous intent make him look ever more like Steptoe's grandson, and he has now added Harold Steptoe's artistic ambition to old man Steptoe's deceit and guile. Tufnell has never been a huge spinner of the ball, but a responsive Oval pitch ensures that he turns it big and often, and his subtle variations in pace and flight are a delight to observe.

Tufnell's polite observations about being a 'reformed character' should not be taken entirely for granted. His regular line about passing his life these days 'wandering round garden centres' can be seen as a winking commentary on society's facile attempts to impose upon him a set of conventional middle-class values, although all those allegations about smoking pot in a disabled toilet in Auckland do make you wonder what he might have been searching for behind the nasturtiums. He did experience a hairy time in the spring when his wife Lisa required an emergency Caesarean, both wife and daughter happily surviving a severely complicated pregnancy in good health. This might well have matured him, but it does not mean that he is about to succumb to a programme of bourgeoisification. In any case, why should he? It is his common, mildly rebellious touch which intrigues his public.

Tufnell's true role is to entertain us by taking wickets for England and to take them with his true character to the fore, and this he does with great skill and panache. With both openers already banked from the first evening – Matt Elliott looking aghast when a sharply turning delivery careered between bat and pad – Tufnell delivers 27 unbroken overs from the Pavilion End. Alec Stewart somehow clings to three catches of great distinctiveness. An acrobatic legside effort accounts for Greg Blewett, the ball flying off the back of the bat as the batsman tries to sweep. Stewart then manages to dismiss his fellow wicketkeeper Ian Healy by trapping an edge between his thighs. Shaun Young, summoned from a productive season at Gloucestershire for an unexpected Test debut, cuts at a delivery which spits out of the rough and Stewart, flinching blindly as the edge strikes his body, spins around to catch the rebound.

England only trail on first innings by 40, but the postscript is hardly encouraging. In the last 27 overs, they lose Atherton, Butcher and Stewart in exchange for a lead of twelve runs. Atherton's fatalistic smile as he walks off, having sliced to gully, encourages a further study in body language, being widely intepreted as another clue that his mind is set upon resignation. His Ashes haul amounts to 257 runs at an average of 23.36, and his return for Lancashire is so mediocre that the members have been shouting 'Rubbish!' at him. The England captaincy is threatening to harm him for good.

Press watch:
the *Guardian* (Frank Keating): 'Although he plays for Middlesex, Tufnell has always seemed much more homely, matey and errand-boy Kennington. "Lord's is for hansom cabs," said Neville Cardus, "you properly go to the Oval by bus."'

Third day: England 180 and 163, 66.5 overs (Thorpe 62, Ramprakash 48; Kasprowicz 7-36); Australia 220 and 104, 32.1 overs (Ponting 20; Caddick 5-22, Tufnell 4-27).
Result: England win by 19 runs.
Australia win series 3-2.

The England team are dashing from the field, grinning broadly at a wonderful prank they hardly dared believe was possible. A crowd that has roared itself hoarse for much of the past hour is cheering wildly. One of the most gripping finishes in recent Test history has fallen England's way, by 19 runs. Australia, requiring only 124 for victory, have tumbled for 104 in a three-day Test of marvellous insanity. The players feel vindicated, the public mostly respond with disbelief, what is left for the media is a mixture of delight, confusion and perhaps even a fleeting trace of guilt.

Moments like these, with Australia despatched for little over a hundred in only 32.1 overs, are not designed for balanced conclusions or for serious examination of the true state of English cricket. The ingredients are dry mouths, suppressed tears and uncurbed celebrations. England, not for the first time this series, have hit the heights, and Atherton is displaying a toothy grin that has not been on show since Edgbaston. But all those who quietly express the wish that this brilliant escapade does not blind English officialdom to the deep-seated faults in our national game have truth on their side. What England have revealed today is the enormous capacity for improvement, and it is this very potential that should make the desire to untap its potential even stronger.

Mark Taylor is as magnanimous as ever, too much the natural sportsman to bleat about the lbw decision which he thought he had hit, or the caught-behind verdict which Blewett thought that he didn't. But Australia's captain has often referred to their 'dead-rubber syndrome,' so it is perfectly appropriate that he does so again. Statistics insist that, just as Australia lift their game when a series is there to be won, they falter when it has been decided. They win when it matters, lose when it doesn't. 'That seems the way of modern Test cricket,' Taylor suggests.

England have regained the heights of early summer because the desire to express their allegiance to Atherton has created a will-to-win far above that of opponents who, their job done, were mentally heading for home. As they wind down over a couple of beers, Nasser Hussain and Alec Stewart, the likeliest candidates to lead England in the West Indies should Atherton resign, discuss how they can help him to stay on.

They deserve their celebration, these young men who have borne England's hopes in this Ashes summer of lurching fortunes, because they have carried these hopes with honesty of purpose, with great concern and with flashes of brilliance. To lose 4-1 would have mocked their attempts at improvement; to fall 3-2 grants them a respectability unmatched since Mike Gatting's side won the Ashes in Australia a decade earlier. No one should deny them that.

England's lead of 123 is largely down to Thorpe and Ramprakash. On their early days as England 'A' tourists, they would talk cricket over dinner for hours, exploring each other's theories and ambitions. Ramprakash's serious presence – he has a Test future to play for – draws from Thorpe one of his most disciplined innings of the summer. His shot selection is high-class. On BBC TV, Geoffrey Boycott is becoming excited: 'Disciplined batting... Australia will be getting worried.... Twenty-five minutes until lunch... Look at the clock... Still there at the interval.' No sooner does he dare to utter these hopeful words than Thorpe edges to slip, one of seven victims for Michael Kasprowicz, who is producing the most unexpected spell of the summer. Warne is troubled by a groin injury, but soon after lunch, Ramprakash envisages a straight six to bring up his fifty and is stumped by a country mile. Australia's subsequent progression to 36 for one leaves the crowd drained of expectation.

Bedlam follows. England's match-winners with the ball are an odd combination indeed. Tufnell's jousting and joshing brings him another four wickets, and 11 for 93 in the match. The pitch, like the bowler himself, is a bit of a rogue – a couple of soul-brothers giving the Australians no respite – and it is entirely apt that the ragamuffin left-arm spinner should have the final say when McGrath chips him to mid-off, where Thorpe holds a tumbling catch. Tufnell has also fooled Mark Waugh into edging to slip, turned one sharply to trap Ponting leg-before, and caused Warne, batting with a runner, to hoist one to mid-on.

What Tufnell does not not achieve, Andrew Caddick does. Caddick, as Peter Roebuck shrewdly observes in the *Sunday Telegraph*, is a 'calculating, sometimes cranky New Zealander, not a chap, it has been supposed, to rise to an occasion.' Even in his excitement, as Australian wickets tumble, The Cad receives congratulations rather awkwardly, a loner slightly unsettled by the sudden emotion of it all. He bowls with craft and spirit, hitting the pitch hard to expose its tendency to uneven bounce to the full. When it comes to the wickets of Taylor and Blewett, luck is on his side – but there are big wickets, too: Steve Waugh, leg-before on the back foot, and Ian Healy, whose return catch is smoothly held at the third attempt.

When it is all over, Atherton fields the congratulations, the backslaps, the expressions of support. From all sides, he is assured, as he has been all year: 'We're right behind you, captain.' To the end, though, he retains a deadpan ability to keep it all in perspective. 'It was a nice way to finish the series,' he says. And, with that, he plans to retreat from public view for a few days, to consider whether he can continue to withstand the most exposed playing role in British sport.

Appendix

First Cornhill Test – Edgbaston, 5–9 June

AUSTRALIA

			(First Innings)						*(Second Innings)*			
			Runs	Balls	FoW					Runs	Balls	FoW
MA Taylor*	c Butcher	b Malcolm	7	16	1-11	(2)	c and	b Croft		129	296	1-133
MTG Elliott		b Gough	6	13	2-15	(1)		b Croft		66	113	2-327
GS Blewett	c Hussain	b Gough	7	15	4-28		c Butcher	b Croft		125	228	3-354
ME Waugh		b Gough	5	25	3-26	(6)	c Stewart	b Gough		1	7	5-399
SR Waugh	c Stewart	b Caddick	12	20	5-48	(4)	lbw	b Gough		33	101	6-431
MG Bevan	c Ealham	b Malcolm	8	21	7-48	(5)	c Hussain	b Gough		24	41	4-393
IA Healy†	c Stewart	b Caddick	0	1	6-48		c Atherton	b Ealham		30	46	7-465
JN Gillespie	lbw	b Caddick	4	8	8-54	(10)	ro Crawley/Gough			0	6	9-477
SK Warne	c Malcolm	b Caddick	47	46	10-118	(8)	c and	b Ealham		32	34	10-477
MS Kasprowicz	c Butcher	b Caddick	17	28	9-110	(9)	c Butcher	b Ealham		0	2	8-465
GD McGrath	not out		1	3	-			not out		0	0	-
Extras	w2 nb2		4				b18 lb12 w2 nb5			37		
Total	31.5 overs		118				114.4 overs			477		

BOWLING										
Gough	10	1	43	3			35	7	123	3
Malcolm	10	2	25	2			21	6	52	0
Caddick	11.5	1	50	5		(4)	30	6	87	0
Croft						(3)	43	10	125	3
Ealham							15.4	3	60	3

ENGLAND

			(First Innings)						*(Second Innings)*			
			Runs	Balls	FoW					Runs	Balls	FoW
MA Butcher	c Healy	b Kaspr'z	8	13	2-16		lbw	b Kaspr'z		14	10	1-29
MA Atherton*	c Healy	b McGrath	2	4	1-8		not out			57	65	-
AJ Stewart†	c Elliott	b Gillespie	18	33	3-50		not out			40	54	-
N Hussain	c Healy	b Warne	207	337	6-416							
GP Thorpe	c Bevan	b McGrath	138	245	4-338							
JP Crawley	c Healy	b Kaspr'z	1	14	5-345							
MA Ealham	not out		53	131	-							
RDB Croft	c Healy	b Kaspr'z	24	56	7-460							
D Gough	c Healy	b Kaspr'z	0	9	8-463							
AR Caddick	lbw	b Bevan	0	7	9-478							
DE Malcolm	did not bat		-									
Extras	b4 lb7 w1 nb15		27				b4 lb4			8		
TOTAL	138.4 overs		478-9 dec				21.3 overs			119-1		

BOWLING										
McGrath	32	8	107	2			7	1	42	0
Kasprowicz	39	8	113	4			7	0	42	1
Gillespie	10	1	48	1						
Warne	35	8	110	1		(2)	7.3	0	27	0
Bevan	10.4	0	44	1						
S Waugh	12	2	45	0						

Toss: Australia.
Umpires: SA Bucknor, P Willey (JW Holder).
Referee: RS Madugalle.
Man of the Match: N Hussain.

Result: England won by nine wickets.

Second Cornhill Test – Lord's, 19–23 June

ENGLAND

(First Innings)

			Runs	Balls	FoW
MA Butcher	c Blewett	b McGrath	5	26	1-11
MA Atherton*	c Taylor	b McGrath	1	24	2-12
AJ Stewart†		b McGrath	1	23	3-13
N Hussain	lbw	b McGrath	19	73	6-62
GP Thorpe	c Blewett	b Reiffel	21	49	4-47
JP Crawley	c Healy	b McGrath	1	17	5-56
MA Ealham	c Elliott	b Reiffel	7	30	9-77
RDB Croft	c Healy	b McGrath	2	13	7-66
D Gough	c Healy	b McGrath	10	10	8-76
AR Caddick	lbw	b McGrath	1	5	10-77
DE Malcolm	not out		0	0	-
Extras	b4 nb5		9		
TOTAL	42.3 overs		77		

(Second Innings)

			Runs	Balls	FoW
		b Warne	87	210	4-202
	hit wicket	b Kaspr'z	77	159	1-162
	c Kaspr'z	b McGrath	13	24	2-189
	c and	b Warne	0	5	3-197
	not out		30	39	-
	not out		29	45	-
	b4 lb14 w1 nb7		30		
	79 overs		266 -4 dec		

BOWLING

McGrath	20.3	8	38	8					
Reiffel	15	9	17	2					
Kasprowicz	5	1	9	0					
Warne	2	0	9	0					
Bevan						20	5	65	1
S Waugh						13	5	29	0
						15	3	54	1
						19	4	47	2
						8	1	29	0
						4	0	20	0

AUSTRALIA

(First Innings)

			Runs	Balls	FoW
MA Taylor*		b Gough	1	15	1-4
MTG Elliott	c Crawley	b Caddick	112	180	7-212
GS Blewett	c Hussain	b Croft	45	70	2-73
ME Waugh	c Malcolm	b Caddick	33	60	3-147
SK Warne	c Hussain	b Gough	0	4	4-147
SR Waugh	lbw	b Caddick	0	1	5-147
MG Bevan	c Stewart	b Caddick	4	7	6-159
IA Healy†	not out		13	23	-
PR Reiffel	not out		1	6	-
MS Kasprowicz					
GD McGrath					
Extras	b1 lb3		4		
Total	61overs		213-7 dec		

(Second Innings)

	Runs	Balls	FoW

BOWLING

Gough	20	4	82	2
Caddick	22	6	71	4
Malcolm	7	1	26	0
Croft	12	5	30	1

Toss: Australia.
Umpires: DR Shepherd, S. Venkataragharan (DJ Constant).
Referee: RS Madugalle.
Man of the Match: GD McGrath.

Result: Match drawn.

Third Cornhill Test – Old Trafford, 3–7 July

AUSTRALIA

(First Innings)

Batsman	Dismissal		Runs	Balls	FoW	
MA Taylor	c Thorpe	b Headley	2	20	1-9	(2)
MTG Elliott	c Stewart	b Headley	40	98	4-85	(1)
GS Blewett		b Gough	8	13	2-22	
ME Waugh	c Stewart	b Ealham	12	27	3-42	
SR Waugh		b Gough	108	175	9-235	
MG Bevan	c Stewart	b Headley	7	16	5-113	
IA Healy†	c Stewart	b Caddick	9	20	6-150	
SK Warne	c Stewart	b Ealham	3	7	7-160	
PR Reiffel		b Gough	31	84	8-230	
JN Gillespie	c Stewart	b Headley	0	8	10-235	
GD McGrath	not out		0	2	-	
Extras	b8 lb4 nb3		9			
Total	77.3 overs		235			

(Second Innings)

Batsman	Dismissal		Runs	Balls	FoW
MA Taylor	c Butcher	b Headley	1	2	1-5
MTG Elliott	c Butcher	b Headley	11	40	3-39
GS Blewett	c Hussain	b Croft	19	35	2-33
ME Waugh		b Ealham	55	81	4-131
SR Waugh	c Stewart	b Headley	116	271	8-333
MG Bevan	c Atherton	b Headley	0	16	5-132
IA Healy†	c Butcher	b Croft	47	78	6-210
SK Warne	c Stewart	b Caddick	53	77	7-298
PR Reiffel	not out		45	87	-
JN Gillespie	not out		28	55	-
Extras	b1 lb13 nb6		20		
Total	122 overs		395-8 dec		

BOWLING

	O	M	R	W			O	M	R	W
Gough	21	7	52	3			20	3	62	0
Headley	27.3	4	72	4			29	4	104	4
Caddick	14	2	52	1	(5)		21	0	69	1
Ealham	11	2	34	2			13	3	41	1
Croft	4	0	13	0	(3)		39	12	105	2

ENGLAND

(First Innings)

Batsman	Dismissal		Runs	Balls	FoW
MA Butcher	st Healy	b Bevan	51	140	3-94
MA Atherton*	c Healy	b McGrath	5	29	1-8
AJ Stewart†	c Taylor	b Warne	30	79	2-74
N Hussain	c Healy	b Warne	13	29	5-110
GP Thorpe	c Taylor	b Warne	3	7	4-101
JP Crawley	c Healy	b Warne	4	26	6-111
MA Ealham	not out		24	97	-
RDB Croft	c S Waugh	b McGrath	7	23	7-122
D Gough	lbw	b Warne	1	13	8-123
AR Caddick	c M Waugh	b Warne	15	57	9-161
DW Headley		b McGrath	0	10	10-162
Extras	b4 lb3 nb3		10		
TOTAL	84.4 overs		162		

(Second Innings)

Batsman	Dismissal		Runs	Balls	FoW
MA Butcher	c McGrath	b Gillespie	28	78	4-55
MA Atherton*	lbw	b Gillespie	21	38	1-44
AJ Stewart†		b Warne	1	5	2-45
N Hussain	lbw	b Gillespie	1	14	3-50
GP Thorpe	c Healy	b Warne	7	29	5-84
JP Crawley	hit wicket	b McGrath	83	151	8-177
MA Ealham	c Healy	b McGrath	9	75	6-158
RDB Croft	c Reiffel	b McGrath	7	13	7-170
D Gough		b McGrath	6	18	9-188
AR Caddick	c Gillespie	b Warne	17	18	10-200
DW Headley	not out		0	4	-
Extras	b14 lb4 w1 nb1		20		
TOTAL	73.4 overs		200		

BOWLING

	O	M	R	W			O	M	R	W
McGrath	23.4	9	40	3			21	4	46	4
Reiffel	9	3	14	0	(3)		2	0	8	0
Warne	30	14	48	6	(4)		30.4	8	63	3
Gillespie	14	3	39	0	(2)		12	4	31	3
Bevan	8	3	14	1			8	2	34	0

Toss: Australia.
Umpires: G Sharp, S Venkataragharan (JH Hampshire).
Referee: RS Madugalle.
Man of the Match: SR Waugh.

Result: Australia won by 268 runs.

Fourth Cornhill Test – Headingley, 24–28 July

ENGLAND

(First Innings)

			Runs	Balls	FoW
MA Butcher	c Blewett	b Reiffel	24	57	1-43
MA Atherton*	c Gillespie	b McGrath	41	143	5-154
AJ Stewart†	c Blewett	b Gillespie	7	24	2-58
N Hussain	c Taylor	b McGrath	26	40	3-103
DW Headley	c S Waugh	b Gillespie	22	32	4-138
GP Thorpe		b Gillespie	15	26	6-154
JP Crawley	c Blewett	b Gillespie	2	13	7-163
MA Ealham	not out		8	24	-
RDB Croft	c Ponting	b Gillespie	6	8	8-172
D Gough		b Gillespie	0	2	9-172
AM Smith		b Gillespie	0	2	10-172
Extras	b4 lb4 w1 nb12		21		
TOTAL	59.4 overs		172		

(Second Innings)

			Runs	Balls	FoW
	c Healy	b McGrath	19	18	1-23
	c Warne	b McGrath	2	13	2-28
		b Reiffel	16	30	3-57
	c Gillespie	b Warne	105	181	5-222
(8)	lbw	b Reiffel	3	17	8-263
(5)	c M Waugh	b Gillespie	15	30	4-89
(6)		b Reiffel	72	214	7-256
(7)	c M Waugh	b Reiffel	4	47	6-252
	c Healy	b Reiffel	3	7	10-268
	c M Waugh	b Gillespie	0	1	9-263
	not out		4	4	-
	b6 lb4 nb13		23		
	91.1 overs		268		

BOWLING

McGrath	22	5	67	22		22	5	80	2
Reiffel	20	4	41	1		21.1	2	49	5
Gillespie	13.4	1	37	7		23	8	65	2
Blewett	3	0	17	0					
Warne	1	0	2	0	(4)	21	6	53	1
S Waugh					(5)	4	1	11	0

AUSTRALIA

(First Innings)

			Runs	Balls	FoW
MA Taylor*	c Stewart	b Gough	0	11	1-0
MTG Elliott		b Gough	199	351	8-444
GS Blewett	c Stewart	b Gough	1	8	2-16
ME Waugh	c and	b Headley	8	18	3-43
SR Waugh	c Crawley	b Headley	4	12	4-50
RT Ponting	c Ealham	b Gough	127	202	5-318
IA Healy†		b Ealham	31	46	6-382
SK Warne	c Thorpe	b Ealham	0	5	7-383
PR Reiffel	not out		54	72	-
JN Gillespie		b Gough	3	18	9-641
GD McGrath	not out		30	30	-
Extras	b9 lb10 nb35		54		
Total	123 overs		501-9dec		

(Second Innings)

	Runs	Balls	FoW

BOWLING

Gough	36	5	149	5
Headley	25	2	125	2
Smith	23	2	89	0
Ealham	19	3	56	2
Croft	18	1	49	0
Butcher	2	0	14	0

Toss: Australia.
Umpires: MJ Kitchen, CJ Mitchley (R Julian).
Referee: CW Smith.
Man of the Match: JN Gillespie.

Result: Australia won by an innings and 61 runs.

Fifth Cornhill Test – Trent Bridge, 7–11 August

AUSTRALIA

	(First Innings)		Runs	Balls	FoW			*(Second Innings)*		Runs	Balls	FoW
MTG Elliott	c Stewart	b Headley	69	117	1-117	(2)	c Crawley	b Caddick		37	40	1-51
MA Taylor*		b Caddick	76	155	2-160	(1)	c Hussain	b B Hollioake	45	100	2-105
GS Blewett	c Stewart	b B Hollioake	50	115	3-225		c Stewart	b Caddick		60	94	4-156
ME Waugh	lbw	b Caddick	68	124	4-311		lbw	b Headley		7	22	3-134
SR Waugh		b Malcolm	75	102	8-386		c A H'oake	b Caddick		14	25	5-171
RT Ponting		b Headley	9	15	5-325		c Stewart	b A Hollioake	45	131	7-292
IA Healy†	c A H'oake	b Malcolm	16	18	6-355		c Stewart	b A Hollioake	63	78	6-276
SK Warne	c Thorpe	b Malcolm	0	5	7-363		c Thorpe	b Croft		20	36	8-314
PR Reiffel	c Thorpe	b Headley	26	48	9-419		c B H'oake	b Croft		22	37	10-336
JN Gillespie	not out		18	34	-		c Thorpe	b Headley		4	19	9-236
GD McGrath		b Headley	1	6	10-427		not out			1	16	-
Extras	b4 lb10 w1 nb4		19				b1 lb11 nb6			18		
Total	121.5 overs		427				98.5 overs			336		

BOWLING

Malcolm	25	4	100	3			16	4	52	0	
Headley	30.5	7	87	4			19	3	56	2	
Caddick	30	4	102	2		(4)	20	2	85	3	
B Hollioake	10	1	57	1		(5)	5	1	26	1	
Croft	19	7	43	0		(3)	26.5	6	74	2	
A Hollioake	7	0	24	0			12	2	31	2	

ENGLAND

	(First Innings)		Runs	Balls	FoW		*(Second Innings)*		Runs	Balls	FoW
MA Atherton*	c Healy	b Warne	27	75	1-106	c Healy	b McGrath	8	32	1-25
AJ Stewart†	c Healy	b Warne	87	107	2-129	c S Waugh	b Reiffel	16	22	2-25
JP Crawley	c Healy	b McGrath	18	44	4-141	c Healy	b Gillespie	33	41	4-99
N Hussain		b Warne	2	22	3-135		b Gillespie	21	37	3-78
GP Thorpe	c Blewett	b Warne	53	118	6-243	not out		82	93	-
AJ Hollioake	c Taylor	b Reiffel	45	94	5-243	lbw	b Gillespie	2	6	5-121
BC Hollioake	c M Waugh	b Reiffel	28	39	8-290	lbw	b Warne	2	25	6-144
RDB Croft	c Blewett	b McGrath	18	34	7-272	c McGrath	b Warne	6	6	7-150
AR Caddick	c Healy	b McGrath	0	6	9-290	lbw	b Warne	0	10	8-166
DW Headley	not out		10	17	-	c Healy	b McGrath	4	26	9-186
DE Malcolm		b McGrath	12	12	10-313	c M Waugh	b McGrath	0	2	10-186
Extras	b2 lb6 nb5		13			b6 lb2 nb4		12		
TOTAL	93.5 overs		313			48.5 overs		186		

BOWLING

McGrath	29.5	9	71	4		13.5	4	36	3
Reiffel	21	2	101	2		11	3	34	1
Gillespie	11	3	47	0		8	0	65	3
Warne	32	8	86	4		16	4	43	3

Toss: Australia.
Umpires: CJ Mitchley, DR Shepherd (AA Jones).
Referee: CW Smith.
Man of the Match: IA Healy.

Result: Australia won by 264 runs.

Sixth Cornhill Test – The Oval, 21–25 August

ENGLAND

(First Innings)			Runs	Balls	FoW	(Second Innings)			Runs	Balls	FoW
MA Butcher		b McGrath	5	24	1-18	lbw		b ME Waugh	13	48	3-26
MA Atherton*	c Healy	b McGrath	8	17	2-24		c SR Waugh	b Kaspr'z	8	21	1-20
AJ Stewart†	lbw	b McGrath	36	73	3-97	lbw		b Kaspr'z	3	9	2-24
N Hussain	c Elliott	b McGrath	35	114	4-128		c Elliott	b Warne	2	50	4-52
GP Thorpe		b McGrath	27	34	5-131		c Taylor	b Kaspr'z	62	115	5-131
MR Ramprakash	c Blewett	b McGrath	4	8	7-132		st Healy	b Warne	48	110	7-160
AJ Hollioake		b Warne	0	6	6-132	lbw		b Kaspr'z	4	10	6-138
AR Caddick	not out		26	35	-	not out			0	37	-
PJ Martin		b McGrath	20	19	8-158		c and	b Kaspr'z	3	2	8-163
PCR Tufnell	c Blewett	b Warne	1	20	9-175		c Healy	b Kaspr'z	0	2	9-163
DE Malcolm	lbw	b Kaspr'z	0	1	10-180			b Kaspr'z	0	2	10-163
Extras	b2 lb6 nb1		18			b6 lb10 nb4			20		
TOTAL	56.4 overs		180			66.5 overs			163		

BOWLING

McGrath	21	4	76	7		17	5	33	0
Kasprowicz	11.4	2	56	1		15.5	5	36	7
Warne	17	8	32	2		26	9	57	2
ME Waugh						7	3	16	1
Young	7	3	8	0		1	0	5	0

AUSTRALIA

(First Innings)			Runs	Balls	FoW	(Second Innings)			Runs	Balls	FoW
MTG Elliott		b Tufnell	12	33	1-49	lbw		b Malcolm	4	3	1-5
MA Taylor*	c Hollioake	b Tufnell	38	42	2-54	lbw		b Caddick	18	34	2-36
GS Blewett	c Stewart	b Tufnell	47	132	5-150		c Stewart	b Caddick	19	36	4-49
ME Waugh	c Butcher	b Tufnell	19	69	3-94		c Hussain	b Tufnell	1	7	3-42
SR Waugh	lbw	b Caddick	22	34	4-140		c Thorpe	b Caddick	6	19	5-54
RT Ponting	c Hussain	b Tufnell	40	96	10-220	lbw		b Tufnell	20	35	6-88
IA Healy†	c Stewart	b Tufnell	2	34	6-164		c and	b Caddick	14	17	7-92
S Young	c Stewart	b Tufnell	0	3	7-164	not out			4	24	-
SK Warne		b Caddick	30	34	8-205		c Martin	b Tufnell	3	5	8-95
MS Kasprowicz	lbw	b Caddick	0	1	9-205		c Hollioake	b Caddick	4	13	9-99
GD McGrath	not out		1	5	-		c Thorpe	b Tufnell	1	2	10-104
Extras	lb3 w1 nb5		9			b3 lb4 w1 nb2			10		
Total	79.3 overs		220			32.1 overs			104		

BOWLING

Malcolm	11	2	37	0		3	0	15	1
Martin	15	5	38	0		4	0	13	0
Caddick	19	4	76	3		12	2	42	5
Tufnell	34.3	16	66	7		13.1	6	27	4

Toss: England.
Umpires: LH Barker, P Willey (KE Palmer).
Referee: CW Smith.
Man of the Match: PCR Tufnell.

Result: England won by 19 runs.

Men of the Series: GD McGrath and GP Thorpe.

Result of series: Australia won series 3–2.

Test averages

ENGLAND

Batting

Player	M	I	NO	Runs	HS	Av
G P Thorpe	6	11	2	453	138	50.33
N Hussain	6	11	0	431	207	39.18
M A Ealham	4	6	3	105	53*	35.00
J P Crawley	5	9	1	243	83	30.37
M R Ramprakash	1	2	0	52	48	26.00
M A Butcher	5	10	0	254	87	25.40
A J Stewart	6	12	1	268	87	24.36
M A Atherton	6	12	1	257	77	23.36
B C Hollioake	1	2	0	30	28	15.00
A J Hollioake	2	4	0	51	45	12.75
P J Martin	1	2	0	23	20	11.50
A R Caddick	5	8	2	59	26*	9.83
D W Headley	3	6	2	39	22	9.75
R D B Croft	5	8	0	75	24	9.37
A M Smith	1	2	1	4	4*	4.00
D E Malcolm	4	5	1	12	12	3.00
D Gough	4	6	0	17	10	2.83
P C R Tufnell	1	2	0	1	1	0.50

Bowling

Player	O	M	R	W	Av	B-B
P C R Tufnell	47.4	22	93	11	8.45	7-66
M A Ealham	58.4	11	191	8	23.87	3-60
A R Caddick	179.5	27	634	24	26.41	5-42
A J Hollioake	19	2	55	2	27.50	2-31
D W Headley	131.2	20	444	16	27.75	4-72
D Gough	142	27	511	16	31.93	5-14
B C Hollioake	15	2	83	2	41.50	1-26
D E Malcolm	93	19	307	6	51.16	3-10
R D B Croft	161.5	41	439	8	54.87	3-12
M A Butcher	2	0	14	0	-	-
P J Martin	19	5	51	0	-	-
A M Smith	23	2	89	0	-	-

Test averages

AUSTRALIA

Batting

Player	M	I	NO	Runs	HS	Av
P R Reiffel	4	6	3	179	54	59.66
M T G Elliott	6	10	0	556	199	55.60
R T Ponting	3	5	0	241	127	48.20
S R Waugh	6	10	0	390	116	39.00
G S Blewett	6	10	0	381	125	38.10
M A Taylor	6	10	0	317	129	31.70
I A Healy	6	10	1	225	63	25.00
M E Waugh	6	10	0	209	68	20.90
S K Warne	6	10	0	188	53	18.80
G D McGrath	6	8	6	25	20*	12.50
J N Gillespie	4	7	2	57	28*	11.40
M G Bevan	3	5	0	43	24	8.60
M S Kasprowicz	3	4	0	21	17	5.25
S Young	1	2	1	4	4*	4.00

Bowling

Player	O	M	R	W	Av	B-B
M E Waugh	7	3	16	1	16.00	1-16
G D McGrath	249.5	67	701	36	19.47	8-38
J N Gillespie	91.4	20	332	16	20.75	7-37
M S Kasprowicz	93.3	19	310	14	22.14	7-36
S K Warne	237.1	69	577	24	24.04	6-48
P R Reiffel	112.1	28	293	11	26.63	5-49
M G Bevan	34.4	6	121	2	60.50	1-14
G S Blewett	3	0	17	0	-	-
S R Waugh	20	3	76	0	-	-
S Young	8	3	13	0	-	-

Acknowledgements

My particular thanks go to all those at Thorner Mexborough CC, who have allowed me to poke fun at them, both in print and in real life (there again, they have given a bit back in their time). Thanks also to the various cricket writers and broadcasters throughout the world whose opinions and company have proved a regular source of stimulation. However much we might disagree from time to time about the details, there are occasions when the 'power of the pack' keeps us all going. Thanks, too, to the players, who have had the talent and commitment to go out and do it. Or, at least, try to do it. Without them, I'd have nothing to write about. And good luck to those who believe that English cricket is worth preserving and can become so much better. Good luck to those, at all levels, who care enough to get involved.

Gratitude also goes to my family, who withstand my constant absences from home because of cricket commitments with great patience; to Tom Jordan, who read the proofs diligently in an idle moment, and who knew what Oxymoron meant; and to Matthew Engel for the Foreword.

And thanks, most of all, to those whose friendship and comradeship has helped to make the game of cricket such a diverting way to while away a disturbingly large part of my life.

David Hopps,
Wetherby, West Yorkshire, September 1997.